HRAC

D1608895

Oklahoma Horizons Series

PRIDE OF THE WICHITAS

A HISTORY OF CAMERON UNIVERSITY

BY

SARAH EPPLER JANDA

FOREWORD BY CINDY ROSS

SERIES EDITOR: GINI MOORE CAMPBELL

OHA

DEDICATION

For My Students

TABLE OF CONTENTS

FOREWORD

Cameron University is very fortunate to have this beautifully written history by Dr. Sarah Janda. It tells the story of the university's past and much more. This book is an important tribute and testimony to those who came before us. It is also a promise to those who will come after us, for it reveals the constant nature of Cameron University and its unwavering commitment to students. Within these pages, you will find powerful stories of students determined to receive an education despite serious hardships alongside delightful stories of student hijinks through the years. You will discover the role administrators and political leaders played in Cameron's development and read stories of caring faculty who go above and beyond the call of duty to teach and nurture Cameron students. You also will find find another key factor in Cameron University's 100 year history – the steadfast support of the community to ensure not only the survival but the continuing growth of the Cameron State School of Agriculture, now Cameron University.

As you read through this book, you will notice a theme: the unwavering commitment carried out by Cameron University to serve students first. One of the many examples of this is the insistence of administrators and faculty that a Cameron education be affordable for all students, including those from disadvantaged backgrounds. You will read story after story, for instance, about the importance placed on supplying nutritious low-cost meals for all students. Another example involves the persistent efforts by administrators and community and state leaders to provide adequate facilities for student housing as well as classrooms for instruction. Without doubt, students always have been the heart of Cameron's commitment.

Cameron's Centennial provided the ideal celebration of these stories. It was also the celebration of the beginning of a promising new century. One hundred years ago, the first Cameron classes were held in the basement of a local bank with only a handful of students. Today, Cameron University boasts some 5,700 students from 50 countries, 49 states, and 48 counties in Oklahoma. The very first graduating class of Cameron State School of Agriculture in 1912 had four graduates – two women and two men. They studied agriculture, manual training, math, English, and domestic science. For our Centennial Commencement, approximately 1,000 students graduated from Cameron University with associate, bachelor, and master's degrees in 50 different programs. And the best is yet to come!

In spring 1911, Cameron moved to its current location – a new campus west of town. And by new campus, it was a three-story building with ten classrooms, all faculty offices, a creamery in the basement, and a blacksmith shop. Today, Cameron University is a modern physical plant of 540 acres and 1.2 million square feet. Completion of the new technology-rich School of Business Building, the McMahon Centennial Complex which will be the hub of campus life, and the 2.6 acre Bentley Gardens will further enhance our beautiful campus.

It was my belief when I became president of Cameron University in 2002, and it remains true today – Cameron University is the students' "University of Choice." Cameron is the hub of the region and the engine driving southwest Oklahoma. In this role, our focus must be clear. The Centennial Celebration helped us honor the past and gave us momentum for the future. The rich history within these pages inspires all of us to envision what Cameron can and must become.

I invite you to read this book and to see for yourself this important record of where we have been and where we are going. Enjoy.

Cindy Ross, *President*
Cameron University

ACKNOWLEDGMENTS

I never thought I would write a history of Cameron University. Or at least I hoped I would not. My training as a twentieth century social historian left little room for the possibility that institutional history could be anything other than boring. I imagined reading assessment reports, dry minutes from countless committee meetings, and the dates buildings were constructed. Little did I realize that the people in those buildings and what this particular institution has meant to them over the past 100 years would be many things, the least of which is "boring." To that end, I owe a good deal of gratitude to Don Sullivan for convincing me to take on the task of writing about Cameron. When I first told Jim Horinek, a PLUS scholar and editor of *The Cameron Collegian*, that I had agreed to write a history of Cameron, he responded by saying what an honor it must be for me. Confused, I had to ask Jim to repeat himself as I tried to hide my surprise and then reluctantly agreed with him. I immediately felt bad because of all the words I would have chosen to describe how I felt—overwhelmed, obligated, and even burdened—it had simply not occurred to me to feel honored to write Cameron's history. As my work on this project progressed, I reflected back on that exchange many times as it has indeed been an honor to write about a place that has meant so much to so many people.

As is the case with any project, I have amassed numerous debts and wish in particular to thank everyone who agreed to let me interview them and who provided me with information I could not have found without their help. Tom Sutherlin, in particular, proved very helpful with university statistics. Terral McKellips deserves special thanks for his insights and because of the wealth of information he has retained after a long career at Cameron. The Cameron University Archives, housed on the second floor of the Library,

was a tremendous resource and I wish to thank Sherry Young, Anna Cory, Jason Smith, and the rest of the Library staff for making the archive records, both processed and unprocessed, available to me as well as for their support of and interest in the project. Records collected and retained for the archive by Sally Soelle were also of great value in my work. Susan Hill and Marge Kingsley generously allowed me access to the collection of *Wichitas* housed in the Department of English and Foreign Languages which helped me a good deal, especially toward the end of the project. Elizabeth Grooms, Heidi Livesay, Jana Gowan, Craig Martin, Josh Lehman, Glen Pinkston, and Jamie Glover also provided me with invaluable assistance for which I am most grateful. Kathy Liontas-Warren generously contributed her beautiful art work, which appears inside the cover. I would also like to thank Gini Moore Campbell, Director of Publications and Education at the Oklahoma Heritage Association, for her guidance.

As a faculty member with many teaching and service demands on my time, it is important to note that this project would not have been possible without the support of my school and my department. I owe a good deal of gratitude to my colleagues in the Department of History and Government for their support, especially Richard Voeltz, Suzanne Crawford, Doug Catterall, and Tony Wohlers. I would like to thank Von Underwood, the dean of Liberal Arts, who offered me encouragement throughout the project. John McArthur, the vice president for Academic Affairs, provided me with the support, including release time that I needed to write Cameron's history. While many people I talked to about this project expressed enthusiasm, like Jim Horinek, others voiced concerns as to what I would actually be "allowed" to write about. To that end, it is, I think, important to note that when I met with John

McArthur to discuss the project, he said simply that he would support me on any issue of academic freedom. Nevertheless, before agreeing to take on the project it seemed prudent to meet with President Cindy Ross to get an idea of her expectations for the book. She said that as president she felt a strong sense of duty to make sure that the history of the school was written but that from her perspective, nothing was off limits and I had the freedom to cover what I saw fit. And so, while I could not have written this book without the help of dozens of people across campus and the community, it is also the case that any mistakes, oversights, or omissions are mine alone.

On a personal note, I would like to thank my husband Lance, who is also a historian and now serves as chair of History and Government. He has been a constant source of support for me and has had his own work interrupted more times than either of us care to recall to listen to my sometimes half-formed ideas or to read a passage that I either struggled with or felt pleased by. Our daughter Sydney has offered much comic relief and joy throughout the process as I have had to explain that some days my work-time consisted of researching or writing rather than teaching. Not to be out-done, even at four years of age, she has often responded to our discussions about work by gathering up her own "papers" and saying she was going to her office at Cameron to work on her own book.

Social historians are seldom arrogant enough to suggest that their work is THE history of a given subject. Rather, we are more comfortable with the disclaimer that our work is *a* history or *one* interpretation, leaving open the often distinct possibility that other perspectives and histories will be written. In the case of Cameron, it is perhaps less likely that a significant amount of scholarship on the subject will ever be written. Given that, I have

tried to be particularly sensitive to offering what I hope is a balanced and reflective history of the university.

The most rewarding part of the project has been being able to work with students and include essays written by students in my 2009 senior seminar in history class in this book. In my entire undergraduate and graduate career, I never sat down in an archive with one of my professors and had them show me how to do research. Broadly speaking, in the discipline of history, student and faculty research is usually separate. Students benefit from the knowledge and skills of their professors, but they do not conduct research together. Yet, the first time I met with my students in the university archive, I began to see the benefits of this sort of approach. I wish to thank Joyce Turner, Kyle Lewis, Kris Underwood, Eric Nabinger, Kevin Chandler, and Tyson Moll for their hard work, enthusiasm, and willingness to contribute to this book. Finally, I would like to thank Jim Horinek. He not only allowed me to see this project from a fresh perspective but he spent countless hours helping me with photographs for the book. He scanned and cropped over one hundred pictures that appear in the book and for that, I am greatly indebted.

Sarah Eppler Janda

INTRODUCTION

Cameron has changed enormously during its 100-year history, from an agricultural high school to a junior college to a four-year university. Yet many common themes connect the past to the present. When Cameron first opened its doors, the primary purpose of the institution was to provide a practical education to the people of southwest Oklahoma. While what constitutes a practical education has certainly changed over time, Cameron's central mission has not. Cameron began offering junior college course work in 1927 because the people of southwest Oklahoma needed local access to higher education. When Cameron added junior level university courses in 1968 and senior level courses in 1969, this again happened because of an overwhelming demand in the community.

Moreover, in every period of Cameron's growth and development, there exist numerous and poignant stories of relationships forged between teachers and students, fortunes changed because of a kind word of encouragement or praise or because a faculty or staff member went the extra mile to help a student. That a Cameron professor made a personal loan to a student for flight courses which eventually contributed to making that student the number two ace in the European Theater in World War II was reflective of Cameron tradition rather than an aberration speaks volumes about the school's history and its relationship to the students it has served for the past 100 years. As Cameron prepares for its second century of educating students, it continues to emphasize providing a personalized education in which students have access to an affordable and quality education and where students get to know the faculty and staff; where students are a name rather than a number.

Early Cameron students considered the school to be the pride of the Wichita Mountains and expressed great enthusiasm for the newly constructed campus. Even students who lived in tents or slept on cots in basements and hallways felt privileged to be at Cameron and to have access to the opportunities it provided. Nearly 100 years after those first Cameron students began taking classes in the basement of a downtown Lawton Bank, State Regent and Cameron alumnus Bill Burgess could still observe that Cameron has "made a bigger impact in the lives of poor people than any institution" he knew of.[1]

Then, as now, the Lawton community made possible the very existence of Cameron as an educational institution, sustaining and nurturing the school's growth. The story of Cameron is inextricably tied to that community. For 100 years Lawton has raised money to support the institution, and has at various points fed, clothed, housed, employed, and even cheered for the students of Cameron. And so, any effort to tell the history of Cameron is by extension a history of the southwest Oklahoma community that made its

In November of 1981 Richard Brawley won a campus-sponsored contest to design a new logo for Cameron University. The logo was adopted as the official university seal at that time. *Photograph by Jim Horinek.*

very existence possible. In many ways, the story of Cameron is a story of the United States. Cameron students have served in every war and conflict the United States has been involved in from World War I to the War on Terror. The Cameron community experienced first hand the pangs of the Great Depression during the 1930s as well as the national shock following the terrorist attacks against the United States in 2002.

Unfortunately, it is simply not feasible to include every aspect of Cameron's history or to know, much less discuss, every student's personal experience. To be sure, there are many omissions in the pages that follow but there is, nevertheless, an attempt to tell a history of Cameron, one that is reflective and representative, if not exhaustive. When all is said and done, what matters most, it seems, is what Cameron has meant to the thousands of students it has educated. In attempting to articulate both the intent and the short-comings of what follows, there seem no better words than

those chosen by the Cameron students who took it upon themselves to write the first volume of their yearbook, the *Wichita*. "If in times of hardship and disappointment, you can sit down and find something in this book that brightens your way," explained members of the Class of 1914 "then our efforts have been worth while." They also added that "If you find things in the book that you do not like, remember that we can never have things quite as we should like them," and that "there are things in the book that we, ourselves, do not like." [2]

The six chapters that follow chart the growth and development of Cameron from its agricultural high school days to those of a four-year institution with particular attention to the experiences of students and to the challenges that Cameron has faced. Each chapter also includes an essay written by a Cameron history major about some aspect of Cameron history because, after all, without the students who choose to come to Cameron, there would be no history to write.

Cameron grew considerably during its first few decades of existence and many of the early buildings on campus were built with student labor and financed by the Lawton community whose efforts helped secure the school's location two miles west of the city. *Courtesy Cameron University Archives.*

CHAPTER ONE

"DEAR OLD CAMERON"[1]

Here's to Old Cameron:
To our dear old School, we'll say
We'll be true every day,
Cameron, we love you—
We're loyal; we'll cheer you.
We'll give a song to cheer
Every loyal heart that's here,
For they know, friend or foe,
We are loyal to you old School.[2]

"The farmer is busy and prosperity is before him and everything looks good" boasted a *Lawton News Republican* article in September of 1904 in celebration of Lawton's third birthday.[3] As the city grew, so too did the optimism about the future of southwest Oklahoma. One local reporter summed up the promise of the county seat, writing "the man who is looking for a good place to permanently locate cannot afford to overlook Lawton."[4] Just a few years later, on November 16, 1907, Oklahoma became the forty-sixth state in the union, and six months after that, the legislature moved to address the educational needs of Oklahoma's rural farm communities. Senate Bill 109 provided "for the establishment and maintenance of Agricultural schools of secondary grade in each supreme court district."[5] Passage of this bill on May 20, 1908 laid the foundation for The Cameron State School of Agriculture to become one of six state high schools charged with the responsibility of educating farm children as well as offering "short courses" to area farmers. Despite the growth of Lawton and the numerous farm families living in relative proximity to it, local citizens worked hard to ensure that they would actually get the school. Lawton business leaders formed a committee and raised money to buy the land necessary to secure Cameron's location two miles west of the city.[6]

Named after Evan Dhu Cameron, the first state superintendent of public instruction in Oklahoma, The Cameron State School of Agriculture held its first classes on November 16, 1909, on the second anniversary of Oklahoma's statehood, in the basement of First National Bank in downtown Lawton. These temporary quarters housed the school until 1911. One estimate placed attendance on that first day of class at a total of 14 boys and girls, but later estimates indicated that first year enrollment increased from 28 to 110.[7] J.A. Liner, an educator from Alabama, came to Lawton as Cameron's first president.[8] Four other faculty members joined him in welcoming the first class of Cameron students.[9] According to alumnus Hugh Corwin, students were not categorized by class until 1910 and even then there were only three high school grades and two preparatory grades.[10]

Enrollment numbers during the first few years proved erratic with students coming and going and with a number of people from the community taking short courses or even enrolling in regular classes to help boost the head count. Indeed, from the time the state legislature passed Senate Bill 109, the citizens of Lawton took it upon themselves to look out for the future of the school. This turned out to be no small task. Nearly every year that Cameron existed as a high school, legislation

In 1901 the "city" of Lawton mostly consisted of tents and hastily constructed makeshift buildings. *Courtesy Hugh Corwin Collection, Cameron University Archives.*

Evan Dhu Cameron was the first state superintendent of public instruction and is the school's namesake. *Courtesy Cameron University Archives.*

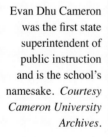

was either introduced or rumored to be introduced which would have abolished the institution altogether. Yet, the community continued to rally around the school, and Cameron faculty, staff, and students reciprocated.

In its first year of existence Cameron established the practice of inviting members of the community to the school for receptions and

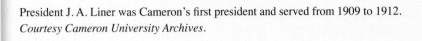

President J. A. Liner was Cameron's first president and served from 1909 to 1912. *Courtesy Cameron University Archives.*

The laying of the foundation for Cameron's first building began in 1910 and was completed in March of 1911. *Courtesy Cameron University Archives.*

entertainment. This tradition later evolved into "Cameron Day," which school officials sporadically celebrated over the next several decades. Apparently some of Lawton's "best citizens" turned out for Cameron's first informal community reception during which Evan Dhu Cameron spoke and Cameron students entertained the crowd with such evocative tunes as "Battle Hymn of the Republic" and "Gypsy Maiden." The subheading in a local paper summed up the successful event for which more than 250 people were in attendance: "Assembly Room Packed—Cameron Speaks—Refreshments Served—Big Time."[11]

While construction of Cameron's first building moved forward, the fall semester of Cameron's second year again opened in the basement of the First National Bank building. Paul F. Orr, who started at Cameron in 1909 and was among the first four graduates of the school in 1912, recalled President Liner telling the students that they had the "distinction of being the first Agricultural school to carry on its operations under ground."[12] The students nevertheless looked forward to occupying their "own beautiful building" while lamenting that their "work the second year was

hard," something future generations of Cameron students continued to echo.[13] Enrollment increased alongside enthusiasm about the school's future. According to President Liner, enrollment increased by one-third during Cameron's second year.[14] In February of 1911 he told a local reporter that Cameron had never had "as bright and enthusiastic [a] crowd of boys and girls" as they had that spring semester.[15] The following month Cameron students moved to their new location. The auditorium of the newly-constructed main building "was crowded with interested listeners, including a large number of Lawton folks," at the official opening ceremony.[16] In what quickly became customary at Cameron, President Liner conducted students as they entertained the crowd with various "musical numbers."[17]

The musical entertainment provided by Cameron students not only became a staple of Cameron public relations, it also reflected the larger pedagogical philosophy of the institution. All students were required to take music. In fact, in January of 1912 Cameron purchased a snare drum for $8.00 and a tuba for $30.00, an amount equal to that spent on feed for cows during the same month.[18] And while vocational and technical training remained the central focus of the school for decades to come, students could expect to receive a solid foundation in such staples as English, history, civics, and mathematics, which were required components of study. According to school officials, Cameron offered "a useful and practical education to the boys and girls of farms, villages, and towns in the Fourth Supreme Court Judicial District" that either lacked the time, money, or educational background to "pursue a regular collegiate course of study."[19] The school also emphasized physical fitness and strong moral conduct. All students were required to undertake "individual work in physical culture" and Cameron sought to "foster all kinds of clean manly and womanly games," which were, of course, "careful-

ly supervised and controlled by the faculty."[20] In advertising Cameron to the public, school officials repeatedly emphasized that students were "surrounded by all proper moral influences." Indeed, school literature indicated that Lawton—with a population of only 9,000 in 1911—had "fifteen churches representing all the denominations."[21]

With parents and local townspeople assured that the youth of southwest Oklahoma would receive a sound education that developed their character, spirituality, moral integrity, and practical

Students who attended a Cameron Short Course posing in front of the first girls' dormitory which was built 1912. *Courtesy Turner Alumni Collection, Cameron University Archives.*

Arda Frans was an instructor at Cameron for a number of years. She taught math as well as English. *Courtesy 1914 Wichita, Cameron University Archives.*

Students in a dairy science class, circa 1920s.
Courtesy Cameron University Archives.

knowledge, the school attracted a growing number of pupils. As important as the literary societies and student associations became to campus life, the minimal expense no doubt influenced the decision of families to send their children to Cameron. In 1911, Oklahoma residents who attended Cameron paid a one-time entrance fee of $1.50 in comparison to out-of-state students who paid $2.50 per month in fees.[22] Prior to the completion of the first dormitories, students—especially female students—boarded with local families, and both male and female students found work to help support themselves.

Students at Cameron took many of the same basic academic courses but the technical training differed for male and female students. Boys took classes in such areas as road making, farm dairying and crops, agricultural botany and physics, soils and fertilizers, carpentry, blacksmithing, and farm machinery. Female students, on the other

hand, learned hygiene, cooking, domestic chemistry, social culture, home nursing, laundering, sewing, and even a particularly specialized course in "invalid cookery."[23]

By the time Cameron entered into its third year of existence, the school already had drawn national attention. As part of its 160-acre farm, which included vegetable gardens, hogs, poultry, and cows, the school operated its own dairy. According to an article in *The Oklahoman*, Cameron could not keep up with the national demand for its butter. Beneath the promising subheading "New Yorkers Scramble for Dairy Product of Lawton School," appeared a plea from President Liner to update the school's dairy plant because it already had outgrown itself.[24] The article pointed out that Cameron had successfully combined student learning with profit making—something that has long since appealed to state policy makers—and added that President Liner did not "want

President Ralph K. Robertson was the second president of Cameron. He replaced Present J. A. Liner and served from 1912 to 1913. *Courtesy Cameron University Archives.*

ABOVE: Minnie Cook, Homer Turner, Ruth Teague, and Paul Orr were the first four students to graduate from The Cameron State School of Agriculture in 1912. *Courtesy Cameron University Archives.*

to disappoint those New York society matrons."[25] The implications of Cameron's emphasis on the value of a practical education did indeed extend beyond the counties of southwest Oklahoma.

The same year, Cameron's butter received national accolades and Minnie Cook, Homer Turner and Ruth Teague joined Paul Orr as the first four graduates of The Cameron State School of Agriculture. President Liner congratulated this first class for their "splendid record" and indicated that he had "high regard and personal esteem" for each of them. Liner further praised the graduates, assuring them of his belief that they would go on to be "an honor to our school, an honor to our country, and an honor to God."[26] The students themselves recognized their distinction as the first graduating class and concluded their class history with the following admonition: "Let all who follow us dig and delve and strive to surpass the class of '12."

While Liner had once expressed great opti-

mism about the future of Cameron and clearly felt proud of its first graduating class, he resigned his post shortly after their graduation. According to a local paper, Liner had grown increasingly discouraged over the lack of funding to build dormitories. The paper cited Governor Lee Cruce's policy of refusing "approval of such appropriations" as a "decided handicap to the progress" of Cameron and the cause of Liner's resignation, which took effect on June 30, 1912.[27]

Ralph K. Robertson, described as "a young man, probably 27 years of age," became Cameron's second president.[28] Prior to coming to Cameron, Robertson taught at the Haskell School of Agriculture in Broken Arrow, Oklahoma. Printing and distributing 3,000 catalogues marked his first order of business as he sought to ensure that "every effort...be put forth to enlarge the attendance at the school" in the upcoming year.[29] In addition, some "3,000 feet of motion picture films" were used to recruit prospective students.[30] Yet, just as Robertson prepared to assume control of the school, a petition circulated in an effort to close Cameron along with several other state schools. This particular push to abolish the schools failed when the Secretary of State determined that many of the names on the petition were fraudulent—some of them appearing two or more times.[31] This incident nevertheless underscored the precarious status of educational institutions in Oklahoma.

That very summer Lawton citizens again rallied around Cameron to protect the school's future. The Chamber of Commerce accepted a proposal by the State Board of Agriculture in which the chamber agreed to raise $5,000 to build a girls' dormitory in exchange for the state providing equipment for the new building and helping recruit more students.[32] As the plan moved forward a renewed sense of optimism took hold. A local paper declared "Dormitory Is Practically Assured Now," and it estimated that construction would likely start soon.[33] While construction eventually got underway, school officials postponed the opening of the 1912 fall semester until September 14th because the dorm had not yet been completed. A further complication arose when President Robertson became ill, leaving J. S. Murray to serve as interim head of the school.[34]

As Cameron students prepared for the late opening of their school, their enthusiasm reportedly remained intact. The much anticipated girls' dormitory offered little advantage to the boys and yet one article described "Farm boys from all over the county" as "taking kindly to the plan for housing them in tents."[35] When the first day of classes got underway, enrollment at Cameron doubled over its first day enrollment from the previous year to a total of 50 students. The girls' dormitory did not open, however, for another month which meant that a number of female students took up temporary quarters in private homes.[36] By the time the girls' dormitory opened in the third week

of October, enrollment had increased to 75, which included 30 girls in the dormitories and 25 boys in tents. Despite the comparatively posh living quarters of the female students, both boys and girls paid $2.50 a week for their room and board.[37] Not surprisingly, the enthusiasm for tents waned when a blizzard hit in January of 1913, forcing the boys to flee to unoccupied rooms on the top floor of the girls' dormitory.[38] When members of the State Board of Agriculture, who acted as the governing board for the school until the 1940s, visited the campus, they praised the growth of the school.

President Robert P. Short became Cameron's fourth president when he replaced President E. M. Frost, who had served from the summer of 1913 until January of 1914. Like Frost, Short only stayed in office briefly, serving from January to December of 1914. *Courtesy Cameron University Archives.*

However, as one article summed it up: the board "seemed pleased with [Cameron's] growth but uncommunicative on possible appropriations;" an observation that would be repeated many times in the school's history.[39]

Concern over appropriations and even outright abolition of the institution continued to cast a shadow over the school's growth. In January of 1913 Cameron again faced the threat of being closed with the introduction of a new bill in the Oklahoma House of Representatives which called for the abolition of the state agricultural secondary schools along with the state school for the blind.[40] The following month the bill won support from the committee on agriculture, although the governor approved appropriations for the schools and the matter subsided.[41] Despite these threats, the students set out to establish new clubs and campus government. Students organized a House and Senate with a system of checks and balances which gave faculty the power to accept or reject

President A.C. Farley was the fifth president of Cameron and replaced President Robert P. Short. He served from 1914 until 1920. *Courtesy Cameron University Archives.*

the measures proposed by students.[42] As the school year came to an end, Cameron bid farewell to the seven graduating members of the class of 1913.[43]

The start of another summer brought more change and Cameron prepared for the arrival of a new president. Robertson resigned to attend law school at Washington and Lee University in Virginia and E. M. Frost became Cameron's third president in its short history. Frost came from Stillwater with experience as the superintendent of Dewey County and head of the Tryon, Oklahoma schools.[44] Yet Robert P. Short replaced Frost shortly thereafter in January of 1914.[45] The *Lawton Constitution* described the twenty-seven-year-old

Short—who already had been teaching agriculture at Cameron—as "one of the best qualified men in the state for the position."[46] Nevertheless, Cameron again received a new president when Short resigned in December of 1914.[47] Short explained his resignation to the State Board of Agriculture saying that he had "private business" that required his "whole time and attention." The board acted quickly, voting at that same meeting to elect A. C. Farley as president at a rate of $1,800.00 per year.[48]

Despite the consistent upheaval of the administration as Cameron's leadership changed five times in a four- year period, the school reached a new level of maturity during the 1913-1914 academic year. Two new literary societies, the Delphic Oracles and the Literati were formed. Students published the first edition of the *Wichita*, Cameron's yearbook, and the *Lawton Constitution* applauded their achievement, saying that it showed "much work and plenty of ability."[49] The yearbook described the "once barren spot where Cameron State School now stands," adding that the "members of the class of 1914 take great pride in naming this volume for the spot no man can hide."[50] Dedicated to their fathers and mothers for making it possible for them to remain in school, the pages of the *Wichita* offer a rich portrait of the lives of these early Cameron students.

Physical fitness and sports remained a staple at Cameron. Students had participated in track and basketball since Cameron first opened in 1909. The school added football in 1912 and by 1914 students boasted of a baseball team "that can't be beaten by anything less than professionals."[51] Involvement in sports for girls proved sporadic but they often played basketball and apparently were "well represented" in the sport.[52] Both boys' and girls' basketball were played outdoors as Cameron had no gym until 1924. Indeed, much of the sports culture at Cameron during its high school years hinged on playing whatever games came their way. The football team often played Lawton

ABOVE: Historically, Cameron has emphasized the centrality of physical fitness to the overall development and well-being of both male and female students and, in fact, still requires physical education courses as part of general education. Female students exercising outside, circa 1920s, provide just one example of this commitment. *Courtesy Sally Soelle Collection, Cameron University Archives.*

Hugh Corwin graduated from Cameron in 1913 and later returned to Cameron as an instructor and band director. He also wrote the first history of Cameron State School of Agriculture. *Courtesy 1923* Wichita, *Cameron University Archives.*

High and even Fort Sill teams, and intramural games of football and basketball became commonplace.

As the school grew, the State Board of Agriculture decided to add a fourth year of studies to the school. Up until the fall of 1914, there were only three high school grades—freshmen, juniors, and seniors. According to Hugh Corwin, himself a 1913 graduate, "vigorous efforts were made to induce the 1912, 1913, and 1914 graduates to return to Cameron for an additional year." He concluded that this "was not very successful."[53] While students may not have been receptive to an added grade, they certainly expressed a nostalgic persistence in completing the original three.

The boys finally got their own dormitory in 1915, although they built it themselves.[54] Despite such apparent progress, administrative problems continued to plague the school. In November of 1915, the *Lawton News* cited a "lack of harmony" at Cameron, as roughly half the faculty and student body went on strike in protest of President Farley's decision to fire O.C. Whipple, the manager of Cameron's creamery, over "differences regarding accounts of the creamery."[55] The paper also indicated that even prior to Whipple's dismissal, the "relations between President Farley and a number of members of the faculty were not congenial."[56] The matter seems to have passed relatively quickly as students and faculty returned to class. Just a few months later J. J. Savage, a member of the State Board of Agriculture, inspected Cameron and concluded that "the best cooperation exists between the entire faculty and the student body." Aside from a lame buggy horse and the need for repairs to the boys' and girls' dormitories, he described everything as being "in splendid order."[57]

Enrollment and campus activities grew and Cameron students expressed pride in their accomplishments while poking fun at themselves and others. Lulu Gray, a 1915 graduate, described herself and her fellow freshmen when they arrived at Cameron in 1912 as "twenty-five specimens of unrefined humanity who were 'fresh from the farm.'"[58] By the time Lulu and her classmates

graduated, their own assessment of one another appeared beneath their photographs in the *Wichita*. Lulu, it seems, was "overflowing with good humor" and would apparently "torment a wooden man." Her hobbies included such things as "creating jealously." Edith Nickell, "one of the fairest Senior girls," possessed "a smile that will win her a home." William Beaver had the distinction of not acting or looking "like any one else." Some of their classmates like Lewis Dennie had "a good appreciation of responsibilities," while others like Benjamin Harrison, had the hobby of "stall-

Lulu M. Gray graduated from Cameron in 1915 and played a very active role on campus. *Courtesy 1914* Wichita, *Cameron University Archives.*

Cameron eventually had a number of barns on the main campus, and in the early years the barns functioned as an extension of the classroom where students learned a variety of both formal and informal lessons. *Courtesy 1914* Wichita, *Cameron University Archives.*

Food remained at the center of campus life for several decades and as such the cafeteria workers, the "Kitchen Mechanics," played a vital and sometimes coveted role. *Courtesy 1918* Wichita, *Cameron University Archives.*

ing," which was perhaps not as bad as Sherman Krisher's dubious hobby of "seeking favor with the faculty." [59] Such descriptions reveal much about the class of 1915, and indeed many more classes to come. In an era that predated television and the proliferation of individual telephones, the small isolated campus flourished with a rich student-led, albeit faculty approved, social and cultural life.

Food constituted a central aspect of student life at Cameron; it brought students together for socializing and remained a strong selling point for decades to come. In 1915 an average meal cost only 11.4 cents and the campus menu committee employed frugality to ensure that students could purchase "good wholesome meals" at a low cost. [60] And with the emphasis on cheap but tasty meals and a practical education, Cameron attracted even more students the following year. The *Lawton News* indicated that school officials expected a record high in enrollment and described Cameron as "one of the best secondary schools in the state," adding that the instructors were all "well fitted for the work in their various departments." [61]

Life at Cameron, however, grew more complicated when the United States entered the First World War in April of 1917. While much of Europe had erupted in war following the assassination of Archduke Franz Ferdinand of Austria on June 28, 1914, United States President Woodrow Wilson pledged to maintain American neutrality. For a variety of reasons—not least of which was Germany's use of unrestricted submarine warfare against American ships—the day came when Cameron students joined other young people from across the country and indeed the world in definitively leaving behind their youthful school days. The 1917 edition of the *Wichita* included a message from President Wilson in which he admonished farmers of the "supreme need" among the allied countries for "an abundance of supplies and especially foodstuffs." The president said that farmers could "show their patriotism in no better or more convincing way…than helping to feed the nation and peoples fighting for [their] liberty and our own." [62]

While Americans did not endure the same degree of food shortages and rationing that their

While Cameron's overall enrollment continued to increase, World War I led to a decrease in the male to female ratio as evidenced by the 1919 graduating class of Cameron. *Courtesy 1919* Wichita, *Cameron University Archives.*

allies did, students at Cameron nonetheless felt the pangs of war deprivation. The cafeteria staff, who called themselves the "Kitchen Mechanics," regaled readers of the 1918 *Wichita* with the challenges of wartime cooking:

> *We rise early in the morning,*
> *We go late to bed.*
> *It takes all the time we have*
> *To get the aggies fed.*
>
> *Uncle Sam is after us*
> *To keep the meatless day.*
> *If it were not for Kaiser Bill*
> *We might make it pay.*
>
> *So the best way we can see*
> *To get the ornary cuss*
> *Is to go and join the army*
> *And let Uncle Sam feed us.*[63]

On a more sober note, editors of the 1918 *Wichita* dedicated that year's annual to "Our Soldier Boys, Once Students of Cameron," adding "Be they here or 'over there' Cameron students reserve a sacred place for them in the still, deep chambers of the heart." The dedication included a list of 39 Cameron students who were in the armed forces.[64]

The war "to end all wars" raged on but enrollment at Cameron continued to increase as classes resumed in the fall of 1919. The school could only "comfortably handle about 125" students and President Farley estimated that more than 50 students were turned away. He added that with adequate facilities, enrollment might well have reached between 300 to 500 students.[65] President Farley attributed this increase directly to the lessons learned in the war, saying that "men in the army found out that it required certain training or education to make advances." He also indicated that young women learned a similar lesson in that if they had the necessary "training and education," they could enter into such fields as civil service and social service work.[66]

At the eleventh hour of the eleventh day of the eleventh month of 1919, the allied and central powers reached an armistice, followed by the Treaty of Versailles which brought the war to an end. The allied victory ensured a dramatic reshaping of Europe with consequences not fully realized until World War II. For Americans, the end of World War I ushered in an intense period of Isolationism and a renewed desire to stay clear of foreign entanglements while focusing on domestic prosperity. As young people in southwest Oklahoma and across the country turned to educational pursuits to achieve their goals, Cameron's emphasis on a practical education held much promise. The 1920 edition of the *Wichita* was again dedicated to "The Boys from Cameron who took part in the World War," while the student body looked for ways to rekindle the more carefree pursuits of youth. That same edition of the *Wichita* contained the usual reminiscences about student clubs and athletic accomplishments. It also gave particular attention to the theft of the campus truck. A poem entitled "The Cameron Truck," detailed how "some of Cameron's bravest boys" took the truck "right out from under Mr. Farley's nose" and believed their feat had gone undetected until the president woke them from their beds after which point the truck "was never seen."[67]

The lighthearted story of the Cameron truck, however, took a backseat to more serious allegations of student misdeeds as female students made loud protestations against false charges of immorality. According to *The Oklahoman*, the governor considered closing Cameron because of "complaints against the management" made by students and some faculty. The "central complaint" cen-

tered on "a number of slanderous remarks" which were made about Cameron's female students. Augusta Shepler, the matron of the girls' dormitory, resigned because of the criticism that she "expelled a half-dozen or more girls each year for several years," causing "unjust suspicions against them."[68] This amounted to an average of more than one-fifth of female Cameron students facing expulsion on an annual basis. The article included ominous predictions that "the whole

President A. E. Wickizer was the sixth president of Cameron. He replaced President A. C. Farley in 1920 and served until 1923. *Courtesy Cameron University Archives.*

staff [at Cameron] may be removed."[69] While that did not happen, five of the nine faculty members, including the president, were replaced by the start of the 1920 fall semester.[70] According to Hugh Corwin, President Farley's decision to resign from Cameron "was not made public until after the 1920 school year closed." Corwin cited Cameron's failure to grow "as anticipated" and said that it "became clear that a change of administration was needed."[71] Whether it was political pressure over Shepler's conduct or the growth rate of Cameron that was to blame, A. E. Wickizer replaced Farley as the president of Cameron.

Wickizer came to Cameron with an agenda which included expanding teacher education offerings and producing "as much food as possible on the school farm" as a way to "lower food costs for boarding students."[72] He also made a notable

A Practical Education in Context: The Cameron-Tuskegee Comparison

by Joyce Turner
History Major • Class of 2010

The concept of agricultural schools began long before the founding of Cameron. In 1860 the People's College in upstate New York opened its doors. Education in agriculture, mechanics, and industrial arts for both sexes set the foundation for the college. Although the college closed within its first year due to poor funding and the impending conflict of the Civil War, the new and revolutionary idea of a practical public education took hold. This concept of a practical education continued to gain ground and two years after the opening of the People's College, Congress passed the Morrill Act of 1862, also known as the Land-Grant Act. The Morrill Act took the previously simple question of public education, which had been under the purview of individual states, and created an unprecedented degree of access to higher education for the common person. Although Cameron began as a secondary school it still followed the same foundation set for the Land-Grant colleges. The desire for a more utilitarian education continued to grow through out the late nineteenth and early twentieth century as students sought access to an education that would take them beyond the classroom and into the evolving industrial society.

One such school was the Tuskegee Institute, founded in Alabama in 1881 by Booker T. Washington as a vocational school for African Americans. Nearly 30 years before Cameron offered its first classes, Tuskegee provided a utilitarian education to its students in the business trades as well as in agriculture. When Washington found his school in need of a new brick building, but without the funds to purchase bricks, he decided that Tuskegee students could learn to make their own bricks and in doing so students acquired a practical skill that would benefit them beyond a scholastic education. Not only did these bricks provide the needed materials for the new buildings, but soon the Tuskegee Institute began selling their bricks to customers outside of the school thereby creating a source of revenue, just as Cameron

students did by operating their own dairy. In fact, Tuskegee students gained much of their education through the same methods as those later utilized by Cameron students. They built many of their own buildings, learned self-discipline, self-reliance, and dedication while benefitting directly from the fruits of their labor. Male students at Cameron, for example, assisted in the erecting of new buildings such as tool sheds and hen houses on the school farm.

While this vocational school for African Americans did not intentionally serve as a model for the agricultural schools later established in Oklahoma, a comparison nevertheless reveals important similarities; a practical education helped both groups of students overcome poverty by providing them skills to get ahead in an increasingly industrialized society and economy. Like Booker T. Washington's Tuskegee Institute, Cameron desired to offer a practical education that afforded its students greater opportunities. There are other similarities between these two schools as well, including the fact that they began in rather primitive accommodations until something better could be built or secured; Cameron started in the basement of a bank building and Tuskegee began holding classes in an old hen house. When these schools discovered themselves in need of buildings they used the need as a learning opportunity to further their students' education by using their labor to erect the needed structures while teaching them architecture, engineering, and carpentry through practical application.

For young women, the 1914 Smith-Lever Extension Act linked home economics to agriculture, and provided an important educational foundation for training female students. The following year, home-economics became a staple in the public education system. Cameron's Domestic Economy class appears to have fulfilled the government requirement to offer instruction in home-economics and included emphasis on three basic needs: food, shelter, and clothing. The collection of classes that fell under Domestic Economy, also referred to as Domestic Science, offered a wide variety of educational opportunities. The most basic class being simple cooking, which was taught as though it were an experiment, allowed the student to learn through practical application how to cook something as basic as an egg to how to prepare food for an invalid or the ill. Students received further teaching and training in society manners, sewing, and household management, as well as some minor education in human physiology in the form of "domestic chemistry" in which the student gained knowledge in how the body digested and used food.

Cameron's early years as an agricultural school offered the students a substantial variety of classes in practical education as well as academic areas. The early Cameron students overcame many obstacles that eventually allowed the secondary school to evolve into the university it is today. In its first 13 years, the only access to Cameron from Lawton was a dirt road which was virtually impassable at times, yet the students continued to trudge on. By providing students an agricultural, mechanical, and domestic education, in addition to both academic and social clubs and activities, Cameron's student body continued to grow and flourish. Cameron's early start as a secondary school for agriculture and the students it attracted is what allowed it to grow and prosper. Without the foundation of the student body, the agricultural and practical education offered to the students, and support the community offered, it is very likely that Cameron would not have continued and subsequently became the university that students from all over the world now enjoy.

RIGHT: Manual Training was an important part of the curriculum at Cameron and gave male students an opportunity to learn in a "hands-on" environment. *Courtesy 1927 Wichita, Cameron University Archives.*

LEFT: The Blacksmithing classes offered at Cameron illustrate the emphasis on providing students with practical skills that would serve them well upon their return to the family farm. *Courtesy 1923 Wichita, Cameron University Archives.*

alteration in living arrangements. Prior to his administration, it had become customary for the president and his family to take up residence in the girls' dormitory. As the shortage of dormitory space became a significant obstacle to the school's growth, President Wickizer decided to rent a nearby home and urged other faculty to do the same.[73] Wickizer worked to carry out his vision for Cameron's growth and even collected 5,000 signatures on a petition that called for additional buildings on campus but, as Corwin recalled, the petition to the legislature failed to yield the necessary construction funds. Corwin attributed this failure to growing political opposition to the agriculture schools, a problem regularly revisited at Cameron during the high school years.[74] Despite the economic challenge of expanding a school

without adequate funding, Wickizer continued to promote the interests of the school. Hugh Corwin joined the faculty at Cameron in 1921 to teach band, which had not been offered since 1916.

And so Wickizer's administration resembled that of many other Cameron presidents; his time in the office was short—only three years—and he faced the seemingly insurmountable problem of inadequate funding coupled with the looming

President John G. March was the seventh president of Cameron. He replaced President A. E. Wickizer and served from 1923 until 1927. *Courtesy Cameron University Archives.*

The first girls' dormitory was built in 1912 and for a number of years it was customary for the president's family to also reside there. Cameron's female students who lived on campus were kept under very strict supervision by the president, faculty, and the dormitory matron. *Courtesy 1914* Wichita, *Cameron University Archives.*

threat of all out closure. Ironically, the persistent problems facing the school seemed out of step with the consistent praise it received from the State Board of Agriculture. When J. J. Savage, a member of the board, visited Cameron to inspect the school in 1922, he said, "I have not one word of criticism of the school to offer." He recognized that some buildings were "badly in need of repair," but called on the citizens of Lawton to meet this need "until aid can be secured from the legislature." [75] Wickizer tried to remain optimistic about the future of the school, saying "conditions are improving," and the *Lawton Constitution* cited a "deep seated interest in rural education problems" as farmers realized that "they have been getting the crumbs instead of the whole loaves in the state provision for their education." [76] As 1922 came to a close, the *Lawton Constitution* again pronounced that Cameron was making "remarkable progress" and indicated that "It has finally become clear to the rural people that this is their school." [77]

The rural students who attended Cameron certainly understood and took great pride in that fact. President Wickizer reminded students that during the 1922-1923 school year they needed to undertake "a little real MISSIONARY WORK" and spread the word about Cameron. He added that "There are hundreds of boys and girls who are now being deprived of the privilege of a good school." He further admonished students that "each one endeavor to make himself the very best man or woman possible," and to help others "to do the same." [78] Paul Bowman, a 1924 graduate of Cameron, recalled that "Wickizer was very strict," but he added this was necessary because of previous problems at the school. Bowman, like most Cameron students, worked his way through school. He eventually was put in charge of the campus dairy, which meant that he had to get up at 4:30 in the morning. One of his duties included delivering milk to the basement of the girls' dormi-

tory which housed the dining room. In recalling this, laughing, he said that this was the closest he ever got to the girls' dormitory. [79] Some 50 years after Bowman graduated from Cameron, students and administrators still haggled over dormitory visitation, but in Bowman's day, students of the opposite sex were strictly forbidden from entering into even the common areas. Vivian Hay Buckwell, who also attended Cameron in the mid 1920s, remembered boys being allowed to walk girls to the door of the dormitory where they were always met by the dormitory matron and promptly sent on their way. [80]

Cameron students regularly attended chapel and had a number of religious-based organizations, like the Hi Y, which promoted Christian values and high moral standards. In 1923 students formed the Demetrian Club, whose membership included all female students at Cameron. This club sought to promote "those social graces so desirable in the education of young women." The Demetrians stood for "high ideals, pure living, sane social habits" as well as "recreation, restful diversion, and wholesome fun." [81] Cameron girls regularly threw parties for their male classmates, including Halloween, St. Patrick's Day festivities, and the occasional banquet.

Campus life thrived as Cameron's enrollment continued to increase. Hugh Corwin attributed this to President Wickizer's "very active student recruitment program" which resulted in "the three largest" graduating classes in 1923, 1924, and 1925. [82] However, in 1923, John G. March replaced Wickizer. Corwin blamed this administrative change on "political upheaval of heads of state education institutions," and indeed, Oklahoma A & M, later Oklahoma State University, went through four presidents in the summer of 1923 alone. When March came to Cameron, he sought to improve the infrastructure of the growing school. Finally, in 1924, his administration "found seventeen hundred dollars surplus from a

Cameron students and employees working on the school's first gymnasium. The use of male student labor to construct new buildings was common during the school's early history. *Courtesy 1925* Wichita, *Cameron University Archives.*

building fund" and began construction on a 60-by-72-foot gymnasium with "volunteer" student labor from manual training classes.[83] The following year President March and Hugh Corwin, then teaching manual training at the school, oversaw the historic graveling of the often muddy road that connected Cameron to Lawton. According to Corwin, "all boys in the school were excused from afternoon classes for a period of two weeks" so they could build the road which ran west from 11th Street and F Avenue to Sheridan and then northwest on E Avenue until it hit 28th Street and then another two blocks north to Cameron's campus.[84]   Cameron English teacher W. E. Armstrong praised President March for these improvements, as well as for overseeing the construction of a new brick dormitory for female students. Armstrong described March as "a splendid man for whom to work" whose "ability to get along with his patrons is unsurpassed" and he further characterized the president as "a Christian gentleman of high social standards."[85]

With a gymnasium, new women's dormitory, and a gravel road, social life at Cameron reached

new levels by the mid 1920s. A large number of students lived on campus and, under close faculty supervision, organizations and clubs served to enhance the school's emphasis on "practical education," which in many ways translated into upholding the ideal social order. All Cameron students were expected to leave the school as well-rounded individuals. In the same way that all female students were required to join the Demetrians, all male students were required to take part in debate. The boys were divided into five debate teams and, as Harry Hammond summed it up, "Some didn't say much and some didn't like it much, but they all had to do it regardless."[86] While many of the students would go on to be farmers, or farmer's wives, as several female alumni were identified, the basic assumption of education centered on a belief in the value of eloquent expression and a traditional liberal arts education in addition to applied vocational and technical skills. For young women, this hinged on an understanding that girls who went to Cameron would go on to fill the all important role of wife and mother. "Who wants a woman that can't sew a button on a shirt, darn a sock, or wash a baby's face" asked an essay in the *Wichita*. The response was "No intelligent young man; hence Domestic Art."[87] Cameron's role in educating the "modern housewife" was summed up with this 1925 poem:

> If you want a wife to cook and sew,
> Or wash and tend the baby.
> Old Cameron is the place to go.
> They're there, I don't mean maybe.[88]

Courses in domestic science provided the knowledge that "each American woman should know to meet the requirements of domestic, social, and business life," explained a piece in the *Wichita*.[89] By the mid 1920s, technological advances had transformed many aspects of American life, including notions about traditional gender roles. Concerns surfaced that the increased

freedom brought by the automobile and modern conveniences like the vacuum cleaner and washing machine would undermine the role of American housewives by leaving them with too much time on their hands. In fact, such advances only increased the duties of housewives as women became responsible for running errands and a higher standard of cleanliness. At Cameron, the emphasis on a more traditional place for women served to counter such social anxiety. One quip in the *Wichita* portrayed an exchange between a husband and wife in which the wife told her husband that they would have to go out for dinner because she had broken the can opener. Proper domestic training at Cameron, it seems, promised to produce a different kind of housewife, one that could ably compete in a pumpkin pie cooking contest—an event which was "looked forward to

Students in a Domestic Art class in which they learned how to sew and other such skills required of housewives during the 1920s. *Courtesy 1927* Wichita, *Cameron University Archives.*

with anticipation by the boys."[90]

The quest to produce future citizens of southwest Oklahoma who possessed good citizenship and applied knowledge meant that in addition to sports, debate, and Christian fellowship, Cameron boys spent considerable time honing their farm and manual training skills. The Cameron farm served many practical functions. The students expressed pride in their "good self-supporting farm," saying they felt "fortunate indeed in being able to put into actual practice the things" they learned in the classroom.[91] The farm included not only a dairy, which among other things supplied the 170-member boarding club with milk, but a fruit orchard, vineyard, hogs, mares, and turkeys.[92] In addition to farm work, the manual training department tried to provide courses of "practical value to the students," in blacksmithing, carpentry, and drawing. The course of study at Cameron had

expanded to include more classes by this time but the fundamental emphasis remained the same: providing a practical education for the farm boys and girls of southwest Oklahoma.

That Cameron State School of Agriculture offered a "practical education" is not surprising as this fulfilled the intent laid out in the legislation which created it and other institutions like it. What seems remarkable, however, is how prolific these high school students were. Year after year, the pages of the *Wichita* are filled with poems, class prophecies, and histories, not to mention the fact that by 1925 the two literature clubs—the Delphic Oracles and the Literati—were engaged in fierce competition with one another. And so while girls cultivated their domestic skills and boys prepared for their future agricultural and mechanical careers or looked forward to furthering their studies in higher education, they did so within the con-

Cameron's band enjoyed considerable success during the 1920s after Hugh Corwin reorganized it. The band participated in two notable trips to Oklahoma City. *Courtesy 1923* Wichita, *Cameron University Archives.*

From Cameron's earliest days, students regularly put on plays for their classmates and members of the community. Cast members from a production of "The Texas Rangers." *Courtesy 1923 Wichita, Cameron University Archives.*

text—and indeed climate—of a classical liberal arts education. The time spent at Cameron marked a pivotal point in their young lives just as their presence at Cameron shaped the early character of the school. "We just really got our foundation at Cameron," explained Alice Fullerton Watson who graduated in 1928. She added that Cameron "was our home away from home."[93]

While the administration and students emphasized the commitment to high moral and personal standards, Cameron students nevertheless seized upon opportunities for pranks. Les Faulkner, a 1926 graduate, participated fully in the activities offered at Cameron. He played football and was in the band and despite "being scared" of President Wickizer, fondly recalled the "trouble" he and others gave to E.G. Moss. Moss served in a variety of capacities at Cameron, from overseeing the prepatory grades to working as the "Poultry Man" and as the campus "Research Man."[94] Students often described him as being among the more popular teachers. Moss lived at the end of Webster

Hall which served as a dormitory for a small group of boys. There were only seven rooms and chicken wire covered the outer walls; students referred to it as living in the chicken coup. Faulkner recalled one weekend when Moss, along with many of the students and other faculty, were away. During that time a group of boys tied a long piece of iron to a piece of wire and ran it the length of the "coup" so that it dangled inside one of the walls of Moss's room. In the middle of the night the boys would, on occasion, pull the wire from the other end causing a loud commotion in Moss's room. Faulkner laughingly described Moss running out, yelling "My dear boys did you hear that? I think it must be the boys over in the south dorm." Faulkner and his friends would agree as they stifled their laughter until they returned to their rooms. The "squeeker," as they called the piece of iron, went undetected until a work crew tore the building down decades later.[95]

Faulkner also recalled a memorable trip that the Cameron band made to Oklahoma City for the '89er Celebration with Hugh Corwin, the band director, and President March. He estimated that between 50 to 60 students made the trip in an old army surplus truck which pulled a trailer with the band equipment. It took the Cameron band twelve hours to travel from Lawton to Oklahoma City because many of the dirt roads were muddy and washed out. The students even had to walk up hills in some places to relieve the straining vehicle. Wearing discarded army uniforms, the Cameron band finally arrived in time to play in the parade. That night it rained so hard that President March decided that the students would return to Cameron on the train rather than face another muddy trek.[96]

The inauguration of Governor Jack Walton also provided an opportunity for the Cameron band to travel to Oklahoma City. Walton came to office promising great things for the state, especially for its educational institutions, only to face impeachment a short time later. Nonetheless, the opportunity to play in his inauguration ceremony prompted much excitement. According to Hugh Corwin, a group of Lawton businesmen "contributed several hundred dollars to send thirty-two members of the band to participate in the inaugural parade." This money allowed the students to take the train to Oklahoma City where they marched for six miles in the parade amidst cold and windy conditions. Corwin proudly added that the band from the University of Oklahoma "completed only about three miles of the six-mile parade."[97] Clinton Far, a member of the band who accompanied Corwin on the trip, remembered the feast that awaited them that night which included bear and buffalo meat. He also remembered sleeping in a barn at the old fairgrounds that night and struggling to keep warm, as did his classmate, Harry Hammond, who used paper found in the barn for extra warmth.[98]

The accommodations of Cameron students during the high school days seem difficult to fathom when compared to the housing concerns facing later generations of Cameron students. In the 1920s, overnight school trips did not necessarily mean staying in a hotel or even having a heated place to sleep. And back on campus, dorm space remained at a premium for many years so that the occasional student might find himself or herself boarding in the loft of the barn or in the dairy. Ernie Crain operated a shoe cobbling shop in the basement of the administration building and he actually slept in a basement hallway during his second year at Cameron.[99] Oakle Best Hilbert, who started her first semester at Cameron six weeks late, recalled having to sleep with a number of other girls in the creamery because the dormitory rooms all were occupied.[100] They did not have any running water inside the building and each student who lived on campus had an assigned day of the week in which to bathe, something students themselves enforced by hazing those who broke the bathing schedule. While later debates centered on the ratio of students to showers, in the 1920s students adhered to their once weekly bath time.[101]

Future Cameron students would no doubt shudder at the idea of only bathing once a week or sleeping in hallways and barns but Cameron students of the 1920s had one noteworthy advantage over later generations when it came to the campus meal plan. The "Kitchen Force" or "Hashers" as they sometimes called themselves, took great pride in the "splendid service" afforded to Cameron students. According to the *Wichita*, "the Cameron Boarding Club serves better meals for less money than any other school in the state," which in 1925 meant that it cost students only $12.00 a month for their meals.[102] In a fashion typical of Cameron students in this era, the *Wichita* staff summed up the valued contributions of the kitchen staff:

> *O take away your flapper girls,*
> *Your Jelly Beans and Mashers,*
> *But Heaven's choicest blessings rest*
> *Upon our Cooks and Hashers.*[103]

As a high school Cameron repeatedly faced funding shortages and the possibility—as one article put it—of "being vetoed out of existence," yet community support and student enthusiasm remained steadfast. The opportunities afforded the children of rural families repeatedly drew praise. An article in *The Oklahoman* explained that "a majority of children attending Cameron return to the farm after graduation," adding that "in nearly every instance the training they received helped them to prosperity in agriculture."[104] Cameron, the article said, was "not a school for the city-bred child." While acknowledging that "all youths" regardless of whether they came from rural or urban areas could attend the school, the author stressed the value of a farm-centered education saying that "Cameron specializes only in subjects which will be of practical use to the children of the farm." And so, while girls learned to cook "the kind of meals a farmer's wife must prepare for a hardworking husband," Cameron boys learned the latest in agricultural and mechanical science.[105]

Many continued to esteem the secondary educational opportunities afforded at a school like Cameron, but as the American economy and society continued to evolve, growing educational needs arose for new generations of students. A junior college movement grew across the country in recognition of the need for modern students to receive more advanced education. Starting in the fall of 1927, Cameron joined the ranks of other emerging junior colleges across the United States. The name was changed from "The Cameron State School of Agriculture" to "Cameron Junior College" and John Coffey became the eighth president of the institution. For many observers of Cameron, the best years still lay ahead but to those who took such pride in the establishment and growth of the high school in what was once "a barren spot," a wave of nostalgic sadness marked the transition.[106] Hugh Corwin was a member of Cameron's second graduating class.

As a faculty member, he founded the band, taught manual training, helped gravel the first road which connected Cameron to the city of Lawton, and, through a long and distinguished life in southwest Oklahoma, held great affinity for the school that shaped the lives and fortunes of so many young people like himself. Corwin focused exclusively on the high school years when he wrote the first history of Cameron in 1976, even though nearly 50 years had passed since Cameron had become a junior college and ten years since the institution gained approval to become a four-year university. In his conclusion he remarked simply that "With no public recognition the Cameron School of Agriculture passed out of existence after serving the people of Southwestern Oklahoma for 18 years."[107]

While Cameron's transition to a junior college marked the distinct end of an era for Corwin, much of Cameron life remained unchanged for several years to come. Cameron continued to offer high school work until 1941. Many of the same faculty stayed on along with a number of the high school alumni who then took college courses. The same Lawton community that raised money to buy the land on which to build Cameron's campus, who paid for the construction of the first dormitory, and whose financial support ironically allowed band members to march six long miles in the inaugural parade of a governor who shortly thereafter tried to abolish the school, continued their patronage of Cameron. The basic function of the school—which was to meet the educational needs of the residents of southwest Oklahoma—did not change but what constituted those needs changed, and so Cameron did as well.

A number of new buildings were commissioned on Cameron's campus at the height of the New Deal in the mid 1930s, including barns which were of great significance for the agricultural program. *Photograph by Jim Horinek.*

CHAPTER TWO

"IT'S CAMERON COLLEGE"

It's Cameron College, it's Cameron College,
The pride of every student here.
Come on you Aggies, come on you Aggies,
It's Cameron College now we cheer.
Now is the time boys
To make a great noise
No matter what the people say,
For there is naught to fear
The gang's all here,
So hail to Cameron College! Hail![1]

Just weeks before Senator Jed Johnson introduced Senate Bill 187, which called for Cameron to add two years of college coursework, the *Lawton Constitution* touted the school as "the 'Mecca' of the farm boys and girls of southwestern Oklahoma," explaining that "most of the students who attend Cameron return to the farm to apply the theory and practical educations they have obtained." The article also pointed out that students could attend Cameron for a full year at a cost of only $132.25 which made it the "cheapest per capita cost of any state institution."[2] Senator Johnson echoed this praise for Cameron but explained that the addition of college coursework would "greatly augment the service of the school to the farm" as well as the other "residents of the southwest section of the state."[3] Others in state government shared Johnson's sentiment and moved to support his bill. In March of 1927, only a month after Johnson introduced the bill, the Senate and House passed it and forwarded it to the desk of Governor Henry S. Johnston for approval.

Nevertheless, Cameron's transition to a junior college evolved slowly as the school struggled to gain the funding necessary to respond to growing demands for access to higher education in southwest Oklahoma.

Initially it appeared that the school would receive adequate appropriations, as one newspaper headline suggested: "Cameron School Fares Well in Legislature." Noting a historically rare occurrence that Cameron "received practically all that was asked" in appropriations, the article added that the legislature also approved $60,000 for construction of new buildings.[4] The following month, the *Lawton Constitution* charted the school's changing fate: "Cameron Hit by Johnston Pen; Fund Cut." As part of a total $310,000 institutional appropriation cut, the governor also eliminated the $60,000 building fund for Cameron.[5] The following day, the paper again reported the latest on Cameron's appropriations, noting that the school would receive "a total of $79,250 for operation

and maintenance during the next two years."[6] And so it seems that the push to transform Cameron into a junior college marked more continuity than change in terms of the obstacles facing the school.

The 1927 spring semester proved volatile as the school gained approval to add college course work amidst budgetary struggles and "disharmony" among faculty, students, and the administration. The tension became public after an altercation between Basil Wilkerson, the captain of the football team, and instructor Hugh Corwin who drafted a petition calling for President March's dismissal. The ordeal eventually came to an end without anyone being terminated, but not before the governor intervened and the entire State Board of Agriculture came to Lawton to conduct an investigation and hold hearings.[7] While the tension seemingly subsided, President March did not seek reappointment and John L. Coffey replaced him in July of 1927. Governor Johnston reportedly said "I am not sure that March is responsible, but things

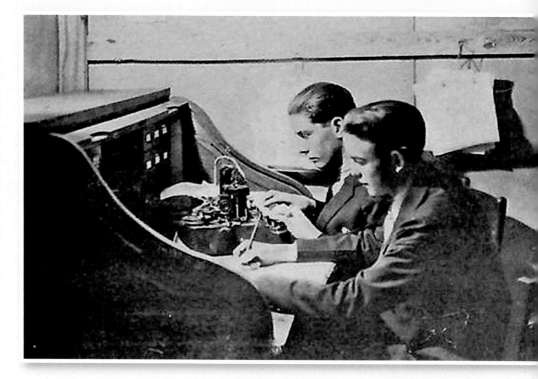

In an era that predated television and other forms of mass entertainment, the yearbook provided students with an important record of their social activities and achievements for the year. Members of the *Wichita* staff working on their yearbook. *Courtesy 1926 Wichita, Cameron University Archives.*

have not been running right at the school."[8] The newly-appointed President Coffey came to Cameron in time to make quick preparations to oversee the addition of Cameron's first college class. In early August, shortly after President Coffey assumed his new duties, State Senator S. G. Thomas visited Cameron and said he expected "a bright future for the school under the present administration" and "highly praised" the renovations of Cameron's campus that summer, largely made possible by the labor of male students.[9]

That same August, just weeks before the official start of the school year, Governor Johnston characterized Cameron as playing a leading role in south-west Oklahoma by providing the latest innovations in agricultural education. He described a "new spirit" at Cameron and "community interest" in the school because the county agreed to help finance a paved road from Lawton to Cameron. The governor explained that "When the community awakens to the fact that this is a community institution and gets behind it wholeheartedly, the community and the school is going to win." He further added that "No governor is going to continue vetoing appropriations" with such strong community support behind the school. While this turned out not to be the case, Governor Johnston correctly identified the centrality of community support to the survival of the school.[10]

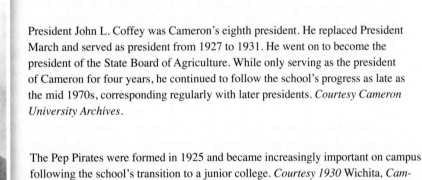

President John L. Coffey was Cameron's eighth president. He replaced President March and served as president from 1927 to 1931. He went on to become the president of the State Board of Agriculture. While only serving as the president of Cameron for four years, he continued to follow the school's progress as late as the mid 1970s, corresponding regularly with later presidents. *Courtesy Cameron University Archives.*

The Pep Pirates were formed in 1925 and became increasingly important on campus following the school's transition to a junior college. *Courtesy 1930* Wichita, *Cameron University Archives.*

With the 1927-1928 school year underway, the Cameron community had much to celebrate. Enrollment increased to just over 250 with roughly half of the students attending high school and half attending college.[11] The college students started a newspaper, which very quickly became an award-winning publication. The students used the paper to promote school pride and spirit, publish official school information, as well as national, and sometimes international news, and of course to entertain the student body. The paper also laid out the code of conduct for students. In the very first edition of *The Cameron Collegian*, beneath the heading "Campus Rules," appeared a list of requirements to which students were expected to adhere. They included a requirement that girls obtain a furlough any time they left campus and that boys do the same after 5:00 p.m. Students also were cautioned that "Any faculty member had the right to correct any student at any time."[12] The addition of a college class in no way meant a loosening of the rules. Students at every level received much oversight from faculty and staff and they continued to regularly attend chapel services on campus.

The *Wichita* described the addition of a college class as Cameron's "crowning achievement." The author, a member of the college freshman class by the name of Jim Thorne, remarked on the many contributions his class made to the school. These college freshmen certainly worked hard to live up to the new level of expectations for the students and the school as a whole.[13] The downside of this addition, however, manifested itself in an equally predictable and colorful dispute between the high school classes and the college freshmen. An editorial in *The Cameron Collegian* tellingly entitled "Petty Quarrels," condemned the growing "factionalism" at Cameron as "all tommyrot" and "a lot of wasteful ballyhoo that would be a disgrace to a third grade school." The editorial described the "college class" as "all stirred up by what it terms insolent impertinence of the high school classes," whereas the high school students apparently viewed them as "overbearing parrots." It concluded by calling on all Cameron students to cooperate with one another and remember that they were "buddies under the skin."[14]

Campus clubs, sports, and student activities flourished as the school's enrollment grew. At the start of the 1927 football season, male students formed the "Hell Hounds" to keep "the athletic teams in good mental condition."[15] In recapping the football season, the *Wichita* described the team as "one of the strongest" in the Junior Collegiate Conference even though they did not win the conference that year. With the Hell Hounds in attendance at both "home and foreign fields," and a "battle cry" of "Ride 'em Cowboys," the students felt that they made a good showing as newcomers to the conference.[16] The membership of the Pep Pirates, established in 1925, grew with the addition of a college class and they worked alongside the Hell Hounds to support the football team, missing only three football games of the season.[17] The girls' basketball team had the distinction of becoming Cameron's first undefeated team during the 1928 season under the leadership of Coach E. C. Reynolds and team captain Anna Japp. The point average for their 16-0 season "totaled more than four hundred to one hundred twenty-eight points" over their opponents. This indeed constituted "a record that would be envied by any team, anywhere."[18]

A growing student body and new college class also meant a need for increased services to the students. At the suggestion of President Coffey the students voted to create a Student Senate which included a representative "from each class and two from the student body at large." The first student senate representatives were elected in "one of the hottest elections that had occurred on the campus for some time," which brought five male and two female students to office in the inaugural

During some years the yearbook identified the girls' basketball team as a club and in others as a sports team with no indication given as to why. *Courtesy 1929* Wichita, *Cameron University Archives.*

student senate.[19] As important as student senate became, its members took a back seat in importance to those students who worked in the dining hall. The student paper described the campus "hashers" as "the happiest group in the whole student body." The hashers were "enthusiastic boys and girls opening their way to knowledge with a can opener" and were "the most envied students" because they constituted the "soul life of Cameron both physically and spiritually." The hashers, it seems, often broke out in song while serving food

and helped cheer students who were having a bad day. They also took care of the football players who received "the proper menu made out by their coach."[20] One student who worked in the cafeteria recalled the extra portions provided to football players, including such coveted treats as bread and karo syrup.[21]

While Cameron periodically still faced the possibility of being closed, the growth in enrollment and local support for the school constituted its best defense against abolition. The start of the

1928 school year brought the addition of sophomore coursework which contributed to the growth of the student body. In an advertisement in the 1928 *Wichita* beneath the heading "Cameron State School of Agriculture Junior College" lay a description of Cameron as "The Coming School of the Southwest," offering four years of high school and two years of college course work. The ad concluded with the theme that had dominated Cameron advertisements since its creation: "A practical and economical school for your boy or girl." [22]

When Cameron again faced proposed legislation threatening its existence in February of 1929, students vocally protested in the school paper. One editorial entitled "To Parents of School Children," suggested that only "criminal indifference would allow [parents] to stand aside" while "certain big interests who are adverse to paying a few more cents school tax" prevailed in their efforts to close the school. The article further admonished parents to contact their representatives to ensure that "Cameron will remain the educational guide

of the generations that follow." [23]

As the spring semester of 1929 progressed, Cameron's enrollment increased and the latest rumors of closure subsided. Cameron had the highest enrollment of any junior college in the state with a total of 433 students. [24] In March of that same semester, Herbert Hoover became the third Republican of the decade to take office as president of the United States. The election itself apparently captured the attention of many in the Cameron community as one letter to the editor in the student paper suggested. For this student the most noticeable post election change came in the form of faculty members having "their days work better outlined because they are no longer interested in 'listening in' on political speeches until the wee, small hours of the night." Students also seemed "better prepared" because they were no longer up late arguing politics with their roommates. The letter concluded on an optimistic note saying that "if everything goes as good as is promised we are sure to have four years of prosperity,

The student orchestra remained a prominent feature at Cameron during this period as they entertained their classmates as well as the Lawton community. *Courtesy 1930* Wichita, *Cameron University Archives*.

happiness, and contentment." The author added "here's hoping this is true and that all our troubles are little ones." [25] This student could not have known that the country hovered on the brink of the worst depression in American history.

America's economy seemingly boomed by the mid 1920s. Productivity soared, reviving the post-war economy, until demand began to slip. Just months after President Herbert Hoover took office the country faced undeniable signs of economic catastrophe. Farm prices had fallen steadily since the end of World War I and the steel and automobile industries were among the early casualties of the growing economic crisis. Between Labor Day and late October of 1929 the stock market fell by 40%. For most Cameron students low farm prices brought on by over production constituted the biggest area of concern. Yet, optimism about the future of farming persisted. Black Thursday followed by Black Tuesday in late October marked the official crash of the stock market and the onset of the depression. However, this had little immediate impact on Cameron. In November of 1929 students geared up for the Thanksgiving holiday and looked forward to the end of the semester—as they did every year. Enrollment only continued to increase the following semester and when classes came to an end in May of 1930 the school stood well poised for even more growth.

Nationally, unemployment soared reaching more than 20% that summer and yet, Cameron seemed unscathed. The *Lawton Constitution* proclaimed "Cameron College Looking Forward to Most Successful Year in History, Twenty-Second Catalog Indicates." [26] The paper also described President Coffey as "enthusiastic" that enrollment would "show large increase over previous years." The article went on to discuss "a new era in the progress of Cameron College as the educational center of the southwest." [27] Another 1930 article described Cameron's enrollment as having tripled since 1927 and praised the "spirit

of democracy" at the school due the ability of almost half of the student body population to "work their way through school" which resulted in "equality for all." [28] This equality of opportunity increased enrollment, but state appropriations for much needed dorm space did not follow. When visiting Cameron's campus in January of 1931, a reporter from the *Lawton Constitution* discovered that rooms designed for two students actually housed three and in several instances that number reached as high as five boys in a single room. Moss Hall's sixteen-room boys' dormitory housed 45 students. Some students took it upon themselves to construct make-shift double bunks which meant that they "strapped and roped cots to the railing of double beds so that students could sleep on the cots above [their] more fortunate" roommates. Moreover, the winter months caused an even greater problem of overcrowding because "sleeping porches" off of King Hall and Moss Hall became unsuitable. [29]

Cramped quarters paled in comparison to the suffering endured by millions of Americans as the country grappled with the ever deepening depression. Not surprisingly, Cameron students enthusiastically took advantage of the opportunity to work their way through school, and they slept wherever they found space. President Coffey's continued enthusiasm about the school's growth proved well founded. By 1931 the school boasted the third-largest enrollment of any junior college in the country. With 762 students in attendance, Cameron's enrollment led other state junior colleges in Oklahoma by 200 in the spring of 1931. Coffey attributed Cameron's growth to two basic factors: "Strict regulation of students at the college" and "economy." The president explained that "Parents like to know that their sons and daughters are closely looked after." Moreover—and perhaps more importantly—students who could "pay ten dollars a month and work two hours a day" could get an education at Cameron. [30] A 1931 study of Cameron conducted for the Oklahoma State Board of Agriculture revealed that a large percentage of Cameron students were indeed employed either on or off campus. Although enrollment increased drastically during Cameron's early years as a junior college, the report described the student population as still small enough to allow the president to "personally know all working students and direct them without formal records." Only 262 Cameron students were listed as not working, and of that number, 194 of them lived at home.[31] President Coffey asserted that "No young man or woman who has ever shown an honest desire to get an education has ever been turned away from this institution for lack of funds."[32]

The ability of Cameron students to pay their way through school by working on and off campus constituted a valuable opportunity in depression-era America. President Coffey worked hard to find employment for his students and contributed greatly to the school's growth. *The Oklahoman*

described Cameron, under Coffey's leadership, as having become the "servant and the fostering mother of hundreds of ambitious students who without the benign help which Cameron has rendered could not have entered college at all." The article credited Coffey for having found "sufficient jobs" for the students and the "hearty and unanimous support of the people of Lawton" for making it possible.[33] Unfortunately for President Coffey, his success at Cameron did not save his job when the governor decided to remove him. According to *The Oklahoman*, Coffey, acting "less spineless and craven than the pitiful board which fired him at the governor's order," refused to vote for the governor's candidate of choice for the president of the State Board of Agriculture. The article concluded that "Nothing done in Oklahoma's recent political maneuvering has been more contemptible or more injurious than this conversion of our institutions of learning into rank and putrid political spoils."[34] Perhaps John Coffey found a measure of solace a few years later when he became the head of the State Board of Agriculture, a move which significantly benefitted Cameron.[35]

President Coffey's departure from Cameron after only four years and considerable progress initially placed Charles M. Conwill in a difficult spot when he accepted the presidency at Cameron. Even the 1931 *Wichita* reflected Coffey's popularity among the students. They dedicated it to him because of his "underlying interest in the welfare of each individual" and his "unwavering determination to offer to the students" the best possible opportunities.[36] Yet, Conwill carried on the progress implemented under Coffey and achieved a strong record of his own. Conwill had more than 20 years of experience in education, having served as "both county and city superintendent of schools" in Atoka. *The Oklahoman* described him as "a practical farmer who has grown nearly every crop common to Oklahoma."[37] Conwill's combined experience in agriculture and education made him an ideal choice to lead Cameron despite the dubious circumstances behind Coffey's dismissal.

Despite being the third-largest junior college in the nation by the 1930s, students nevertheless enjoyed a relatively small close-knit environment in which to study and form life-long friendships. *Courtesy Mildred H. Bleinett Collection, Cameron University Archives.*

As Americans celebrated the start of a new year in January of 1932, optimism about the economic future of the country proved elusive. The American people had now been in a depression for more than two years and President Hoover's low approval ratings reflected the mood of the country. An early indication of economic hardship at Cameron came in 1931 when President Conwill announced that Cameron would not publish a yearbook that year because of a shortfall in subscriptions.[38] Not until after World War II did Cameron publish the *Wichita* again. Cameron did, however, benefit from the difficult economic times in that enrollment kept increasing. The student paper attributed the rising numbers to "the transfer of many students from larger institutions to those known to be more economical."[39] An article entitled "Unemployment's Greatest Enemy Found to be Education, Aggie Instructor Says," claimed that only 3% of students who had graduated in the last decade were unemployed, putting them far below the state and national unemployment figures which hovered between 20-25%. These figures, interestingly, placed housewife as the "vocation chosen by the largest percent of high school graduates," followed by school teacher, farmer, and book keeper respectively.[40] While hardly scientific, this cursory study revealed a strong sentiment at play throughout much of the country; if possible, students should stay in school. This kept both high school and college students from competing for jobs with family bread winners and it afforded a degree of optimism about future employment opportunities. Attitudes about traditional gender roles, however, underpinned notions about the acceptable place for educated women in the American work force and society. The kinds of jobs open to female students at Cameron, for example, remained highly gender specific—sewing, working in the laundry, as well as on and off-campus domestic service.

Despite a warning in the student newspaper

President Charles M. Conwill was Cameron's ninth president. He replaced President John Coffey and served longer than any other president to that time, overseeing the school from 1931 to 1946 when he stepped down for health reasons. *Courtesy Cameron University Archives.*

that "Co-Eds Get Less Chance to Marry Than Other Girls," Cameron's female population remained quite comparable to the male population. Citing a survey conducted by "some committee on research," *The Cameron Collegian* article indicated that the "modern" female student had to choose between "a college diploma or a marriage license; a cap and gown or wedding veil; a typewriter or an eggbeater; babies or books." One bit of "comfort" for female students came in the notion that among older women, the "college old maid" had better odds of "teaming up" than did her less educated counterpart. Ultimately, the article revealed that these marriage statistics referred only to students attending exclusively female institutions. "Belles of co-educational colleges (like dear old Cameron)," it seems, said "'I do' about as often as the girl who stayed home to wait until Johnnie got his raise."[41] Perhaps the continued popularity of majoring in home economics spoke to the cultural assumption of the proper place of women in American society. As the *Wichita* explained, "In the consideration of the various educational departments for women and their respective merits, there is perhaps none that is quite so important as that of Home Economics."[42]

The emphasis on female graduates of Cameron going into presumably female enterprises such as getting married and taking care of their families was not new in the 1930s but it took on a heightened significance during the Great Depression. Increased hostility toward women who worked in the same occupations as men led many employers to adopt policies of firing married women in order to save the jobs of men who were, after all, viewed as the bread winner. This trend held true even in instances when the husbands of these women already were unemployed. Historian Susan Ware pointed out that female employment actually remained stable during the 1930s, even increasing a percentage point by the end of the decade. She attributed this to the fact that male-dominated jobs in heavy industry were hardest hit by the depression and that men did not typically move into "female" jobs when they became unemployed.[43] Nevertheless, social unease about the educated woman persisted amidst difficult economic times, particularly in the socially conservative Cameron community which prided itself on strict discipline and moral conduct among the students. A poem appearing in the 1931 *Wichita* entitled "Nonfeminist," captured this tension well:

Although with vigor they profess
A yen for science, business, fame,
Old human nature, none the less,
Remains the same;

For many a female Ph.D.,
Master or Bachelor of Arts
Would very much prefer to be
The Queen of Hearts.

Let critics point to what they will
Of matrimonial disasters,
The favorite degree is still
A Lord and Master's![44]

Whether or not the central aspiration of most female students at Cameron boiled down to receiving their "Mrs. Degree," the depression seriously jeopardized educational opportunities for both male and female students. While Cameron's enrollment remained high, keeping students in school proved a challenging task as economic hardship continuously threatened the school's already meager appropriations. When democratic presidential candidate Franklin Delano Roosevelt soundly defeated Herbert Hoover in the 1932 presidential election, economic relief became increasingly realistic for millions of Americans, including young people from southwest Oklahoma who could not afford to attend Cameron unless given the opportunity to pay their own way. Quite simply, Cameron enrollment hinged on the ability of the school and the Lawton community to provide part-time jobs to students.

Home Economics remained one of the most popular majors for female students at Cameron for several decades. *Courtesy Clements Alumni Collection, 1938-1939, Cameron University Archives.*

Cameron's football team was well known throughout the region and had a reputation for being difficult to beat. The 1933 Cameron football team enjoyed a coveted status on campus. *Courtesy Mildred H. Bleinett Collection, Cameron University Archives.*

Shortly after taking office in March of 1933 President Roosevelt launched the New Deal, which among other things, created a number of agencies designed to create jobs across the country. The Civil Works Administration (CWA) employed millions of Americans and this included students. An article in the *Lawton Constitution* indicated that Carl Giles, the state head of the CWA, pledged $28,200 for Oklahoma college students which he estimated "would keep 1,424 students in college and permit 475 others to enter." CWA money paid students $15.00 a month for working part time.[45] This money went even further at Cameron because the school's tuition consistently remained below that of other state institutions. Cameron's share of the CWA money amounted to $2,300 which benefited "nearly fifty students" by employing them at "clerical, library, and research work, as well as at other odd jobs" on Cameron's campus.[46] Like many of the New Deal work relief programs, the approach to job creation centered on

the identification of needs based public works. CWA funds, for example, paid for the construction of Cameron's football field and running track in 1934.[47]

As New Deal relief money poured into the state, Cameron students reaped the benefits. In the spring of 1934 Cameron set a new school record with 132 college students graduating.[48] Enthusiasm for the New Deal at Cameron paralleled praise for President Conwill. When the State Board of Agriculture announced Conwill's reappointment in April of 1934, an editorial in the student paper described him as "Cameron's best friend," saying that Conwill took "advantage of every opportunity to lend assistance" and that he was "never too busy to talk to a student."[49] Conwill's commitment to the Cameron student body included plans for increased facilities, something he had in common with most, if not all, of his predecessors. He recognized the added difficulty in attaining construction funds during the depression, noting that "new dormitories and new classrooms" would "be built sometime in the future."[50]

Nevertheless, President Conwill continued to protect the school's interests by promoting growth when possible. He also served as president of the American Association of Junior Colleges, which brought even greater visibility to the school. Cameron continued to be the largest of Oklahoma's 23 junior colleges and much of that had to do with the administration's commitment to keeping tuition low and part-time employment high.[51]

In many ways, the implementation of New Deal Programs at Cameron marked a degree of continuity; historically, Cameron's survival depended on community support and creative economic solutions to offset inadequate state appropriations. Plans by the local director of the Federal Emergency Relief Agency (FERA) to launch ground improvements at Cameron, including "paving curbs and gutter construction," mirrored earlier approaches to campus work. In this case, the State Board of Agriculture provided the materials and FERA paid for the work.[52] Additional money became available to Cameron when the federal government approved educational relief in the amount of 22,275 for Oklahoma.[53] President Conwill also enlisted help from the Lawton Business and Professional Women's Association and the Rotary to help find jobs for Cameron students which would be financed by the National Recovery Administration (NRA). He pointed out that a similar program in Stillwater provided jobs for 150 students. He also reminded Lawtonians that working "four hours a day would furnish board and room for the average college student."[54]

By 1936 President Roosevelt had launched a second New Deal in an effort to increase work relief programs and provide greater assistance to those still suffering from the depression. Cameron students continued to benefit through work programs and through efforts to improve Cameron's infrastructure. After considerable effort, President

During the 1930s a group of boys posed in front of a 1925 campus monument which recognized Cameron's roots as an agricultural high school. *Courtesy Mildred H. Bleinett Collection, Cameron University Archives.*

Conwill secured a $100,000 New Deal grant out of Public Works Administration (PWA) funds to construct much needed dormitories on the school's campus.[55] Initially the plan President Conwill submitted called for two fireproof boys' dormitories which would each house 100 students, which later changed to one boys' dorm and one girls' dorm.[56] Several New Deal buildings eventually gained funding on Cameron's campus, including present day West Hall, originally a girls' dormitory, and two physical facilities buildings which initially served as barns.

New Deal construction and jobs for students meant that Cameron flourished amidst a bleak economic outlook for the country. One 1935 article boasted that only eight of the 1934 graduates were unemployed, a figure far below the national average.[57] While these informal employment statistics included those who had continued on to four-year schools, returned to their parent's farms, or female students who had gotten married, the significance lies in the hope and optimism embodied in a celebration of the value of higher education. Cameron's core mission continued to center on providing a practical and affordable education to the rural residents of southwest Oklahoma. In 1936, 130 college sophomores graduated, making it Cameron's largest graduating class up to that point. While the number of high school students had begun to dwindle to smaller and smaller numbers, college enrollment remained high. Parents of Cameron students were employed in 60 different occupations, yet a majority of these parents continued to work as farmers, just as had been the case when Cameron first opened its doors in September of 1909.[58]

Support for Cameron's ongoing commitment to educating the children of rural farm communities increased when John Coffey became president of the State Board of Agriculture in January of 1937. Cameron stood to benefit in a variety of

Cameron instructor Pansy Robertson working in one of the campus gardens. The plots became increasingly important during the Great Depression because they provided both food and employment for students. *Courtesy Mary Knowles Collection, Cameron University Archives.*

Barns financed by President Franklin Roosevelt's New Deal in the late 1930s are just one example of the New Deal construction that took place at Cameron and across the country. *Courtesy Mary Knowles Collection, Cameron University Archives.*

ways. Coffey continued to have high regard for the school over which he had presided. *The Cameron Collegian* described Coffey as "in a position to understand thoroughly the problems of such educational institutions."[59] While at Cameron, Coffey focused heavily on helping students find jobs so that they could work their way through school. As president of the State Board of Agriculture, he brought that same approach to all of the agricultural schools in the state. In 1937, for example, he implemented a plan which he first tested while at Cameron, which included schools making garden plots available to students. Coffey explained that this meant that "students could raise vegetables, cook and can them, and serve them too to work their way through our agriculture colleges."[60] This proved popular among students during a period in American history when both malnutrition and unemployment had become all too common place.

Through various work relief programs more than 250 Cameron students found employment in 1937 alone. One hundred of those students, 50 male and 50 female, worked in the area of "campus and dormitory beautification" financed by the National Youth Administration (NYA), which among other things included an "extensive irrigation project" necessary for the student garden plots as well as the growing agriculture program.[61] By the spring of 1938, 200 acres of crops had been planted by Cameron students employed by the NYA. The gardens included beans, peas, onions, okra, lettuce, spinach, and a variety of other vegetables, most of which were used to feed Cameron students in the dining hall, with "any surplus" going to the "NYA girls" to can.[62] NYA girls at Cameron also made clothing for local public institutions, so long as the institutions provided the girls with the necessary material.[63] NYA student workers also constructed two tennis courts at Cameron, which doubled the number of total courts on campus, a much needed addition according to President Conwill.[64] Yet another NYA

project funded the construction of a new 50-by-100-foot shop for Cameron students.[65] One NYA project that benefitted both male and female students was the construction of a $10,000 "training building" for female students. Cameron boys did all of the work including "plumbing, electrical fixtures, and other technical types of work."[66] Once completed, the project enabled female students to rotate in and out of the apartment style living accommodations where they received practical instruction on home-making.

New Deal-financed student labor clearly led to many improvements across campus. Despite the graveling of some of the roads on and around school property, one article in the student paper offered a humorous assessment of "Back-To-Nature" roads on campus. People at Cameron, explained the article, seem to think that "if nature did not give us good roads to start with, there is no use trying to make them." The article further quipped that while often roads destroyed natural beauty, at Cameron "little discrepancy" existed between actual roads and "the hard dirt prairie."[67] Nevertheless, excitement and pride characterized many attitudes toward campus improvements. An editorial entitled "Cameron the Beautiful" praised the many improvements on the school's campus, noting that five new buildings were constructed between 1935 and 1939. The editorial nicely summed up the role of the New Deal in improving the campus: "the WPA [Works Progress Administration] works to give us buildings that add to our comfort and the college's recognition."[68] In addition, Cameron had a new telephone system installed that consisted of eleven phones strategically placed across campus with "two trunk lines between Cameron and Lawton." This modern convenience also meant employment for half a dozen female students who operated the switchboard.[69] These sorts of improvements were a double victory for the institution because not only did students gain access to employment, but the work they did often

The Hell Hounds were formed in 1927 and quickly became one of the most prestigious organizations on campus where they sought to boost support for the sports teams. *Courtesy 1930* Wichita, *Cameron University Archives*.

directly and visibly benefitted the school and the community.

Indeed, New Deal-funded student jobs made it possible for hundreds of Cameron students to stay in school in the 1930s, and the spirit of equality of opportunity permeated the school's culture in many ways. While Cameron boasted four pep organizations by the mid 1930s, some feared that the lengthy pledging process worked to the detriment of school spirit. One editorial in the school paper proposed a "new deal system" to increase the number of students able to participate in pep clubs. In turn, this would "magnetize the majority of the entire student body in a movement that would restore the old school spirit."[70] The rituals involved in initiating new pledges into esteemed clubs like the Hell Hounds included such dubious activities as "olive oil eating," followed by drinking a unique concoction of mineral oil and pepsin salts. At dinner, pledges found themselves treated to raw liver, lard, and oysters. The "slimes," as the new pledges were called, used a "daily hair tonic composed of lard and catsup."[71] Despite the cry for increased student participation in pep clubs, the elite Hell Hounds remained small in numbers, no doubt proud of their lofty achievements. Cameron's pep clubs, along with the football team, had much to cheer about when Roosevelt Field opened in the fall of 1937. Both Lawton High and Cameron used this new football field for many years. Construction of the field took two years and received financing through the Works Progress Administration (WPA), the largest and most extensive of the New Deal work relief programs.[72]

To be sure, New Deal programs immeasurably aided Cameron students in their quest for an education during this period and many no doubt realized how lucky they were to be in school at all. After graduating from a small southwestern Oklahoma high school in 1937, Lloyd Mitchell

Cameron's Early Belief in Instructing Morals

by Kyle Lewis
History Major • Class of 2009

The role of morals in educating America's youth remains as valid today as ever. The Duke of Wellington's statement that "education without instruction in morals breeds only clever devils" mirrored the belief Cameron's founding members applied to the early days of the school's education. Instruction in both religion and morality from the school's beginning through the decade of the 1920s reflected the issues that many small communities faced. By the early twentieth century, the morals of small communities became less regionalized with the invention of the automobile, the radio, mass syndicated columns, and increased immigration. National concepts of morality began to filter into the small communities throughout the United States. Nevertheless, for many, education still included instructing American youth in such areas as morality, religious thought, Bible study, public worship, ideals of manhood and womanhood, courtship, and faith-based social service.

State education institutions and promoters of religious studies had three elements to ensure proper spiritual growth: the school, faculty and students, and the Church. Schools could maintain chapel exercises but chapel did not have the same meaning throughout the United States. Some educational institutions that exercised chapel meetings held daily, semi-weekly, or weekly services. Attendance, voluntary or mandatory, depended upon the school. Chapels in some schools offered no singing of hymns, no prayer, and no scripture reading, while other schools conducted some or all these activities. Even in Oklahoma, the length of chapel services varied greatly from daily services that lasted thirty minutes to those occurring only once weekly. For example, the University of Oklahoma held one chapel service a week, and early on Cameron, as a secondary agricultural high school, held daily chapel services at the start of each school day. The chapel service typically had a guest speaker; many of the speakers came from strong religious backgrounds or local ministers and at Cameron both students and faculty participated in leading chapel services from time to time.

Yet, the advent of new technologies brought a change to the moral beliefs of small communities across the United States. The mass production of new technologies made them more affordable to the population and the automobile and radio undermined small town isolation by exposing the youth to greater degrees of outside thought, and by extension, some feared a loosening of morality. Increasingly, the smaller communities came to possess more national, seemingly progressive ideals regarding morality. Young people of the period flocked to new inventions. The birth of the flappers, jazz, and public dances gain popularity thanks to these technological advances. Like many other young Americans of the period, Cameron youth wanted a radio set. In May 1925, the sophomore class presented a comedy, "Daughter of the Desert," to raise proceeds to purchase a radio set.

Following this sophomore play, plans got underway for deciding the day and location of the Junior Banquet which was held in honor of all graduating seniors. Various churches took part in bidding, each seeing their church and location as best for the event. A celebration for the graduating class ended up being held in the school's auditorium. All the heartwarming events showed the camaraderie and fidelity among students. The program included the history of the class being read aloud and the class prophecy acted out in a parlor scene with the announcement coming from the school's new radio.

Chapel attendance on campus, as well as off-campus church activities, were expected of students at Cameron and the school administration regularly reminded parents of the high quality of moral instruction their children received at Cameron. Mildred H. Bleinett, along with other Cameron students, in front of a chapel in the early 1930s. *Courtesy Mildred H. Bleinett Collection, Cameron University Archives.*

The Christmas party of 1927 represented another typical celebration of the era as being wholesome and innocent. The parties always had a matron or sponsor, and generally had more than one faculty member in attendance to help chaperone. The holiday party included reception rooms in Reinwand Hall to entertain friends. The reception rooms had the typical Christmas decorations of mistletoe, holly, and Christmas tree. A receiving line at the beginning of the party with a female representative from each class signified the beginning of the festivities. For entertainment the students played lively games along with less active games, such as cards or dominos.

Advice columns in magazines and newspapers gave counsel to American youth regarding what to wear, proper courtship, and how to conduct ones' self in public. The syndicated columns of mass media influenced southwestern Oklahoma residents as with the rest of America. The youth at Cameron knew of the conduct of their peers across the country. The likelihood of an isolated or insolated area for

students to be instructed in the absence of the impressions from larger communities with larger problems became increasingly less possible. The impressions of other schools, their activities and the conduct of their students made their way to Cameron during the 1920s as well, but the impact on Cameron proved more limited in scope.

Notions of proper morality at Cameron were founded on more conservative values compared to larger institutions of learning, but minor changes that impacted the school throughout the 1920s resembled those across the nation. The school, maintaining instruction in religious ideas and morals, changed as the school grew in academic credentials and the average student age grew older. The major changes that affected larger academic institutions of the 1920s, however, resulted in much smaller changes at Cameron. The depression that halted the moral revolution in large cities and schools also affected the changes taking place on Cameron's campus. Among other things, the financial collapse that began in 1929 undermined the purchasing power of the young which in turn curtailed their ability to buy goods and engage in behavior that many considered immoral. In fact, the Great Depression caused numerous Americans to return to their religious roots to find the solace that many at Cameron never left.

PRIDE OF THE WICHITAS

began working for the Civilian Conservation Corps (CCC) north of Altus. After working there for about a year and a half, the assistant camp engineer asked him if he had ever considered going to college. Mitchell responded that while there was "nothing in this wide world" that he would rather do, his family could not afford it. His boss said that he had a good friend at Cameron to whom he would write to see if the school could give him a job so that he could attend classes. Clarence Breedlove responded to the letter, saying that Cameron could, in fact, offer Mitchell a part- time job. Following this news, "on a cold, cold January day" he "walked down to Hollis" and "hitch-hiked a ride to Cameron" where he found "really very friendly, warm, nice people."[73]

Robert S. Johnson, another Cameron graduate and World War II Veteran, recalled his football experience during the Great Depression. He described Coach Jess Thompson as having "a neck like a bull" whose "bellowing made him sound like an enraged steer." Coach Thompson, it seems, "didn't waste time with the recommendations of the state athletic manuals" in training his players. Rather, he would "drag the team out to the plowed fields where furrows were long and deep" and then Thompson would "roar" at the players to "run!" Johnson, who later served with great distinction in the war, credited Thompson for giving him advice on which he often reflected during his flying missions. Thompson simply reminded Johnson that the opponents he faced were really no different from himself. And so, while he nostalgically recalled his old coach yelling "Run boy! There's an old lady leading a cow wants to git by," the time Johnson spent at Cameron helped prepare him for the turbulent years that lay ahead.[74]

Nevertheless, football games, club initiations, class rivalries, social gossip, and cramming for exams dominated campus life during the depression much the same as it had in the previous decade, but the student body was larger and heavily

subsidized by the New Deal. Yet even as the life of Cameron students grew increasingly intertwined with national events, students still focused on the issues so clearly belonging to the young.

Upper-classmen warned incoming students that the "standards of Cameron College are of the highest type," adding that new enrollees were expected to "maintain these elevated Aggie ideals."[75] Student clubs grew as well during the depression years. In 1935 Cameron started a German Club as well as its "first Indian Club" which consisted of 13 members from five different tribes.[76] *The Cameron Collegian* described the purpose of the Indian Club as "to promote a better understanding of the American Indian, the part he played in the history of America, for the sake of truth, of deeper appreciation, of a broader, more statesman-like Americanism of those to whom long before ourselves this was the 'Sweet Land of Liberty.'"[77] Even as the depression worsened in some areas of the country, especially for farmers hurt by the dust bowl, enthusiasm for campus clubs, mixers, religious assemblies, and intramural dorm competitions thrived.

Student life in any era contains both continuity and innovation but in the 1930s it seems particularly remarkable that for many Cameron

Intramural games were commonplace on campus and dorm rivalries received much attention. *Courtesy 1930 Wichita, Cameron University Archives.*

Martha Wingfield, Elma Rose Carley, Elner Mc-Clarty, and Thelma Nelson were members of the Girls' Quartette known as "The Blackbirds" around campus. *Courtesy 1931 Wichita, Cameron University Archives.*

students, the suffering of the Great Depression could, at least for short periods of time, be put to the side as they found opportunities for amusement. Charles Graybill graduated from Lawton High in 1937 and began taking classes at Cameron that fall. While Graybill only attended Cameron for one year, his affiliation with the institution has spanned more than 70 years through his work with what later became the Cameron University Foundation.

Graybill recalled how rural the campus remained during the depression era. Like a number of Cameron students from local families, he lived at home and often rode his bike along Gore Boulevard, passing farm land as he rode west along Gore to the campus. He recalled that on the north side of Gore, now the site of Comanche County Memorial Hospital, an open field often served as a landing area for small airplanes. While Graybill recalled some of his favorite professors, like Clarence Breedlove and Helen Cavanaugh, he especially remembered the fun of campus socializing. A number of Cameron students, Graybill included, would pass the time between their classes at a café across the street from Cameron listening to music and dancing. Graybill said that they listened to "Glenn Miller and Tommy Dorsey records"

and would "get out in the middle of the floor and dance and really have a good time." Even in the midst of the Great Depression, as Graybill's account reveals, student life still centered on many of the same things as both before and after the worst economic decade of the twentieth century; they would "hang out" and "their favorite thing was just listening to music."[78]

Nevertheless, a fundamental preoccupation with both real and imagined changes in gender roles lay at the center of much of the social discourse among students in the 1930s. One article posed the worrisome question: "Is chivalry a thing of the past?" Even campus professors weighed in on the debate. Professor K. B. Cornell indicated that chivalry had, in fact, died. He blamed the depiction of young women in cigarette advertisements and said young men were "drifting in the direction of the gigolo and jelly bean type." He said that young men feared being called a "sissy" if they were chivalrous but he said that girls were "still old fashioned" and even girls "taking part in the business world" still wanted "the same tender and thoughtful manners of men." Professor W. J. Becker, on the other hand, disagreed that chivalry had gone by the way side. He pointed out that "young men are still sacrificing for the fairer sex," citing a recent occurrence at a campus dance where many a Cameron man surrendered his coat in the freezing cold to keep his date warm. Professor Becker added though that "if women are often treated unfair it is due to their own faults." Women who "work among men in business," he argued, "have taken the lead too much" by not waiting for men to come to their assistance.[79] While unable to definitively solve the chivalry question, students did overwhelmingly concur with a 1935 "ruling" in favor of students bringing dates to Student Senate parties. In past, it seems, male students without dates had to pay a quarter to attend. Not everyone agreed with the new rule. One student described it as "a gyp" because a guy could conceivably get "stuck with a gal that can't dance," which he said would be "an injustice."[80]

As male students grappled with such potential injustices as girls who were bad dancers, fair-haired female chemistry students confronted their own indignities: "I once was blonde—A face of which to dream—And now behold—My face, oh I could scream" chanted a group of girls, according to *The Cameron Collegian* after fumes from an experiment with nitric acid changed "the color of certain types of powder to a very dark shade."[81] An article on the ability of men to cook appeared in that same edition of the student paper, reporting that only 22 out of 70 Cameron males, both faculty and students, indicated that they could not cook. While home economics instructor Edith McKinley "declined to express" her professional opinion, she did indicate that "men who can cook well generally have great pride in their art." She added that men "who cannot" do it "look upon cooking as a shameful task." Answers ranged from Professor W. J. Becker who said that he could "cook as well as anybody" to Cameron student Arthur Cavanaugh who answered simply "Why, heck no!"[82]

While a minority of male students scoffed at the idea of learning how to cook, believing

women alone suitable to such a vocation, emphasis on food in depression era America took on new significances. A number of male Cameron students worked in the kitchen as cooks or "hashers" or played other roles in food preparation at the school. As an agricultural school, Cameron could offer students better food at a cheaper price than many institutions across the country. Cameron already had remarkably low tuition in comparison to other institutions of higher education both in and out of Oklahoma, in addition to a high rate of student employment opportunities. The fact that Cameron students had access to good meals at a low price made the institution all the more appealing. Many articles in the student paper during the depression focused on food consumption at the school.

Given that Cameron operated a sizable garden and dairy, raised poultry, hogs, and cattle, food in the school cafeteria not surprisingly

The annual Cameron picnic remained an important campus tradition for a number of years as students looked forward to this much celebrated social event. For some, it even included a dip in Wolf Creek. *Courtesy Clements Alumni Collection, 1938-1939, Cameron University Archives.*

evoked much attention from these depression era students. According to one estimate in the student paper, 450 students consumed 400 pounds of beans a day, 729 eggs, 1,800 biscuits, and 75 to 80 pounds of bacon in a single meal. The article also estimated that it took students only two meals to consume a "cow weighing approximately 300 pounds" and it concluded that "if you don't get fat while you are at Cameron, it'll be a surprise!"[83] In recognition of "a new swine barn" built at Cameron, another article pointed out the importance of the new modern facility which made "work at the swine barn a pleasure." Because "The little piggies of Cameron do not go to the market but to the breakfast table of the Cameron dining hall" explained the article, the pigs "must be properly cared for until fattened."[84]

As the 1930s neared a close, increased challenges loomed for Cameron. In 1938 Cameron set a new enrollment record with 919 students, a 13% increase over the previous year, but that number fell to 736 students in 1939.[85] School authorities attributed the decline in enrollment at least in part to a decline in NYA appropriations.[86] Cameron suffered a 40% loss in NYA funding in 1939, bringing the total number of students employed through the program from 125 in 1938 to only 75 that next year. Moreover, actual wages paid to the remaining 75 students also decreased from approximately 32 cents to 26 cents per hour.[87] While overall enrollment still remained relatively high, the number of secondary students had steadily declined since Cameron became a junior college. By 1939, only about 4% of Cameron's total enrollment came from the high school and perhaps, not surprisingly, Cameron dropped all high school work from its curriculum two years later.

Declining NYA funds were not the only financial shortages facing the school by the end of the decade. In April of 1939 Cameron suffered a 20% cut in salaries in addition to the abolition

of $7,500 in student aid.[88] In response to the news of proposed cuts in higher education, which were estimated to cut the overall appropriations of many state schools by close to 30%, President Conwill said "We are not complaining, but will operate as efficiently as possible under the amount allotted us."[89] The following October school authorities again received word of another salary cut of 10% which dropped salaries from a range of $101.00 to $114.00 per month to approximately $90.00 a month. The budget cut also included a 25% cut in school maintenance.[90] By 1939, the strategy of New Deal deficit spending had brought relief to millions of Americans but by no means had it brought the depression anywhere near to an end. Cuts in federal programs and in state education appropriations constituted only a small part of a much larger—and gloomier—economic outlook.

The year 1939 meant more than continued economic problems in the United States; it also marked the start of a second world war. Adolph Hitler came to power in Germany in 1933 just as President Roosevelt took office and began implementing a "New Deal" for America. Hitler's popularity in depression riddled Germany grew as he pledged to restore and expand Germany's empire. At first his expansion moved slowly: rearming the Rhineland, annexing Austria and eventually the Sudetenland, the latter of which came after the Munich Conference which ended with France and Great Brittan agreeing not to oppose Hitler's move into the Sudetenland so long as his expansion stopped there. Shortly thereafter Hitler violated this agreement and annexed Czechoslovakia. Once this happened, Great Britain and France began preparing for the growing possibility of war, which they declared against Germany following the German invasion of Poland on September 1, 1939. Yet, American attitudes toward the outbreak of war in Europe largely reflected a desire to mind their own business.

A majority of Americans had remained

Cameron intermittently put together a boxing team during years when they had enough students to partic-ipate, as was the case with the 1939 team. At times, Cameron's boxing team realized a good deal of success. *Courtesy Cameron University Archives.*

staunchly opposed to getting involved in another global conflict following the experience of World War I. Isolationism gripped the country through-out the 1920s and 1930s, and this trend held true at Cameron as well. In a 1933 article in the stu-dent paper Homer Specht posed the question, "Is the World Safe for Democracy?" He pointed out that a single ruler controlled "nearly every country in Europe" which included "Hitler for Germany, Stalin for Russia, [and] Il Duce for Italy." While some from Cameron said they would support any declaration of war, others voiced caution reflec-tive of the time. Professor E. C. Reynolds said that he opposed war and that "all methods should be used to prevent war." He added that "more stress should be placed on the man who prevents war than the man who wins the war." Bill Levy said he "would not fight unless he knew the country would benefit from it." Lloyd Wallis said he would not volunteer if it were "a war of aggression,"

whereas Bill O'Neil indicated that he would only "fight if attacked," and added "and then with as little effort as possible." [91] The threat of war per-haps seemed very far off to most of these young men in 1933.

Yet, as the decade unfolded, increased dis-cussion of war ensued. Two years later, in 1935, one student noted that some European countries seemed to be preparing for war and asked "Shall we again go to war or shall we think back on that Armistice?" The student added that "the cost of war in money and men can never be fully estimat-ed." [92] Another article from the same year pictured a woman wearing a gas mask beneath a headline which read "Let War Come, She's Ready." The cap-tion explained that the "busy little fingers of this Italian Steno will keep clicking out letters whether or not war comes." [93] In response to criticism of the Munich agreement, Cameron students defend-ed the effort to avoid war despite "pot shots" taken at the pact which referred to it as "peace at any price." According to an article in *The Collegian*, Cameron students "would not care to join in another war to save democracy unless the threatening element actually invaded this country." The student writer dismissed the notion that those of fighting age would "respond as enthusiastically to the sound of drums [and] sight of the waving flag" as the previous generation had simply because the "powers that be" decide young men should "give their all for 'God, country, and Wall Street.'"[94] Less than six months later Hitler invaded Poland and the Allied Powers declared war against Germany. Cameron students, like millions of Americans, remained leery of United States involvement.

The student paper continued to chart the attitudes of those who had the most to lose should the country go to war. A campus survey conducted the month after the war started found that while

Cameron students had "no great love for Hitler," most also favored America's cash-and-carry policy. As Cameron student Jerry Adair explained the workings of the policy, "Let any country come after material, pay for them, and have their own boats sunk." Other students like Margaret Lee Slover felt strongly that the United States should "keep her nose out of all foreign affairs." When asked if the United States should assist the allies, responses ranged from "Hell yes!" to playing it safe and yelling "at a distance, Sic 'em, England!"[95]

Not until the Japanese attack on Pearl Harbor on December 7, 1941 did Cameron students, along with the rest of the American public, overwhelmingly endorse joining the allied cause. For Cameron students the coming of World War II would mean great changes. Many male students volunteered or were drafted, enrollment declined, and the ratio of female to male students became

Students playing baseball at the Engineers' Picnic in 1939 with J.C. Campford pitching. *Courtesy Mildred H. Bleinett Collection, Cameron University Archives.*

decidedly unbalanced. But the onset of American involvement in the war also meant a growing economy and ultimately the end of the Great Depression. Over the course of a little more than a decade, Cameron had gone from being a high school to one of the largest junior colleges in the country and the school successfully weathered the depression and political maneuvers that threatened to shut it down. Charles Conwill presided over much of this period after coming to office in 1931, and he worked hard to protect the interests of the school. Many challenges lay ahead as faculty and students alike left the school for the war, but Cameron's mission persisted. Those students who remained continued to offer commentary on the war's progression and school officials busied themselves adjusting to war-time changes that altered the scope of the school for a number of years to come.

The O-Club, 1940-1941, included male athletes who lettered in basketball, football, and boxing. *Courtesy Cameron University Archives*.

CHAPTER THREE

"WE'RE FROM CAMERON": STUDENT LIFE IN AN ERA OF WAR AND PROSPERITY

*We're from Cameron, good old Cameron
Where the football players grow;
Where the girls are pretty,
And when you see their smiles
You'd know the reasons why
We'd walk a thousand miles
Back to Cameron, good old Cameron
Where the skies are blue
There's a lot of good old friends
We can't forget
Cameron, we're strong for you.* [1]

Robert S. Johnson signed autographs for a group of young women at Cameron following his safe return from Europe in the mid 1940s. *Courtesy Cameron University Archives.*

When Cameron students prepared for graduation in May of 1941, they could not have known that in less than six months their country would be at war. Student debate about the possibility of American entry into the Second World War had become commonplace in the campus paper, yet to many, the possibility perhaps seemed far away as sophomores prepared for final exams and looked forward to the next phase of their lives. That same May also marked the official end of Cameron's high school program.[2] The school had steadily decreased high school offerings, and the 1941 high school graduating class consisted of only 14 students in contrast to the 180 who received associate degrees that same year. While many commencement addresses focus on the potential and promise of the future, Cameron students graduating in 1941 instead heard that they were "entering a world that is in confusion." Henry G. Bennett,

the president of Oklahoma A & M, described the war in Europe as "a fundamental challenge" to American democracy. In his commencement address he further warned students that the United States was "moving slowly and surely in the direction of war."[3] Sure enough, the Cameron students who gathered with their friends and family to celebrate their graduation soon found themselves grappling with the reality of war. Yet, during the spring and summer of 1941, Cameron's future seemed brighter than it had been during much of the depression. The administration announced plans to pave Cameron roads and that an increase in faculty salaries and operating expenses appeared probable.[4] Cameron employed 23 faculty members as of the fall of 1941 and the school's enrollment of 879 students made it one of the largest junior colleges in the southwestern United States.[5]

Students in front of the Cameron College Shop in the early 1940s. Shortly after this photograph was taken the ratio of male to female students began to sharply decline because of America's entry into World War II. *Courtesy Mary Knowles Collection, 1941-1942, Cameron University Archives.*

When classes started that fall students nevertheless turned their attention once again to the war raging in Europe. The Germans had rolled through much of Western Europe and France's surrender to Germany in June of 1940 left Great Britain fighting for its survival. One student editorial addressed the fall of France, saying that America could learn "a valuable lesson from this ill-fated nation." The editorial blamed divisions in France and "non-support, strikes, and even treachery" for France's defeat.[6] Another student editorial admonished the student body to pay more attention to politics and dangers confronting the country. The editorial started out by saying "We of Cameron are nearer being men and women than children" and should therefore, reject ignorance. "We are Americans. We are citizens of the greatest country in the world," asserted the editorial before criticizing those students who apparently passed "choice bits of gossip back and forth" rather than listening to a radio address by President Franklin Roosevelt being broadcast in the auditorium.[7] The following month another editorial told students to "Wake up!" and "realize the danger that our country and our civilization faces." The article mentioned that just the week before a Cameron student had been drafted and that "as students our nation expects us to work hard so that we will be better able to serve our homeland."[8]

While Cameron students could not have known exactly when or if their country would go to war, some certainly felt a pending sense of concern over world events. Their identities as Cameron students and American citizens often seemed inextricable. One article which started by emphasizing that there were "no Communists on Cameron's campus," went on to explain that "Cameronites love America—they love the land; the labor, the Lord." The article described "Cameronite Patriotism" across campus and said that students at Cameron learned about their government and "how to be patriotic" which seemingly

Seemingly carefree students engaged in a snowball fight just as the United States began heavily mobilizing for entry into World War II. *Courtesy Mary Knowles Collection, 1941-1942, Cameron University Archives.*

explained why "no red taint tints the mind of Cameron students."[9] The anti-communist sentiment espoused in the article reflected many attitudes among Cameron students, or at least those in Professor W. J. Becker's English class. Professor Becker's class wrote essays about the International crisis unfolding in Europe and the student paper described the attitudes of Cameron students about communism as "quite definite" in their opposition to it.[10] "Having learned how to use their mind, their tongues, and their hearts," Cameron students were "not anxious to forfeit their use to a Red Ruler."[11] The students whose writing appeared in the campus paper clearly defined themselves in stark contrast to their understanding of communism and living under dictatorial rule. Indeed, to millions of Americans living in the mid-twentieth century being an American first and foremost meant not being a communist.

"What is an American?" asked one piece in the student paper. The article went on to say that an American could "feel equal to any, pauper or king" but that an American must "believe in the American way of life." It described an American as a "symbol of high standards of living, of strength, of manhood," who "is a Christian" and "believes in God." An American "feels a surge of patriotic pride and unlimited joy as he salutes Old Glory" while feeling "warm sympathy" for "his depressed brothers who salute a swastika." The article concluded that "a true American thanks God, not a dictator!"[12] The following month, in November of 1941, the student paper again raised the issue of possible American entry into the war. Nestled beneath editorials on study anxiety and the importance of friendship, a member of the editorial staff said "I believe—as do many other people like myself—we shall be into the present conflict in the near future." This particular piece focused not on Japan's continued expansion into the Pacific or the breakdown in American-Japanese diplomatic relations but instead on the likelihood of war with Italy and Germany because, as President Roosevelt said in a "world address," the United States "will not tolerate the sinking of our ships," which became a growing concern following the adoption of Lend-Lease the previous spring.[13]

While articles in the campus paper clearly reveal a preoccupation with the potential of war, it remained largely hypothetical until the Japanese attacked Pearl Harbor on Sunday, December 7, 1941. When this happened, the Cameron community along with the rest of the country quickly discovered how much their world had changed. Less than a month before the attack on Pearl Harbor, Cameron graduate Robert S. Johnson had reported for Army cadet training at Kelly Field in San Antonio, Texas. When Johnson and the other cadets heard the news he recalled that "all sound died" and "not a man in the barracks spoke." As the reality of the situation began to sink in, Johnson said that he "felt the sudden change" and he realized that "everything was different."

He described himself and the other cadets as "young men with limited practical experience in the world" and added that "residence and schooling in a town like Lawton, Oklahoma, with a life filled with study, sports, flying, social, and family activities, were perhaps not the best crucibles for forging a sensitive appreciation of wars that were being fought many thousands of miles away." As Johnson put it, he and the others "lacked—by the very isolation of geography, by the inadequacy of newspaper and radio commentary and descriptions, and by our limited experience—an intrinsic grasp of the roles we were destined to play in the new war."[14]

As news of the attack continued to filter across the nation, Americans braced for the possibility of another attack. The following day military recruiting centers across the country found themselves flooded with men volunteering to serve and President Franklin Roosevelt addressed Congress describing December 7th as "a day that would live in infamy." Congress quickly moved to approve the president's request for a declaration of war against Japan, and shortly thereafter Germany declared war on the United States. Ten days later, the *Lawton Constitution* reported news of the first Cameron death in the war. United States Navy Seaman First Class Henry Lee Hutchinson had died in action in Honolulu, Hawaii.[15]

News of Hutchinson's death marked the start of what became all too commonplace as newspapers continued to track war casualties with local ties for the remainder of the war. The impact of military service on enrollment, especially of male students, came quickly. By March of 1942 Cameron's enrollment had decreased by 32 percent from the previous semester.[16] Jay Bee Crosgrove, a twenty-one-year-old Cameron football player from Frederick, became the 50,000th man processed through Fort Sill when he enlisted in the Air Corps three weeks after the Pearl Harbor attack. When asked about his feelings regarding the Japanese attack, he said the United States should "shoot 'em and get it over with," and he expressed a desire to fight in the Philippines.[17] Three months after Crosgrove enlisted, Dean A. L. Jackson reported that according to school records a total of 87 former Cameron students were serving in the armed forces.[18] President Conwill cautioned students to "remain in school until they were drafted." According to Conwill, students who continued with their education "would be better qualified to serve" their country when called to duty.[19] The campus paper echoed Conwill's sentiment. One articled concluded by saying "defend your country by getting an education."[20]

President Conwill instructed students that they should decrease socializing, "work hard, and keep calm" and that the school would do its part to support the war effort.[21] In keeping with this pledge, school officials added defense courses to the curriculum and Cameron, along with other schools in the state, shifted to a twelve-month school year so that students could receive their degrees more quickly and take their place in both civilian and military posts to help America win the war. Cameron students began providing entertainment to troops at Fort Sill and in Lawton.[22] In addition, Cameron students took a pledge to support the war effort by conserving materials that would benefit national defense, pledging their "time and talent" in support of defense programs, conserving electricity, and buying war bonds. By the third week of January, 1942, school officials estimated that Cameron already had purchased more than $3,000 in stamps and war bonds and 189 students had made pledges totaling $197.45 a month.[23] "Every stamp, every bond helps defeat enemies of democracy," reminded an article in the student paper. The paper pointed out that the Unites States faced a "formidable combination of Japan, Germany, and Italy and their stooges in a war to the bitter end," therefore making the actions of every Cameron student relevant to the cause so that students could not afford to "laze around" in their "own selfish orbit."[24]

The Cameron Collegian continued to inundate students with similar messages for the duration of the war, and for their part many students responded to calls to serve their country in one way or another. One former Cameron student serving in the military wrote a letter back to his

Jay Bee Crosgrove at Sheppard Field, Texas in the early 1940s after enlisting in the United States Army at Fort Sill just a few weeks after the Japanese attack on Pearl Harbor. *Courtesy Cameron University Archives.*

old classmates in which he said that in 1941 he too "was a Cameron Aggie" who now fondly remembered his membership in the Hell Hounds and "dancing, playing cards" and "doing algebra assignments at the last minute." He went on to say that after the war started he left to serve his country and by the time his letter appeared in an October 1943 edition of the paper, he already had "been in three major battles" and had "seen things too horrible to talk about." The letter contained no signature. Instead, the author wrote: "My name isn't important. I am just one more boy fighting for America who misses his old alma mater and his friends a heck of a lot." He admonished fellow Aggies to "please invest in War Savings Bonds" and concluded by saying "Look into your heart before you let me down." [25]

Cameron students were not alone in leaving the campus to join the war effort; by April of 1942, nine faculty members had left their teaching posts to serve in the armed forces. Louie C. Turney resigned his position as head of Cameron's engineering department to work as a mechanical instructor in the Air Corps and Commerce instructor Paul Cochran joined the Navy. Clarence H. Breedlove, a former Cameron chemistry professor, dean, and later president, had taken a leave of absence

even before American entry into the war to engage in advanced study of chemical warfare with the Air Corps. Other former faculty members included band director Howard Way, athletic director Jess Thompson, chemistry professor Melvin Johnson, Engineering professor Ira Dykes, and Civilian Pilot Training (CPT) instructor Leon Tisdale. Two female faculty members, speech instructor Ruby Ruth Vincent and home economics instructor Edith Mckinley, also left Cameron for war employment. And so, life at Cameron for students as well as faculty and staff included a constant reminder of the on-going war. Cameron men faced the possibility of being drafted or found themselves compelled to volunteer while others stayed in school believing their studies at Cameron would in time make them better prepared to serve. [26]

While the administration sharply curtailed campus social activities, some aspects of student life remained consistent with the traditional college experience. *The Cameron Collegian* won best junior college student newspaper in the state for its sports reporting and editorials in 1942. [27] The Pep Pirates still held their annual banquet for the football team that same year. [28] Club initiation rituals continued much as they had before the war. Those "slimes" anxious to join the legend-

"The Sisters" posed together on the edge of a campus fountain. *Courtesy Mary Knowles Collection, 1941-1942, Cameron University Archives.*

The Cameron bus
made it much easier
for students who lived
in Lawton with their
families to commute
to campus. It was
especially popular
during the Great
Depression and World
War II. *Courtesy Mary
Knowles Collection,
1941-1942, Cameron
University Archives.*

ary Hell Hounds endured such "tests" as wearing
their clothes inside out in addition to having to
"bark at trees, wear dresses" and even dog collars
during pledge week while knowing at any time
they might hear the dreaded phrase "grab your
ankles, slime" which preceded being "paddled"
by members of the club.[29] Most Cameron students
were, after all, still teenagers. They found time for
the occasional dance and to keep track of campus
gossip. Beneath the apparently tongue-in-cheek
headline, "History Class Shows Pride in Its Citizenship" appeared a short article about students
dozing in class during a citizenship lecture only
to be disrupted by "the buzzing of a fly" to which
one "lazing" student quickly closed his mouth
"with the speed of a steel trap" to avoid catch-
ing the fly.[30] While moments of levity came less
frequently than they once had and the reminder
of war seemed ever present, students nevertheless
found ways to still *be* students.

As the war dragged on, Cameron continued
to evolve in response to the reality of the fighting
overseas. The 1942 summer term included course

offerings in "motor mechanics, nursing training,
[and] airplane assembly" in addition to regular
course work. Cameron's Civilian Pilot Training
Program, which started in 1939, grew in size and
the summer program increased from 20 to 40
students.[31] As some Cameron students used the
new summer semester to expedite their progress
toward finishing their degrees and took advantage
of defense course offers, former Cameron dean
Clarence Breedlove arrived in London, England as
a captain and adjusted to life in the service.[32]

News of those leaving school for military
posts as well as those who became war casualties persisted. Cameron graduate Joe R. Reed, Jr.
received a commission as a second lieutenant
in the Service Pilots Division of the Air Transport
Command. Reed had been a classmate of Robert
S. Johnson and the two had spent many hours of
their youth watching planes take off and land at
Joe's father's flight school in Lawton.[33] Kenneth
Anquoe joined the Marines. Anquoe, who was
half Kiowa and half Creek, had been a lightweight
boxer for Cameron and an amateur featherweight

boxer, as well as an artist, before going into the service.[34] Former Cameron student Bill O'Neil's plane was shot down in the sea just off the African coast. He managed to swim two and a half miles to shore even though he suffered injuries in the attack.[35] Another former Cameron student did not fare so well. Wallace Moseley suffered fatal injuries when his plane crashed in Pensacola, Florida. The twenty-two year old had majored in agriculture and the paper described him as having been "prominent in campus activities." The 1940 graduate had been married less than one year when he died.[36] The stories of young men like Moseley and O'Neil were repeated far too often for the duration of the war.

While it is impossible to discuss every story in detail, it seems significant to note that Cameron felt fully the impact of the Second World War. Only 51 students graduated from Cameron in 1943 in comparison to 111 in 1942 and 180 in 1941. Of the 23 male graduates in 1943, Roy Kennedy, Clayton Shiflett, Eldon Littlefield, and James Webb left school early to enter into military service.[37] In the spring of 1943 President Conwill noted that half of Cameron's students were military, either in the reserves or at Cameron taking technical training courses for the military. Conwill also remarked that Cameron students were "in all parts of the world" and that they were "winning fame and glory for themselves and their homeland."[38]

Conwill's words accurately summed up many of the wartime achievements of Cameron alumni. For example, former Cameron football player, Lieutenant Richard Balenti received the Air Medal for distinguished service for his work as a Navy dive bomber pilot. Balenti's squadron on Guadalcanal "attacked 94 Japanese war ships and sank or damaged 18 of them."[39] Another account of Balenti's feats near the end of the war indicated that he received a second Air Medal for seeing action at Stewart Island in 1942. It described

During World War II a number of soldiers from all over the Untied States came to Cameron for training courses. These soldiers became a fixture at Cameron for the duration of the war. *Courtesy Cameron University Archives.*

him as caring "less about medals than any man" on his carrier, adding that Balenti had neglected "even to claim the Purple Heart after he had been badly shot up during action over Guadalcanal."[40] Captain Pervis Youree, a Cameron graduate who went on to serve as a bomber pilot, won praise for "saving his plane and crew from enemy hands" during a raid in Bremen, Germany. Youree managed to return to England with only one engine. His family reported that to date he had received the Oak Leaf Cluster and two other ribbons for his war efforts.[41] Two other former Cameron students, Lieutenants Loyd D. Griffin and Guy H. McClung, also received Air Medals for heroism in the war.[42] Another Cameron war hero, Lieutenant Commander Gordon N. Owens, received acclaim for "extraordinary heroism during a navy air attack on Truk Atoll in February of 1944."[43]

Roughly 16-million Americans served in World War II and yet some former Aggies overcame the anonymity often associated with serving in the constantly-expanding armed forces and found themselves reacquainted with one another through their war service. Three 1937 Cameron graduates, who also attended Cache High School together, "made captain together the same day in the same B-26 Marauder group in France." By coincidence, Githen Keith Rhoades, Laddie J. Elling, and Robert O. Woodward met up with each other in England before being assigned to their B-26 Marauder group.[44] Two other former classmates, Marvin E. "Cuffie" Waid, Jr. and Alvin A. Boyd both enlisted in the air corps in the summer of 1943, and by March of 1945 both had been promoted to the rank of Sergeant in the same bomber squadron. The *Lawton Constitution* noted that the pair had traded attending classes together for "'attending' bombing raids over Europe."[45]

Reports of Cameron students receiving promotions and being awarded for their heroism no doubt sparked pride in their local communities, but the stories were all too often accompanied by stories with a tragic ending. George Gutshall graduated from Cameron in 1943 before entering the service. He went overseas with his infantry unit in August of 1944 and earned the Purple Heart as well as the Combat Infantryman's Badge. He later died in combat just seven months after leaving the United States. He was nineteen years old.[46] Sergeant Charles M. Finnigan, another former Cameron student, became the "first Lawton casualty of the battle of Iwo Jima" when he died in action within a week of Gutshall.[47] Staff Sergeant Calvin Kelly died in December of 1943 while serving with the 45th Infantry Division in Italy.[48] Sergeant John Carney died in action in Germany the following December and news of their deaths—though occurring one year apart—appeared under identical headlines: "Former Cameron Student Killed."[49] Both Kelly and Carney left behind wives and children under the age of one. These four stories alone provide a microcosm of the global nature of the war, and of the cost to those who fought.

While Cameron students played many roles in World War II, serving and fighting in both the Pacific and European theaters in all branches of the armed service, a good number of them were pilots. Cameron's Civilian Pilot Training Program gave some Cameronites their first taste of flying. President Roosevelt first announced plans for this new program in December of 1938 in hopes that the Civilian Pilot Training Program would increase American preparedness for wartime flying missions, should they become necessary. The Civilian Pilot Training Act of 1939 created aviation training programs at a number of educational institutions around the country. Under the new program, students combined college course work with air training and either participated in the ground unit, which included 72 hours of study in such areas as flight theory, engines, and navigation or the flight unit which required between 35 to 55 hours of flight instruction.[50] Cameron quickly moved to apply for the program and when the school became the first one in the state to gain approval, the *Lawton Constitution* hailed it as "one of the most important events in the school's recent history."[51] This certainly proved to be the case as the performance of Cameron students in the war demonstrates. Yet, as 1941 Cameron graduate Lloyd Mitchell recalled "we were just kind of naïve kids" who thought that "they just wanted to be good to us and let us get the pilot classes," but he added "they were training us for World War II."[52]

Though many served with distinction, Robert S. Johnson remains one of the best known Aggies to have fought in World War II. In 1928, at the age of eight, his father took him to his first air show at Fort Sill.[53] His love of planes grew from there; he had his first opportunity to fly at age 12 and by the time he turned 16, he had logged 35 hours of flight time.[54] After Johnson graduated from Lawton High, he began taking college classes at Cameron and when Cameron received approval for the Civilian Pilot Training Program, Clarence Breedlove encouraged Johnson to sign up for it. When Breedlove told Johnson that the program would cost approximately $50.00 to $55.00, he knew he could not afford it. Johnson contemplated selling his 1929 Model A Ford, which he thought would get him about half of the money he needed. Breedlove told him that would not be necessary and offered to make him a personal loan. To pay Breedlove back, Johnson took up several odd jobs and even worked doing window dressings in a women's clothing store and as a firefighter.[55] Breedlove spent his money well; by the end of World War II, Johnson had the distinction of being "the second highest scoring ace in the European Theater," an especially remarkable feat given that he only served in Europe for a year. During that time he destroyed at least 28 German aircraft.[56]

During World War II, the United States government awarded 464 Congressional Medals of Honor, the highest distinction for bravery, and George Dennis "Den" Keathley received one of them.[57] Keathley graduated from Cameron's high school class in 1930 and took college courses at Cameron for another two years before transferring

to Texas A & M. A letter from President Roosevelt recognized Keathley as standing "in the unbroken line of patriots who have dared to die that freedom might live, and grow, and increase its blessings." Roosevelt added that "Freedom lives, and through it, he lives—in a way that humbles the understanding of most men."[58] Keathley, like a majority of Medal of Honor winners, posthumously received the award. He was a Staff Sergeant in the 85th Infantry Division and died in action on September 14, 1944 "on the western ridge of Mount Altuzzo, Italy." As a result of substantial casualties, Keathley had assumed command of the First, Second, and Third platoons and as his men grew low on ammunition, he "crawled from one casualty to another, collecting ammunition and administering first aid" and then passed out the materials to his remaining men, all the while under enemy fire. Even after a hand grenade inflicted "a mortal wound on his left side" Keathley "rose to his feet"

After flying combat missions for only one year, Robert S. Johnson returned home as the number two ace in the European Theater. *Courtesy Robert S. Johnson Alumni Collection, Cameron University Archives.*

George Dennis "Den" Keathley was posthumously awarded the Medal of Honor for courageously giving his life in the line of duty during World War II. Having graduated from Cameron's high school division in 1930, he was much older than a number of the young men he served with which earned him the nickname "Pops." *Courtesy 1930* Wichita, *Cameron University Archives.*

The Cameron Infirmary provided basic medical care to sick students, which was especially important in 1939 when officials ordered a ten-day quarantine because of an outbreak of scarlet fever on the campus. *Courtesy Mary Knowles Collection, 1941-1942, Cameron University Archives.*

and continued firing his rifle and "shouting orders to his men" for another fifteen minutes before he died. According to this account Keathley's "heroic and intrepid action so inspired his men that they fought with incomparable determination and viciousness." Had Keathley instead "sought a sheltered spot and perhaps saved his life," then quite possibly "the remnants of three rifle platoons of Company B might well have been annihilated by the overwhelming enemy attacking force."[59] In honor of Keathley's service Cameron later named its ROTC drill team "The Keathley Rifles."[60]

Even as news of Cameron students in the service like Johnson and Keathley continued to make its way home, the school grappled with enrollment and funding concerns. Prior to American entry into the war Cameron enrollment had reached more than 800 but it dropped to a little more than 200 students in 1942.[61] Despite such challenges, Cameron continued to have the lowest

operational costs of the agricultural junior colleges in the state. Based on an analysis of five years' worth of costs conducted by the newly formed Oklahoma State Regents for Higher Education (OSRHE), Cameron's expenses totaled only $96.67 per student.[62] School officials received a pleasant surprise when fall 1943 enrollment proved higher than anticipated with 110 female and 72 male students attending the college.[63] The following semester the school learned of a 10% budget cut for the next two years and the administration feared continued enrollment challenges due to the ongoing war.[64] The number of graduates remained quite low for the rest of the war. In 1944 Cameron granted only 32 associate degrees. That number increased to 43 the following year.[65]

The campus community watched as even greater war transformations to their campus unfolded. During the spring 1943 semester a detachment of Army privates arrived at Cameron

The male to female ratio of students declined significantly at Cameron during World War II and the remaining students found their social activities curtailed. Nonetheless, shared dormitory space created an atmosphere of camaraderie. *Courtesy Cameron University Archives*.

to attend a new program for administrative clerks. This increased military presence on campus meant an adjustment in dorm space as the soldiers took up quarters in West Hall and South Hall.[66] Meal times for students also changed to accommodate the military schedule and increased rationing resulted in "sharp revision" in the campus menu.[67]

In April of 1943 President Conwill announced plans to suspend Cameron's football program until the end of the war.[68] Yet, Cameron still found ways to maintain its community ties and support the war effort. The school started a community cannery that allowed local citizens to use Cameron facilities for purposes of canning fruits and vegetables in support of the war food preservation program. The cannery could handle approximately

500 quarts a day.[69] The community cannery at Cameron continued to operate for the duration of the war through the combined partnership of local and school officials.

While Cameron remained in the throes of its wartime routine, President Conwill began looking to the needs of a post-war community and school. He tried at length to gain approval for Cameron to become a four-year school but despite support among some law makers and regents, the proposal failed. Conwill had come to Cameron in 1931 and had served more than twice as long as any other president in the school's history by the end of World War II. The student paper credited President Conwill's "wise smile" with creating "an atmosphere of strength and stability" even during difficult times when "things don't seem quite right."[70] Indeed, Conwill presided over some of the most turbulent years of the school's history—the depression era budget cuts and near catastrophic drops in wartime enrollment. Despite Cameron's failure to secure a change in status to a four-year institution, President Conwill nevertheless focused on expanding existing programs to fill the post-war educational needs of returning veterans. In particular, Conwill stressed the need for the expansion of vocational agriculture and vocational shop courses.[71]

In June of 1944 under the direction of General Dwight D. Eisenhower, Supreme Commander of Allied Expeditionary Forces, the allies launched the largest coordinated air, land, and water attack in history at Normandy, and former Cameron president, John Coffey joined in the assault. Though Americans in particular suffered a high casualty rate, the D-Day invasion ultimately marked a turning point in the war. The following spring Germany surrendered and that August Japan surrendered following America's use of the atomic bomb on the Japanese cities of Hiroshima and Nagasaki. Robert S. Johnson summed up his own sentiment—and perhaps that of many others—about the end of the war: "The moments of the fighting, of the courage and skill, the exultation of victory and despair over close friends lost, remain alive and clear only in the minds" of those who were there. Johnson concluded by saying that those moments "were the proudest of my life."[72] And so began the immense process of bringing soldiers back home to reacclimate to civilian life. Not long before his death, President Roosevelt signed the Montgomery GI Bill, also known as the Serviceman's Readjustment Act. Among other things, this legislation made it possible for returning veterans to pursue their college education. The GI Bill resulted in unprecedented college attendance as schools across the country faced overcrowded classrooms and inadequate dorm space.

The Montgomery GI Bill allowed thousands of returning veterans the chance to attend college, which led to overcrowding on campuses nationwide. This in turn changed the face of the student body for the next several years with the creation of new clubs like the Cameron Veteran's Club. *Courtesy 1947* Cameron Roundup, *Cameron University Archives.*

Keeping the Faith:
Religious Organizations and Student Life

by Kristopher Underwood
History Major • Class of 2009

Many changes occurred on college campuses and in the lives of college students during the mid twentieth-century. Events that occurred in the United States and the world necessarily shaped how college students viewed life outside of school. In the 1930s, the Great Depression moved the country away from the conservative principles of less government interference to the liberal principles of government intervention. The country continued down this path until after World War II, when the threat of communism moved the country back to greater conservatism. The 1960s and 1970s embodied the growth of modern liberalism, but even so, religion continued to hold a dominate place in the lives of Cameron students. In fact, even though changes occurred in religion, many studies show that students did

not abandon their faith, as some have suggested. Rather, students gravitated toward more nontraditional modes of expression. While the nation on the whole experienced significant changes in religious expression on college campuses in the three decades following the end of World War II, at Cameron change came more slowly and played out less dramatically.

Numerous campuses across the country went from having mandatory chapel for all students to shunning religion on campus. Even though secularization of students on college campuses flourished by the 1960s, records show that Cameron students differed in the way they approached life outside of school. Students at Cameron held on to traditional religion longer than students in other parts of the nation. They also did not stray as far from traditional religion as others. This can, in part, be credited to the relationship between Cameron and local churches as well as to the religious organizations on campus.

Three main Christian organizations dominated religious life and expression among Cameron students during the mid-twentieth century. In 1939, the Baptist Student Union (BSU) organized at Cameron for the first

The Baptist Student Union became one of the largest student organizations at Cameron and played a very active role on campus and in the community. *Courtesy 1957* Wichita, *Department of English and Foreign Languages.*

Student members of Cameron's Church of the Bible Chair worked in conjunction with other faith-based organizations on campus to facilitate Christian fellowship and Bible study activities. *Courtesy 1973 Wichita, Department of English and Foreign Languages.*

time. Accounts show that students themselves participated in the establishment of the Baptist Student Union because they felt the need for religious extracurricular activities and found them in the BSU. The BSU continued to grow in the 1940s and 1950s and did not slow down in the 1960s even though many students across the nation moved away from traditional religion. In 1954 the Lawton Churches of Christ established the Bible Chair at Cameron and it served students in many of the same ways that the BSU did. Like the BSU, the Bible Chair continued to influence students during the chaotic 1960s and encouraged them to grow spiritually as well as mentally and physically. The third religious organization that developed at Cameron and influenced students throughout this period was the Methodist Wesleyan Foundation Center, which eventually became Cameron Campus Ministry in the 1970s. Like the BSU and the Bible Chair, the Wesleyan Foundation sought to develop the spiritual lives of students at Cameron. Even though the BSU, the Bible Chair, and the Wesleyan Foundation operated independently, they worked closely with the school.

While a large portion of the nation moved away from mixing religion and academics in the 1960s, Cameron welcomed religious organizations working with students. Religion remained important for many at Cameron well into the 1970s, and as such these religious organizations not only served as a place for the students who visited their buildings to develop spiritually, these organizations also helped keep religion on campus by bridging the gap between students and churches. In 1960, for example, the student handbook still contained a list of churches, and it encouraged students to find a church of their choice to help them develop a well-rounded life. The school also encouraged religious activities

on campus. In 1961, the different organizations took turns presenting a devotional on campus. Cameron offered classes on the Bible, including Old Testament, New Testament, and the writings of the Apostle Paul. In 1962 alone, Cameron offered nine different religious classes taught by three different professors. The classes developed into popular electives among students with an enrollment of 200 students that same year. The professors for the classes were each affiliated with one of the three main religious organizations on campus, and as such the classes provided yet another way for these organizations to acquaint students with the churches and what they viewed as the fundamental beliefs of Christianity.

Clearly, religion had played a dominant role at Cameron from its very beginning, but by the mid-twentieth century, as schools across the country experienced a decline in religious based activities, organizations like the BSU, Bible Chair, and Wesleyan Foundation enhanced the ties between Cameron students and Christianity. They not only influenced students who participated in them, but they shaped the campus environment as well through the devotionals, classes, and other activities that they sponsored. The relationship between Cameron and Christianity stayed strong amidst the larger social changes and political upheaval that took place in much of the country during the 1960s and 1970s in part because of the religious organizations that ministered to the students. In many ways, it appears that the violent and turbulent 1960s passed Cameron by. While many colleges disassociated themselves with religion, religious organizations at Cameron bridged the gap between students and churches and retained their influence on campus for decades to come.

The campus "Sugar Bowl," where couples could sit together in relative seclusion, was likely a popular spot on campus given the virtually nonexistent visitation opportunities in the dormitories. *Courtesy Mary Knowles Collection, 1941-1942, Cameron University Archives.*

Cameron was no exception. Although Cameron's enrollment already had started to increase again by 1944, once the war ended the following year, enrollment grew even more.

Prior to the start of the fall 1945 semester, the *Lawton Constitution* described Cameron's future as "bright," indicating the school's administration believed the school would "come back stronger than ever now that the worst of the wartime slump in enrollment is over."[73] In fact, school officials predicted as much as a "100 percent increase over last year's enrollment by the end of the spring semester."[74] While this did not happen, enrollment did increase steadily. At the end of the first week of the fall semester, enrollment totaled 218 students and predictions dropped to an increase of 25% over that of the previous fall semester.[75] By January of 1946 Cameron listed 100 veterans as having enrolled in the school which brought the total enrollment up to 372 students.[76] Enrollment

only continued to grow, as did the job of cafeteria workers in trying to feed a seemingly ever increasing number of students. According to one estimate from October of 1946, an "average" meal served to 750 students consisted of 300 pounds of meat, 200 pounds of potatoes, 300 pounds of cabbage, 60 pounds of tomatoes, 20 loaves of bread, 25 gallons of ice cream, 40 gallons of milk, and 12 pounds of butter" at a cost of $180.00. The meat and butter, at least, came right from the school's own dairy and livestock department.[77]

The increased enrollment and a loosening of wartime restrictions contributed to a growth of the social life on campus. Students created three campus political parties as they vied for their classmates' support in the student senate elections for the upcoming year. The Carpetbaggers, the Bottle-Stoppers, and the Atomic-Bombers reflected the post-war optimism among students who longed for a return to the more carefree pursuits of college life. Cameron also resumed their pre-war athletic schedule. While the school continued to play basketball during the war, only intramural football had been played since the end of the 1942 season.[78]

The ratio of male to female students declined sharply during the war but that trend quickly reversed itself when the war came to an end. The *Lawton Constitution* published a story about an apparent attempt to reassert male authority on campus, or at least to make sure that everyone understood that Cameron was "strictly a 'he-man' campus where men wear the pants and the women are glad of it." A group of male students decided to "show their disgust at women wearing masculine attire" by making a rule that "any violations" would be met with "a trip to the fish pond." The article concluded that "one series of 'dunkings' proved sufficient to send all females scurrying for dormitories to don skirts."[79] While this seems to have been an isolated incident—or simply successful, depending on one's perspective—the story certainly speaks to a larger trend of gender role readjustments that occurred following the end of World War II. Some women felt pressure to trade typewriters for aprons as the country moved into the demographic anomaly of the baby boom where more Americans got married, stayed married, had more children, and did so at a younger age than their parent's generation had done. That said, college campuses provided a fertile ground for the new marriage trends as many young people met their future spouses while attending school. A perusal of post-war editions of the *Wichita* reveal much attention to campus couples as well as married students.

As the Cameron community adjusted to the various aspects of post-war campus life, these changes coincided with another significant change on the college campus: the retirement of President Conwill. After having presided over Cameron for 15 years, health problems prevented him from

remaining in office. He and his wife moved to California in hopes that the milder climate would improve his failing health. President Conwill died just a few months later, in September of 1946 at age 58.[80] Clarence Breedlove replaced Conwill as president of Cameron, something which apparently "greatly pleased" Conwill.[81] The two had worked together closely while Breedlove served first as a science faculty member at Cameron and then as dean of the school. Lieutenant Colonel Breedlove took an extended leave of absence from Cameron during the war while he served in England as head of the chemical warfare section of the Eighth Air Force. In the summer of 1944 he

President Clarence Breedlove was Cameron's tenth president. He replaced President Charles Conwill in the summer of 1946 after Conwill resigned because of his failing health. President Breedlove resigned six months later to accept a commission in the regular Army, something he had long aspired to. *Courtesy Cameron University Archives.*

President Vernon C. Howell was Cameron's eleventh president. He replaced President Clarence Breedlove in January of 1947 and served for the next decade, until he resigned in 1957. *Courtesy Cameron University Archives.*

BELOW: Native American students at Cameron formed the Ittanaha Indian Club which sought to promote greater understanding and appreciation of Indian history and culture. *Courtesy 1947 Cameron Roundup, Cameron University Archives.*

received the Legion of Merit for developing a device which aided the Eighth Air Force in "dropping bombs on cloud-obscured targets in Germany." His "initiative, skill, and foresight" in developing this device were credited with significantly improving "the effectiveness of bombing through clouds."[82] He returned to the United States in the summer of 1945 and the following summer he returned to Cameron as president. Breedlove pursued many of Conwill's initiatives; he tried to get increased funding for new school buildings and much needed repairs as well as an increase in the school's operational budget. Just as his predecessors had done, President Breedlove pointed out

that students at Cameron were provided with "a wholesome social schedule without the extravagant cost encountered in some institutions."[83]

During his brief presidential tenure at Cameron, Breedlove oversaw numerous changes at the school, including construction projects, such as new veteran housing on campus, an increase in enrollment, and the addition of a flight course which was open to both male and female students.[84] Cameron's enrollment totaled 702 students on the first day of classes in the fall of 1946, which marked an all-time high in first day enrollment numbers in the school's history.[85] Perhaps the rapid increase in enrollment helped convince the regents of Cameron's dire economic need. The school literally ran out of space; classes were overcrowded, the dorms surpassed their occupancy limits, and more faculty positions were needed to cover all the classes. In November of 1946, the regents approved a 35% increase in Cameron's operating budget.[86] While this increase did not include money for badly needed new buildings, it certainly alleviated some of the strain on the school.

After having served as president for just six months, Breedlove resigned his post for an appointment in the regular Army. When leaving office, he expressed his desire that the plans for the school's growth continue to be supported. Breedlove identified numerous issues that still needed to be addressed, including a campus beautification effort, a resumption of the school's irrigation project, the re-establishment of the school's orchard which had been devastated by a drought and not replaced, as well as a new gym, library, labs, a golf course, and expansion of the agricultural facilities.[87] Vernon Howell replaced Breedlove as president and adhered to the blueprint for progress provided by his predecessor. *The Oklahoman* described Howell as the "Guymon boy with the effervescent smile" who "stepped into no bed of calla lilies" when he "came to the walnut desk in the administration building" at Cameron in January of 1947. The article called him a "good administrator" with "vision and enthusiasm."[88] President Howell predicted record enrollment for Cameron at the start of the fall 1947 term but indicated that more housing was necessary to accommodate all the students desiring to attend the school.[89]

When the fall semester actually got underway, Cameron's dormitories were, in fact, full and an estimated 100 students took rooms off campus in Lawton homes as a result of housing shortages.[90] The school's continued growth reflected well on Howell, the "aggressive president," who "injected a high degree of esprit into Oklahoma's

greatest junior college," indicated the *Lawton Constitution*.[91] Indeed, Howell's vision of growth for Cameron included a renewed emphasis on the agriculture program and a plan to "develop the finest dairy herd and beef herds in the state" which would, in turn, benefit student learning in one of the school's largest programs.[92] Howell also announced plans to add a new infirmary to the campus after receiving approval to reassemble an old Army building from Frederick which had served as living quarters for Army nurses during the war.[93]

While the flurry of progress on the campus no doubt generated a degree of excitement among students, nothing proved more pivotal to student morale than the news that Cameron's football team—who enjoyed its first undefeated season in 17 years—had been selected to play in the Junior Rose Bowl in Pasadena. In anticipation of the forthcoming announcement, students even skipped classes but President Howell made the Student Senate promise that if Cameron did in fact win their bid to play in the Rose Bowl that they would "not stage another walk out."[94] When Coach Billy Stamps heard that Cameron had been selected to play in the Junior Rose Bowl he said "I am happy and proud for Lawton and Cameron College and especially for the boys who deserve it so much."[95] The Student Senate quickly moved to plan a campus dance in celebration of the news and school spirit soared.[96]

Cameron first joined the Junior College Conference in 1930 and since that time had won 11 championships, only losing 25 games in 17 years, and Cameron's quick post-war comeback on the football field sparked more than just campus enthusiasm; it rallied support from the local community.[97] In keeping with a long history of supporting Cameron, the chairman of the Chamber of Commerce College committee, Ewell Lacy, called a meeting to discuss raising funds to send the football players to Pasadena. The meeting included

Cameron boosters, railroad representatives, and others who expressed interest in making the trip possible. They outlined plans to ensure that all members of the team would be "assured an opportunity to travel" to the Rose Bowl.[98] Less than a week after the meeting, Coach Stamps announced that almost half of the $5,000 goal for the "On to the Rose Bowl" fund had been reached. The Junior Rose Bowl committee only covered expenses for 33 players and two coaches, which left the need to cover expenses for an additional 15 players and eight women who were married to members of the team.[99] Cameron students and fans also made travel plans to attend the game "by just about every mode of travel," including at least one chartered plane, chartered busses, private cars, and trains as the Aggies prepared to face Chaffey College in the Rose Bowl.[100]

A headline in the *Wichita* poignantly captured the result of the 1947 Junior Rose Bowl: "Aggie Bowl Hopes Crushed as Chaffey Smells Sweet Roses" in a game watched by an estimated 60,000 fans.[101] The final score of 39-26 left Cameron players and fans disappointed, but the fact that

Cameron even made it to the bowl remained a strong source of pride in the coming years. A message from Oklahoma Governor Roy Turner that appeared in the front of the *Wichita* recognized the "members of Cameron's great football squad" for their achievements.[102] Thirty-five members of the 1947 football team received letter jackets for their performance although Coach Stamps indicated that he "regretted that every member of the squad" who traveled to the Rose Bowl "could not be awarded a letter jacket."[103]

Following the loss of the 1947 Rose Bowl, news for Cameron's football team got even worse. Commissioner L. B. Bruner announced that an investigation revealed Cameron's use of an ineligible player. This resulted in Cameron being forced to forfeit five Oklahoma Junior Collegiate victories from the 1947 season. Cameron team member Leonard L. Logan had played for another junior college before coming to Cameron in 1946 which meant that he was ineligible to play during the 1947 season as conference rules limited players to a total of two years eligibility. Coach Stamps criticized the decision, saying that all players had to provide

The Cameron football team was quickly reconfigured following the end of World War II. The 1947 squad made it to the Junior Rose Bowl and while they lost, it nevertheless generated a lot of school spirit. *Courtesy 1948* Wichita, *Cameron University Archives.*

was their high school records and that it would be impossible to "check all 1,500 schools in the nation to see if our men had played before." [104] Darwin Richardson replaced Stamps as the football coach before the start of the next season. [105]

As the spring semester of 1948 came to a close, the setback for the football program retreated from the limelight and Cameron students looked forward to continued possibilities in the upcoming year. Despite sanctions against Cameron's football team, it is significant to note that when a film of the 1947 Rose Bowl became available in the spring of 1948, two showings of the film were planned—one at the USO building in downtown Lawton and the other in Cameron's auditorium. [106] Moreover, 34 of the 35 lettermen from the football team were freshmen, which seemed to bode well for the next season and other campus sports grew in popularity as well. The completion of a new gym gave a significant boost to the basketball program and Coach Harvey Pate dedicated himself to "sending his roundball artists through" rigorous workouts in preparation to build a strong program. [107]

Cameron student culture flourished, yet some of that culture very much reflected the unique post-war baby boom. For a number of years following World War II, several pages of the *Wichita* were dedicated to a section called "Mr. and Mrs." which pictured Cameron married couples, often with children. [108] The national post-war boom in marriage and child birth altered Cameron much the way it did the rest of the country. It remains significant, for example, that eight members of Cameron's 1947 football team already were married. While Cameron in later years would cater more to non-traditional students, many of whom were often married with children, this marked a significant shift from pre-war attendance patterns. An estimated 40 married students lived on campus during the spring of 1948 alone. The school provided separate facilities to married students with

children and those without. [109]

Cameron again prepared for increased enrollment for the following term as school officials awarded 210 diplomas to the 1948 graduating class, making them the largest graduating class in the school's history at that point. [110] President Howell increased recruitment efforts during this period as well. As part of that effort, Cameron sent copies of the award-winning newspaper, *The Cameron Collegian*, to every graduating senior in a nineteen county radius. The Chamber of Commerce donated money to Cameron to help finance a twenty-four page booklet entitled "Life at Oklahoma's Largest Junior College" which school officials also sent to the same group of graduating seniors. [111] Despite new concerns in the summer of 1948 that the National Draft Act would hurt enrollment of male students, Cameron again started a new term with high hopes. [112] The construction of a new library slated to open by the spring of 1949, which also included classroom space, brought much enthusiasm from the administration who viewed the library as central to meeting the educational needs of a growing student body.

Yet, enrollment took a substantial hit in the fall of 1948. Enrollment totals for the fall of 1947 came in at 806 in comparison to 644 students a year later. President Howell attributed the drop in enrollment to a large number of graduating veterans who left to attend four-year institutions and to female students getting married or taking jobs. [113] Since the end of World War II the ratio of male to female students had increased drastically. Prior to the war the ratio hovered around 60/40, but male attendance dropped during the war and afterward male students significantly outnumbered females. Of the 644 students at Cameron in the fall of 1948, 514 of them were male with female students accounting for the remaining 130. Despite decreased enrollment, students nonetheless met the new term with characteristic enthusiasm. They planned a pep rally and bonfire to kick off

RIGHT: Despite concerns by some that World War II would turn women into "she-men," Cameron co-eds adhered to a strict dress-code which included modest dresses or skirts. *Courtesy Mary Knowles Collection, 1941-1942, Cameron University Archives.*

Cameron cheerleaders were an important feature of post-war campus life. As sports teams were reconfigured and able to engage in regular season competitions, the cheerleading squad helped foster greater school spirit. *Courtesy 1951 Wichita, Cameron University Archives.*

the football season following the first assembly of the term, during which the faculty—and perhaps quite tellingly—the football team were introduced to the student body.[114]

As the decade of the 1940s came to a close, Cameron, along with the rest of the country, confronted the duality of post-war optimism and the seemingly omnipresent possibility of being drawn into another global conflict. The United States and the Soviet Union emerged from World War II as the only remaining super powers and both dedicated substantial resources to shoring up their respective spheres of influence, significantly with entrenched opposition to one another. In fact, cold war hostilities between the two countries infused both foreign policy and domestic politics

for the next several decades. For American college students, educational opportunities often were characterized as an extension of a larger effort to contain communism by instilling youth with both job skills needed to prosper in a capitalist society and a commitment to citizenship necessary to advance the largest democracy in the world. Oklahoma State Senator Bill Logan told the 152 students graduating from Cameron in 1949 that the United States had "begun the defense of Democracy" and that "battle lines" had been formed across the world between "those who believe in democratic government" and "those who believe in some form of totalitarianism, usually communism."[115] This sober message continued to be reiterated during the following decade.

In 1950 President Howell reminded Cameron students that the school's original purpose remained "true" and that their "opportunities were never greater." Yet he also reminded them that "greater opportunity for skill and wisdom and greater need for sincere devotion to country and our fellow men have seldom, if ever, faced the youth of America." [116] In 1949 the Soviet Union had successfully tested its first atomic bomb which, among other things, meant that the United States no longer had sole claim to this devastating technology. That same year, Mao ZeDong and his supporters succeeded in installing a communist government in China and to millions of Americans, the communist threat of world domination had never seemed more real or more possible. And so, when communist North Korea invaded South Korea the following year, the United States responded by sending troops into Korea to stop communism from spreading into the south, something that remained a distinct possibility if the recently divided country should unify under northern control. As in previous wars, Cameron students quickly felt the impact of their country once again at war. The 1951 *Wichita* opened with a picture of the American flag and an inscription that read "In honor of those students who have left this college this year to serve in our Armed Forces, we wish to show our appreciation by dedicating this 1951 annual." [117] While the Korean War was by nature a limited war and involved far fewer troops than did World War II, Cameron students nonetheless enjoyed only a short respite from wartime tensions.

Cameron enrollment reflected the growing international tension as the number of students attending the school dropped sharply. Cameron had 540 students enrolled during the fall of 1950 but that number dropped by close to 30% the following semester. The ratio of male to female students dropped and the *Lawton Constitution* described the declining enrollment as being "traced directly

to the international situation" because "male students anticipate they may be called into the service" which led some to volunteer in the hope that they might "obtain favorable consideration toward assignment to better positions and promotions." [118] While enrollment rebounded the following fall and even surpassed enrollment numbers from the fall of 1951 by 10%, the school remained in a difficult spot as the Korean War raged on and as the United States continued its commitment to stopping the spread of communism, which included a military build up.

Despite such challenges, President Howell worked to modernize the school's administrative structure. In 1949 he laid out plans for improving communication and responsibility across campus, which included division heads holding "regular meetings with the instructors," and the submission of annual reports from each division head as well as "the dean, the nurse, and the librarian." President Howell also indicated that the designation of departments listed in the catalogue would be replaced with a list of the six divisions on campus in future catalogues.

Students, perhaps taking a cue from their president, followed suit in their own campus organizations. In 1950 they created a constitution for the "Student Association of Cameron State Agricultural College" and laid out the rules of membership as well as the electoral process. The new constitution included the creation of a Student Activities Committee and a Social Committee. Amendments to the constitution required approval of two-thirds of the Student Senate and, not insignificantly, approval of the Administrative Council. [119] The Student Senate also requested a budget of $700.00 to cover such expenses as the school picnic, homecoming prizes, three dances, the intramural sports programs, and publications. [120]

As Cameron matured, the school codified both administrative and student governance procedures. Despite continued obstacles, the school grew significantly during the 1950s. Enrollment for 1954 totaled 845 students and by the following year Cameron finally broke the 1,000 barrier with a total of 1,054.[121] Growing national emphasis on the importance of a college education, Cameron's continued claim to having among the lowest cost of tuition among junior colleges in the country, and an unprecedented degree of prosperity in the nation all contributed to the school's success. While efforts to make Cameron a four-year school had failed to come to fruition in the post-war years, the school nonetheless had a thriving campus and played a vital role in the development of southwest Oklahoma even as global threats continued to loom on the horizon.

No decade has been more romanticized than that of the 1950s with popular television shows like "Father Knows Best" and "Leave It to Beaver" venerating American ideals of the traditional family where men made the money and women made the meals, yet the reality of the 1950s did not readily correspond to such idealism. The Cold War created an atmosphere of global anxiety and

school children practiced duck and cover drills so that they could protect themselves in the event of a nuclear attack. The post-war consumption patterns certainly helped spur a stronger national economy and the proliferation of television sets contributed to a seemingly homogenous culture. However, global events and unrest did not necessarily infuse the everyday experiences of college students. Peggy Long who attended Cameron in 1955 and 1956 described her generation as just about "the last innocent generation." She recalled the camaraderie on campus and said that "the kind of smallness that we had as a campus" meant that "we knew everyone really well."[122] Eugene "Gene" Thompson, a 1957 graduate, had a similar recollection of the small campus. He came to Cameron on "an Indian scholarship" and got a job in the cafeteria to help with his expenses. His uncle taught at Cameron so he "couldn't do anything without him finding out about it," which included times when Gene pulled the sorts of "pranks a freshman does." Gene met his future wife at Cameron and said simply that they had

Hell Hound officers, including Gene Thompson, who served as president during the 1956-1957 term. *Courtesy 1957* Wichita, *Department of English and Foreign Languages*.

"a lot of fun memories" from their time at the school.[123] To be sure, for hundreds of young people, time spent at Cameron during the 1950s corresponded more to typical college experiences rather than distress over world events. Nevertheless, such events had a way of permeating the complacency of light-hearted school days. Not only did the Korean War and the ongoing possibility of escalating hostilities with the Soviet Union undermine the calm facade of the nation, race relations in the United States teetered on the brink of disaster.

The landmark Supreme Court ruling in the *Brown v. Board of Education of Topeka* in 1954 called for the desegregation of public schools "with all deliberate speed" and while Oklahoma already had been in the process of dealing with segregation challenges in higher education, this ruling shored up the inevitability of desegregation in multiple aspects of American life, including that at Cameron. President Harry S. Truman had ordered the desegregation of the Armed Forces by executive order in 1948 and while this

process unfolded gradually rather than immediately, it nonetheless set the stage for ongoing desegregation efforts. Not until the 1960s would Lawton become embroiled in city-wide desegregation efforts, but even during the 1950s the ramifications of troubled race relations became increasingly clear.

Although new challenges soon faced the school following the resignation of President Howell in 1957, he left the school in good shape. One article credited Howell's "energetic and positive leadership" for the school's success and said that it was "with considerable regret that we witness his departure from such an important post." In particular, the article praised him for his work with the agriculture program and for improving the dairy and beef herds.[124] When Howell left Cameron after serving as president for ten years, he held the record for the second longest stay of any president in Cameron's history—second only to Charles Conwill who oversaw the school during the most trying period in twentieth century American—and Cameron—history.

There is where we always gather
Here to ponder, laugh and talk.

In those sweet solemn nights
When the moon is at its height
We are dreaming of the time
When our life's joy shall be sublime.

This is where we tell our pleasures
Or enumerate stored up treasures;
Here no grief consumes our lot
And we love this sacred spot.

This is where we study hard,
Of our lessons we ne'er are tired;
Something new each day we learn
As o'er the page of life we turn.

From this Campus we loathe to go
And leave the grass we all love so.
If to a distant land we fly
Still in this spot our hearts shall lie.

When school term ends we all go home
Some few of us, perhaps will roam
The most of us I dare say
Will wander back on opening day.

—*Lulu Gray, Class of 1915* [1]

Several generations of Cameron students have enjoyed
and reminisced about the beauty of campus during the
springtime when flowers are in full bloom. *Courtesy
Cameron University Office of Community Relations.*

CHAPTER FOUR

"There Is Where We Always Gather": Tradition and Progress in an Era of Change

As Cameron prepared to welcome its newest president in 1957, the campus community looked forward to many new possibilities. Clarence Davis assumed the office of president following the resignation of Vernon Howell, who left to take a position as vice president of a local bank.[2] At 46 years of age, Davis brought both experience and enthusiasm to the office. Even before he officially assumed his new role, Davis began actively following campus life at Cameron. In a letter to the students and faculty which appeared in *The Cameron Collegian*, Davis praised the "policy of progress" under Howell's administration and said that he hoped that Cameron would "always provide adequate opportunities to meet the needs of the students in the area."[3] When the fall semester got underway, Davis wrote a welcome letter to the Cameron students which appeared in the first issue of the student paper that term. He proposed a "powerful vitamin called enthusiasm" to help students meet the challenges of the upcoming year and urged them to be active in the life of the school and to take pride in Cameron.[4]

President Clarence C. Davis was Cameron's twelfth president. He replaced President Howell in the summer of 1957 and served until June of 1960 when he suffered a heart attack. Davis died just a few weeks later. *Courtesy Cameron University Archives.*

President Davis came to Cameron at a crucial period as the school tried to undertake the progress necessary for growth while maintaining a sense of tradition and identity—a dilemma with which the school continued to struggle for the next several decades. In Davis' first letter to the Cameron faculty and students in May of 1957, he told them that they were "to be commended for the progress in the direction of affiliation with North Central Accreditation," but reminded them that that there remained "much to be done before this important goal is reached."[5] Still, enrollment reached over 1,100 and continued to grow.[6] With increased enrollment came renewed discussions of Cameron becoming a four-year school—something that had periodically been proposed since the mid 1930s but that would not come to fruition until the late 1960s. According to a 1956 survey completed by 96.3% of Cameron students, a large majority of them planned to continue their education beyond the two-year degree. Nearly 83% of those who had completed their first two years at Cameron said they would continue their education. Over half of the students surveyed also

indicated that they had some type of employment, a statistic that served as a strong reminder of the need for quality inexpensive education in southwest Oklahoma. *Collegian* staffer Charles Wilson humorously summed up the socio-economic implications of the finding that some 54.5% of Cameron students worked, writing: "if you consider yourself a slave, don't feel lonesome."[7]

The centrality of Cameron to a vibrant southwestern Oklahoma became all the more clear when the Governor's Commission on Higher Education visited Cameron in the spring of 1958 and found that while "Cameron College is one of the finest junior colleges in the nation," the school had substantial shortages of teachers, classrooms, and housing. Joe C. Scott, the chairman of the commission, also noted that appropriations for higher education had failed to keep up with enrollment increases, making it all the more likely that Oklahoma parents would have to pay higher tuition rates, higher taxes, or not send their children to college.[8] Nearly seven months later, state Senator Fred Harris described Cameron as having been "slighted among state colleges when the appropriation pie was being divided," citing the fact that Cameron ranked eighth in the state for enrollment but twelfth in appropriations and number of faculty. Senator Harris urged the Board of Regents for Agricultural and Mechanical Colleges to add two more years of course work to Cameron's curriculum and to drop the word "agricultural" from the school's name because less than ten percent of the students studied agriculture. Harris argued that the "growth of Lawton and other southwestern Oklahoma cities makes the four-year curriculum a necessity for Cameron."[9] Clarence Davis' son, Don Davis, who later followed in his father's footsteps to serve as president of Cameron, recalled traveling around the state with his father over the summer to "scrounge" for paint and other supplies for the underfunded institution.[10]

As the 1958 spring term came to a close, the

Cameron's Aggiettes were a staple of campus life and school spirit even as some disparaged the "aggie" image, this spirit organization promoted tradition and pride. *Courtesy the 1962* Wichita, *Cameron University Archives*.

The 1958 Boys' Basketball Team won the National Regional II Championship. *Courtesy 1958* Wichita, *Department of English and Foreign Languages*.

student newspaper staff took stock of Cameron's accomplishments during Davis' first year as president, describing his "adroit and far-sighted presidential guidance" during "these two semesters [which] have proved to be the happiest, more progressive, and most achieving in the school's history."[11] President Davis described his first year at Cameron as "a most pleasant" one and said he hoped that the next year brought "increased numbers, more enthusiasm, new ambitions, and higher hopes."[12] President Davis also announced that all new faculty members hired at Cameron would be required to have a master's degree, something that proved vital to accreditation efforts.[13] According to a report compiled by President Davis for the 1958-1959 school year, Cameron employed ten staff members with Bachelor's degrees, and 41 with Master's degrees but had none with Ph.D. degrees.[14] While this issue became increasingly important as the school looked toward becoming a four-year institution, there remained a strong sense that students received a high quality education by dedicated and well-trained faculty. The optimism regarding Cameron's future appeared again in Davis' welcome to students as they started the fall term. He reminded them to stay enthusiastic and to "Let everyone know we have the best of everything to offer to students of Southwest Oklahoma—and then we can enjoy watching Cameron grow."[15]

With the start of the new semester Cameron faced a particularly important challenge as the campus readied itself for a visit from the North Central Accreditation Association of Secondary Schools and Colleges. Among other things, accreditation meant that Cameron students could transfer their work to other institutions of higher education without what the student paper described as the "red tape" students had to go through of getting letters from faculty and catalogues to explain the merit of Cameron work.[16] After the North Central visit, President Davis said that the school would not receive an official report until April of 1959, but that "even if we are deferred accreditation at this time, we have already achieved a great deal" because of the work already being done. "The criticism of the committee," explained Davis, "pointed out no more weaknesses than had already been identified" in the self-study survey undertaken by campus personnel.[17]

In hindsight, Davis' comments seem prescient given that North Central did in fact deny Cameron accreditation in their April report. While President Davis emphasized the experience as positive, saying that the Cameron delegation to the North Central conference in Chicago "were received royally"

and that it "almost felt good flunking," this nevertheless marked a significant disappointment for the school.[18] Admittedly, gaining accreditation for first-time applicants appears to have been "rare," but the school had to wait another two years to re-apply while doggedly addressing the shortcomings on campus. North Central identified "certain vital areas" which required improvement, including low faculty salaries, greater educational emphasis across campus, and increased faculty participation in both campus policies and activities.[19]

While the student paper certainly identified the significance of accreditation for many students at Cameron, their attention lay elsewhere. During Davis' administration, students were required to live on campus, space permitting, unless they lived at home and a majority of students continued to attend the "voluntary" monthly chapel service held on campus.[20] Much attention to morality and student life characterized the dialogue on campus conduct—sometimes in celebration of the high moral quality of campus life and sometimes in opposition to the decline of civility periodically identified by students. One student wrote a letter to the editors of the school paper decrying the rash of students who seemed to be in "training for a talking marathon" which made it impossible to hear what teachers said. The "Irate and Frustrated Student" suggested that others learn "common decency and politeness" before it was too late.[21]

Campus discussion of student conduct and educational aims often came couched in the context of cold war fears over communism. When the Soviets launched the first satellite into outer space in 1957, this fueled educational concerns that the Soviet students were outpacing American students and the "softness" of American students endangered national security. While the Russian satellite, *Sputnik*, was about the size of a basketball and posed no immediate threat, it nonetheless fueled Cold War discourse on preparedness and citizenship obligations. And, despite the fact that the economy boomed during much of the decade and the county avoided any additional full scale conflicts over communism following the end of the Korean War in 1953, the perception of a communist threat loomed large in the minds of many—and Cameron proved no exception. One campus editorial emphasized the necessity of cultivating both strong minds and strong bodies as a central defense against communism. "We are all aware of communistic aims," explained the editorial, before adding that "The salvation of our country lies in the strong bodies and resultant healthy minds of its citizens." The piece went on to explain that "Here at Cameron, our principal objective mission is instructing and studying," but added that this could only be upheld "through the help of healthy bodies." The article concluded by suggesting that Cameron students had a duty to themselves and their country to develop and maintain themselves in mind and body.[22] Another editorial also emphasized the notion that "mental health and physical health go hand in hand" while still another reminded Cameron students to "be alert or be conquered."[23]

The notion that physical and mental fitness provided an important defense against communism included increased emphasis on math and science education, especially in the wake of *Sputnik*. Oklahoma Chancellor of Higher Education, E. T. Dunlap said that the launching of *Sputnik* "excited the whole world" but also "served to trigger a frustration throughout the Western countries in the field of education." This frustration resulted in a flurry of studies into the American educational system, including a state wide "self study" of higher education in Oklahoma. In short, Dunlap explained that "typical of the American way" a demand arose for a study into the "weaknesses and shortcomings of our system."[24] To many contemporary observers of Cold War politics this essentially meant that if the Russians achieved a technological advance before the United States, the educa-

tional system had failed the American people and threatened to undermine national security. This resulted in heightened attention to technology as well as science and math instruction at Cameron just as it did at schools across the United States. In 1959, for example, Cameron sent its first faculty member to the University of Oklahoma to become a "Saturday Student" and learn how to use a computer. Dorothy Tobias, a science instructor at Cameron, indeed represented an important trend in cold war education.[25]

As the decade of the 1950s came to a close, Cameron redoubled its efforts to prepare for a second try at North Central accreditation, even hiring a consultant to help with the process while also focusing on campus growth.[26] Construction of a new student union marked a key aspect of President Davis' vision of a more modern campus. Since first coming to Cameron in 1957, he had prioritized raising funds for the project. Yet, after serving just three short years as president of the

President Richard Burch was Cameron's thirteenth president. He replaced Dean James C. Taylor who served as acting president following the death of President Clarence Davis. President Burch served as president of Cameron from the summer of 1960 to 1969. *Courtesy Cameron University Archives.*

growing institution, in June of 1960 Davis suffered a massive heart attack and died the following month. Richard Burch became Cameron's next president and when the new student union finally

Cameron's 1961 Junior Rose Bowl Championship Football team beat Bakersfield College 28 to 20 with nearly 50,000 fans in attendance. *Courtesy 1962* Wichita, *Cameron University Archives.*

opened in February of 1962, he endorsed naming the building after Davis in honor of his efforts to secure its construction. Forrest McIntire, who served as the administrative assistant for the A & M board of regents described Davis' death as "a great loss to higher education in Oklahoma."[27]

Davis' popularity during his short tenure at Cameron, along with his untimely death, left a void on the campus. James C. Taylor, the dean of administration, had been filling in for President Davis since his heart attack and the regents named him acting president following Davis' death.[28]

Burch's official appointment as Cameron's thirteenth president came at a special regent's meeting on August 2.[29] The following September the regents passed a memorial resolution in which they described Clarence Davis' death as a "dark tragedy and serious loss," adding that he "completely gave his heart to the high public cause which he served."[30] At the end of Burch's first year at Cameron, the regents passed a resolution commending the new president for his work at Cameron, saying that Burch had "been confronted with many sensitive and significant problems arising out of the transition period." They praised Burch for his "wise and considered recommendations," and said that he "exhibited sound judgment, courage, and tactfulness."[31] In fact, Don Davis who was only fifteen when his father died, said that President Burch had been kind to the Davis family and that Burch even gave him a scholarship his freshman year at Cameron.[32]

Despite the vote of confidence Burch received from the regents, he nonetheless struggled during his first few years at Cameron. He found himself at odds with Dean Taylor, who had briefly served as acting president. Burch eventually requested Taylor's resignation in what became a rather public showdown. According to *The Oklahoman*, somewhere between 50 and 100 students gathered on the lawn of President Burch's home to protest the removal of Taylor during which time the students "hung a dummy from a tree," set it on fire, and yelled "We want Taylor!" President Burch went outside to address the students, saying simply: "I am standing by my original decision."[33] The following day, classes apparently resumed as usual and the matter subsided.[34]

The Taylor incident came on the heels of two other important developments. In a letter dated April 2, 1962 President Burch received official notification that Cameron's second bid for North Central accreditation had succeeded.[35] The public announcement that Cameron had received accreditation coincided with an announcement about athletic program cutbacks, something that sparked on-going discussion.[36] An investigation into Cameron's athletic programs resulted in substantial sanctions against the school. Charges against Cameron included the use of ineligible players and financial aid to athletes in violation of conference rules. During the 1961-1962 term, Cameron won 11 football games, which included the 1961 Junior Rose Bowl, and 27 basketball games. As a result of the investigation, the school had to forfeit all of the regular season games played in the Oklahoma Junior College Conference, leaving only the Rose Bowl title intact.[37] In addition, the Oklahoma Junior College Conference placed Cameron on probation for the following year, which meant that the school could not play in any championship or bowl games, regardless of its record that year.[38] Leroy Montgomery, Cameron's football coach and athletic director, responded with frustration to the sanctions against Cameron but said "We've got a long tradition of athletic championships," adding that "it will take something worse than this to break down the fine tradition Cameron has."[39]

Despite the setbacks to the athletic program in the early 1960s, the decade proved to be an important one for Cameron's advancement in a variety of areas. In fact, the football team continued to do quite well and as one headline summing up the 1964 season explained: "New Coach, New System—But Tradition Is Same." During Coach Bear Jensen's first year at Cameron the football team won ten regular season games before losing the Junior Rose Bowl.[40] Enrollment continued to increase as well so that approximately 2,000 students attended Cameron during the 1964-1965 school year, more than a 25% increase over the previous year. Faculty and staff positions increased to 90 by the same period.[41] Enrollment increases at Cameron during the 1960s paralleled that at other institutions in the state, although Cameron

growth outpaced that of many institutions.[42]

Increased enrollment, Cold War anxiety about educational standards, and a growing push to change Cameron's campus to a four-year school all contributed to tension between the school's traditions and its future role in southwest Oklahoma. Reminiscent of the local support Cameron had historically enjoyed, a group of respected community and business leaders in Lawton, including the president of KSWO television and the publisher of the Lawton Constitution, wrote a letter to the Board of Regents for Oklahoma Agricultural and Mechanical Colleges urging them to make Cameron a four-year school. They cited the fact that Cameron already "operated at a most minimal cost" which they anticipated would continue even with the addition of two more years of study. They also argued that transforming Cameron into a four-year school would help "lighten the demand" on other state institutions and would allow "hundreds of young men and women" from the region who were being "deprived of a college education because of high costs" to receive the training they needed.[43]

While their arguments mirrored those made by other advocates of changing the school's status, the proposed shift did in fact have a downside. Cameron enjoyed a reputation as one of the best junior colleges in the country, a reputation which would not automatically transfer with a shift to four-year status. Speaking on behalf of President Burch, Dean Charles Elkins acknowledged the need for a four-year school in southwest Oklahoma, but cautioned that achieving accreditation could take another three to five years after the transition. He also pointed out the need for faculty members with Ph.D.s, especially those serving as department chairmen, should such a shift occur. Even as late as 1965, President Burch was the only Cameron employee with a doctorate. Among the faculty an estimated 54 of them had yet to complete their master's degrees. Ultimately, Elkins concluded that Cameron wanted "to do whatever the people in our area feel that we should do." He added that if Cameron's status did change, the school community would "try to perform satisfactorily the task handed to us."[44] Elkin's characterization of Cameron's "willingness" to do what its constituents wanted is noteworthy for two reasons. First, it illustrates the historical relationship between the school and the community in that the needs of the community have provided the primary force behind each major transformation Cameron has undergone. Second, Elkin's words clearly denote the recognition that the proposed transformation included substantial challenges and risks.

The Oklahoma State Regents for Higher Education wrote to President Burch on March 2, 1967 telling him that they had adopted Resolution Number 423 which revised Cameron's function to include two additional years of college course work. The letter included a provision to add third-year students in the fall of 1968 and fourth-year students in the fall of 1969.[45] Reasons for changing Cameron's status included the anticipated increase in the total number of college students in Oklahoma from 71,982 in 1966 to an estimated 120,000 by 1975. The fact that Comanche County had the third-largest population of any county in the state, as well as the belief that the shift would help relieve "enrollment pressures" on other universities in the state, also were cited in the resolution. Finally, the resolution acknowledged that baccalaureate degrees would now become "geographically convenient to a much larger segment of the state's expanding population" which included "providing more adequately for the post-high school education needs of the personnel stationed at Fort Sill." Cameron received approval to "begin immediately the planning of the new educational programs to implement the revised functions" of the school.[46] And so the process began, but it did so in fits and starts and not always

with great enthusiasm or success.

The appearance of the 1967 *Wichita* illustrated the transition that lay ahead. President Burch described Cameron as "an emerging four-year college" with great "flexibility" in its ability to "offer new technical and occupational programs for tomorrow." Burch optimistically described Cameron's potential, saying that "the future growth of Cameron College can become greater than the most fantastic story ever printed." Yet, in a rather unfortunate—and perhaps painfully accurate—choice of words, Burch asserted that Cameron was "not bound by tradition," which for him meant that they could chart their "own course

As Cameron prepared to transition from a junior college to a four-year institution in the mid-1960s, students did not immediately feel the impact as student life continued to center on sporting events and socializing. *Courtesy Cameron University Archives.*

Professor Mickey Cooper taught at Cameron from 1964 to 2000. Cooper's career at Cameron resembled that of a number of faculty in that there was a large influx of young faculty from the mid-1960s to the early 1970s, a lot of whom spent the remainder of their teaching careers at Cameron. Cooper's photograph, taken in 1971, was reprinted in a later edition of the yearbook. *Courtesy 1991* Wichita, *Department of English and Foreign Languages*.

Cameron's legendary mascot, 'Ole Kim, has gone through many incarnations and during the school's transition to a four-year university provided an important symbol for those who advocated maintaining school traditions. *Courtesy 1972* Wichita, *Department of English and Foreign Languages*.

into the future."[47] The yearbook staff shared in this optimism and dedicated the 1967 *Wichita* to their "confidence in Cameron's future," saying that "a college must grow with its students or it will be lost in the past forever."[48] For the next several decades, however, generations of Cameron students, as well as faculty and staff, would struggle with the conflicting notions of tradition and progress, grappling at times with whether one must be surrendered to save the other.

And so, as Cameron underwent the transformation to a four-year institution, the tension between tradition and progress grew. At the start of the 1969 school year, Cameron's school colors were changed to red, white, and black. This change proved unpopular and short lived as the student senate voted to change the colors back to black and gold in October of 1969. In an article tellingly entitled "Black, Gold, and Beautiful,"

one writer for the student paper explained that the black and gold colors "have built a legacy that is as vital as 'Ole Kim." In a rather lively defense of Cameron's past, the author declared that "the spirit of progress is not stimulated by the destruction of every tradition" and concluded with the admonition that the colors "must be maintained and continued in order to provide the school an honest history and a fighting school spirit."[49] In the next edition of the student paper, another piece addressed the identity crisis facing the school. It explained that "transition, change, a search for campus identity—all these are reflected in Cameron's homecoming theme—Odyssey 1969."[50]

The struggle over Cameron's identity did not play out over night. At the core of debate, it seems, lay a sense that the emphasis on "finally" attaining the status of a four-year university denigrated the school's past. Perhaps one signifier of this mounting tension came with a dramatic change in faculty recruitment methods. In years past, many potential faculty members at Cameron heard about job openings through word of mouth and some were hired without any official interview. In instances when an interview did occur, it often involved only the school president and the candidate. For example, in 1964 James Mickey Cooper was a graduate student at Oklahoma State University when he heard about a position open at Cameron from a former Cameron faculty member. Cooper wrote to Burch about the position and then met Burch at a hotel in downtown Oklahoma City. Cooper summed up the interview, saying "I liked him and he liked me and so we agreed that I would come to Cameron." Burch told him the salary for instructors with no experience was $5,000. When they walked outside and Burch saw Cooper's wife and young son waiting in their car—a '56 Ford—Burch turned to him and said "you are a young man with a family and you need a little more money; I'm going to give you $5,200." A good investment on Burch's part, it seems, because Cooper eventually finished his Ph.D. and taught at Cameron until 2000.[51]

Terral McKellips' career at Cameron started in 1968 when he was hired to chair the Department of Mathematics. He eventually served as a division head and dean before becoming the chief academic officer for the university. He retired in 2001. *Courtesy 1969* Wichita, *Department of English and Foreign Languages.*

Nationally, many college students during the volatile 1960s challenged the status quo in one way or another, yet at Cameron a much more conservative atmosphere prevailed. *Courtesy Cameron University Archives.*

Once Cameron began its transition to a four-year school, however, it became necessary to codify recruitment and hiring procedures, especially as the school increasingly sought faculty with terminal degrees. So when President Burch requested approval from the regents for out-of-state travel to "recruit new faculty members" during March of 1967, times were, in fact, changing.[52] While Cameron continued to hire a number of new faculty from Oklahoma and neighboring states like Texas and Kansas, the process changed dramatically in just a few short years. By the time the decade of the 1960s came to a close, Cameron had hired a number of faculty with terminal degrees, including such long time faculty members as Terral McKellips who was hired in May of 1968 as chair of the math department.[53] McKellips went on to fill many important roles on campus including division head, dean, and chief academic officer. During his first semester at Cameron he chaired the Salary, Rank, and Tenure Committee and helped devise the first uniform code for "Faculty Personnel Policies" for the *new* Cameron State College. Yet, McKellips recalled his "shock" when he learned that Cameron officials believed they would soon gain four-year accreditation by North Central. When McKellips came to Cameron, he said he was one of only four faculty members on campus with experience teaching at a four-year institution and that he could not imagine the institution actually succeeding in its bid for accreditation at such an early stage.[55]

Cameron student life, however, felt little direct impact from the new hiring practices and accreditation efforts. Instead, students confronted some of their own challenging demographics. Historically, a large number of Cameron students have worked, but once Cameron became a four-year school, many of those students seemingly became less involved in campus life. In a survey conducted by the student senate in November of 1968, only 9% of students questioned identified themselves as

"very interested" in student government in contrast to the 24% who said they were "not particularly" interested in it. Perhaps even more tellingly, 45% of students responding to the survey said that they spent no time pursuing extracurricular activities on campus. Additionally, 85% said that they had not participated in any student organizations at all.[56] In the fall of 1969, the first semester in which Cameron offered all four years of college course work, 400 hundred students responded to another student senate survey in which they overwhelmingly said that the student body should be consulted before the student senate issued a "statement on an issue of national importance."[57] Without making too much of these surveys, they do at least reveal a perceived decline in student participation on campus yet a desire for the student body to be consulted on weightier issues. In other words, a lack of campus activity did not necessarily reflect widespread apathy.

Student protests and a rejection of authority often appear inextricably linked to the 1960s, yet on the comparatively conservative campus of Cameron this seldom seemed to be the case. Instead, the school exercised tremendous control over student conduct. At the height of the "free love" movement in the late 1960s, three female Cameron students were suspended for violating school regulations and having male visitors, who were not their brothers or fathers, in their dormitory room. In one instance, a female student was suspended for simply failing to report that she witnessed a male visiting another female student's room. Despite letters of appeal written to President Burch, he refused to overturn the ruling of the disciplinary committee.[58] Other issues of concern on Cameron's campus in the late 1960s included such student infractions as using profanity, using someone else's meal ticket in the cafeteria, and drinking on campus property. One student who refused to remove his ball cap after being told to do so by the dean received a one-week suspension from the student union. And, in another instance, the committee debated what to do regarding a male student who refused to shave his beard.[59]

Yet, concern over protests and extremism on college campuses persisted in Oklahoma and across the country. The Board of Regents for the Oklahoma State University and Agricultural and Mechanical Colleges actually passed a resolution which sharply curtailed the "sort" of person who could be brought to campus to speak. The resolution said that since campus facilities "were paid for by the taxpayers of this State from their earnings in our society based on law and order" that they could not be available to anyone who advocated the following:

a. lawlessness and disregard for the laws of this country;

b. any change in the laws of this country, other than by peaceful means; and

c. the violent overthrow of our government.[60]

When the regents issued this resolution in late 1967, the United States was embroiled in perhaps the most divisive war in the history of the country. While substantial numbers of American troops did not arrive in Vietnam until March of 1965, the United States had been intervening—financially and covertly—in Vietnam since the end of World War II. When Vietnamese leader Ho Chi Minh issued a declaration of independence for Vietnam in the fall of 1945, American leaders correctly inferred that this meant that Vietnam would fall to communism under Minh's leadership. After the French failed to retake Vietnam, the country was divided at the 38th parallel into North and South Vietnam, with Ho Chi Minh and his communist supporters controlling the north, and the south ostensibly in need of protection from communism.

When Congress passed the Gulf of Tonkin Resolution in the summer of 1964, which essentially gave the president the power to take all necessary measures to combat further aggression

During the 1960s strict dress codes prevailed on Cameron's campus. Female students were expected to wear skirts that covered their knees and male students were expected to remove their hats indoors and to be free of facial hair. *Courtesy Cameron University Archives.*

in Southeast Asia, they set the framework for the war in Vietnam. While the Vietnam War remains a sharply contested event among historians, veterans, and policy makers, one cannot ignore the divisive nature of the conflict. By 1968 American anti-war protests reached a high water mark and confrontations between law enforcement and protestors grew increasingly volatile. In October of 1969 when many students observed a moratorium to protest the continuation of the war in Vietnam, Barbara Driver, the editor of *The Cameron Collegian*, wrote to the governor telling him that Cameron would not participate. She wrote: "We hate war; we hate dying; we love America and will keep Old Glory flying."[61] Governor Dewey Bartlett responded that it was "especially noteworthy that the students of Cameron College stand united with others to keep Old Glory flying." In a student senate survey regarding the war and a proposed moratorium for November of 1969, 49% of Cameron students responding to the survey indicated that they thought the school should participate while 41% opposed Cameron participation and 9% remained undecided.[62]

And while Cameron did not participate in the moratorium, the uneasiness over radicalism on college campuses continued to shape administrative discourse on student conduct. Yet, as Dr. Cooper recalled, "Dr. Burch was a white side wall kind of guy" so there were "no hippies and that kind of thing because he was not of that nature."[63] Even the team from North Central commented on the lack of radicalism at Cameron, saying that "student agitation has been minimal" and that

"there seems to be a ready acceptance on the part of students of the rather stern, restrictive campus life at Cameron." North Central evaluators also commented on the number of speakers invited to Cameron's campus, noting that "very few are controversial."[64] At first glance, this assessment might appear positive, but in fact factored into North Central concerns about student life on campus.

In their 1969 report, North Central identified several areas of student life about which they felt the campus too rigid. They recognized the challenging role played by the dean of students because he had to maintain the "confidence of students" while also conveying to them "the administration's extreme conservatism about anything that threatens to be controversial or uncontrolled."[65] The report further noted that even among a largely conservative student body, students tended to find

At Cameron the ROTC program remained in high esteem, even at the height of the national anti-war movement. President Richard Burch, himself a strong supporter of the military, participated in an ROTC commissioning ceremony during the mid-1960s. *Courtesy Cameron University Archives.*

Cameron Student Reaction to ROTC During the Vietnam War: 1971-1975

by Second Lieutenant Eric Nabinger
History Major and ROTC Graduate
Class of 2009

During the Vietnam War anti-war activist groups turned up at colleges across the nation and, for the most part, these groups manned by students at the school where they made their home, encouraged people in the United States to stand up against the war. Schools such as Berkeley, Michigan, Harvard, Kent State University, and many others all had some form of anti-war activist groups on their campus. While these schools were spending their time dealing with protests against the Vietnam War, some did not go along with the trends set by these schools. One such school is Cameron University, which proved to be the exception to the perception that colleges were nothing but a hot bed of protesters and activists.

The ROTC program at Cameron had played an important role in both student life and learning since its installation on campus in 1951. From the start, the ROTC program played a central role on campus, in part because it was compulsory but also because Cameron already had strong ties to the military due to its close proximity to Fort Sill. The program participated in school functions such as football games, student senate, homecoming competitions, and other important aspects of campus life. ROTC cadets also participated in activities on Fort Sill that allowed many students to see and understand the operations of the United States Army. The program maintained its position on campus throughout the 1960s and even had their own drill team called the "Keathley Rifles." This elite group often marched in the homecoming parade in remembrance of those who had served their country, including George Dennis Keathley, a World War II Medal of Honor Winner who died in the line of duty. At the height of enrollment in Cameron University's ROTC, the program consisted of two companies with four platoons in each company. The fact that Cameron ROTC had been mandatory allowed the program to become the largest ROTC program in Oklahoma with a corps of cadets that numbered approximately 600 by 1970.

During the 20 years Cameron's ROTC remained mandatory, the program had made a name for itself on campus. Not until 1971 did the Student Senate conduct forums so that students could voice their opinion about Cameron's mandatory ROTC policy. Then, after reviewing student sentiment, they "unanimously accepted removal of compulsory two-year ROTC from the school." After the Board of Regents approved changing Cameron's compulsory ROTC program to a voluntary one, enrollment not surprisingly fell. Yet, this did not stop the ROTC from thriving at a time when ROTC programs on other campuses faced ridicule and numerous schools dealt with sometimes violent protests against their Reserve Officer Training Corps. Instead of being the type of school that Richard Nixon referred to when he complained that American students were determined to spend their time "not in learning, but in 'blowin' up buildings [and] burning books,'" Cameron University proved the exception.

Even as ROTC became voluntary, the program maintained their prominence on campus. For many years they voted for an ROTC queen and crowned her at the homecoming games. ROTC continued firing their cannon during home games every time the football team scored a touchdown until Cameron shut down the football program in 1992. Overall, the ROTC held an important place both on campus and in the community, teaching students who participated in the program about the "traditions and military profession, the role of the professional officer in our country, and the maneuvers of the army units."

Even as much of the country grew divided over the war, support for the Cameron ROTC program and the Vietnam War appeared numerous times in *The Cameron Collegian*. Many students voiced opinions about both anti-war demonstrators and media coverage in letters to the editors, and other newspaper articles. For instance, Cameron student Rick Mitz decried the fact that "1,785 demonstrations took place on college campuses, 313 building seizures and sit-ins, 281 anti-ROTC demonstrations, 246 arsons, and 7,200 student arrests, resulting in more than $9.5 million in dam-

Cameron's ROTC program became nationally renowned and enjoyed a positive image on campus throughout the late 1960s and 1970s. Cadets played an active role in student organizations and in campus life even after compulsory ROTC was discontinued in 1971. *Courtesy Cameron University Archives.*

age." Articles like this one frequented *The Cameron Collegian* from 1971 to 1975, more often than not condemning the actions of the anti-war protestors and the news media for reinforcing the stereotype of college students.

Unlike the students at schools such as Kent State, the University of Oklahoma, and Berkeley, the students at Cameron seemed unwilling to protest the war. In fact on October 15, 1969 nine campuses in the state of Oklahoma participated in protests on what had been called Vietnam Moratorium Day. The Vietnam Moratorium provided an opportunity for the nation to demonstrate against American involvement in Vietnam in hopes of forcing the government to pull the soldiers out of South Vietnam. A report published in the October 16th edition of *The Oklahoman* explained that the demonstrators gathered on the campuses of the former Phillips University, University of Oklahoma, Oklahoma State University, and Tulsa University. This report details how each of these schools held rallies and discussion boards. While these schools were protesting

against the war, Cameron University used the Vietnam Moratorium Day to demonstrate with a "Love America Parade." This made Cameron and Lawton just one of a few schools and towns to answer the governor's call for a counter demonstration against the Vietnam Moratorium Day, and fly their flags at full-staff in rebuttal of the actions of those schools that acted against the government on that day.

The close relationship that the students and campus had with Fort Sill, as well as the relationship the school had with the ROTC, helped to fuel the discontent that many students felt toward the anti-war activists. The ROTC's place in campus life kept them from becoming a target of students that might have viewed the ROTC as a tool of a corrupt government. It is clear that the ROTC maintained its prominence at Cameron through out the Vietnam War, and despite pressure from the anti-war and anti-ROTC activists, the students stood up for the ROTC and government that they believed in.

the school "tight in its control of student life and its discouragement of controversy on campus." The "brightest and most adventuresome students" apparently conveyed to the North Central visiting team their "concern about censorship of the student newspaper, screening of campus speakers" as well as "the interception at registration of students whose skirts are too short or whose hair is too long."[66] While North Central recognized the difficulty of substantiating some of the student claims, they also said that such reports did "not appear to be altogether apocryphal." In their conclusion on student life, North Central asserted that Cameron would "become a strong educational institution only when it welcomes, or at least tolerates, debate, dissent and difference," which included allowing for "greater variation in student appearance, and discussion in class of ideas that may sound suspect to the Lawton community."[67]

And so, while in the late 1960s and early 1970s many institutions of higher learning felt themselves being pulled apart at the seams by

Cameron students with their parade float themed "A United America," which was especially notable during the mid-1960s when the country faced some of the worst divisions of the twentieth century. *Courtesy Cameron University Archives.*

Cameron's theatrical productions reached audiences across campus and throughout the Lawton community during this period. Theater students posed on their production set in 1966. *Courtesy Cameron University Archives.*

student protests, at Cameron the apparent conservatism sheltered the school from such unrest but came at no small price. Cameron confronted an enormous transition, and one which fundamentally challenged its identity, mission, and future.

After North Central's first visit to Cameron in 1968 for purposes of accrediting the institution as a four-year degree granting school, they denied preliminary accreditation and told school officials to stop offering upper division work or they would completely lose their accreditation.[68] North Central cited a host of problems at the school including a lack of faculty with graduate training, a lack of adequate funding for adding third and fourth year curriculum, and a general lack of attention to what niche the school might fill within the state. According to the North Central report, "there was little evidence in any area of careful planning based on hard data and no significant long-range planning."[69]

Despite being told to discontinue teaching upper division classes, North Central noted that the State Regents, A & M Regents, and Cameron were all "going ahead with plans for the full development of the four-year program" for the 1969-1970 school year.[70] The 1969 North Central report criticized the State Regents for their "unwillingness" to "use their suasive powers to ensure more positive implementation" of the four-year curriculum.[71] To further complicate the matter, the A & M Regents fired President Burch in January of 1969, just a month before North Central's campus visit. While Burch remained in his position until the next president officially took over the following summer, this sequence of events contributed to the perception of the school as "the embattled Cameron State College" and did little to transmit a feeling of security on campus.[72] North Central referred to this "abrupt change" as "unfortunate," saying that, "progress had been made" during Burch's eight years as president. They noted that the new president had a "formidable task" ahead.[73]

The faculty as well as state newspapers also recognized the pivotal role the new president would play. In a letter to the A & M Board of Regents, Cameron's Faculty Affairs Committee urged the Board to allow faculty to assist in the search for a new president. The committee explained that "No single decision could have more influence on the morale and welfare of a college faculty than the election of a new president, especially at a time when the school is under the scrutiny of an agency like the North Central Accreditation Association."[74] Terral McKellips recalled that the regents responded with a rather brisk and definitive "No!" to the committee's request for input into the presidential search. Two days after John Murphy, chairman of the Faculty Affairs Committee, sent the letter to the regents, a brief blurb in the *Oklahoma City Times* commented on the situation at Cameron. It admonished the regents to "avoid the temptation to appoint just some other 'good old boy' superintendent of schools" and instead "appoint a joint regents-faculty committee to shape the selection." The piece explained that with the selection of a new president, Cameron had "the chance to either become a real four-year college, or just a sort of super junior college."[76]

President Don Owen was Cameron's fourteenth president. He replaced President Richard Burch in the summer of 1969, although both men maintained offices at Cameron, while sharing some of the presidential responsibilities during the spring of 1969. *Courtesy Cameron University Archives.*

Forest McIntire, Executive Secretary to the A & M Regents said that "Candidates should have an earned doctorate degree" and that they should be "between the ages of 30 and 55" in addition to having education administrative experience.[77] Forty-one year old Don Owen, a former Cameron student who held a doctorate in education left his job as superintendent of Shawnee Public Schools to become Cameron's next president.[78]

While Burch technically remained president until the following summer, Owen began taking on increased responsibilities at Cameron in the spring of 1969. On April 1, President Burch received a letter from North Central reminding him that their board had "voted to remove accreditation from the entire institution at the end of the 1968-1969 academic year, if upper division work leading to the Bachelor's degree had not been discontinued by that time." The letter also served as official—if unsurprising—notice that North Central had denied Cameron preliminary accreditation as a "Bachelor's degree granting institution." Summing up what they considered some of the most serious problems at Cameron, Norman Burns, the executive secretary for North Central, wrote that these included:

> inadequate provisions for faculty participation in the development of academic policies in institutional governance; lack of sufficient faculty and staff development for upper division work, inadequate conditions of faculty service, particularly in regard to rank and tenure policies; and, insufficient development of library resources.[79]

Don Owen, rather than Burch, responded to the letter. Owen said that because both the legislature and the State Regents had changed Cameron's function to that of a four-year school, they did in fact plan to proceed. Owen explained "As we see it, we have no alternative, only to proceed, in that funds have been provided, faculty recruited, and we are sufficiently resourced to begin this pro-

gram." He then requested "permission to withdraw from the North Central Association before it is too late." Owen closed by saying that Cameron would reapply in a few years after completing their conversion.[80] Much had changed in just a few short years. After Cameron received accreditation from North Central as a junior college in the spring of 1962, Cameron proudly publicized that fact, and even had it printed along the bottom of official school letterhead. Yet just seven years later Cameron opted for a complete withdrawal from the association rather than face the certainty of losing complete accreditation of their programs and degrees.

As predicted by North Central, Owen did indeed face a difficult task in carrying out Cameron's transition to a viable four-year institution. Cameron's historically strong community support became strained during these transitional years. On the one hand, it seems abundantly clear that Cameron's change in status had the support of the local community. On the other, there appears to have been some disconnect between *wanting* the transformation and understanding what it entailed. North Central's 1968 report indicated that while Cameron reported "that much of the impetus for the move came from the Regents," there existed "many indications that considerable pressure for the move came from the local community of which the Regents were doubtless aware."[81] In a report commissioned by the Chancellor of Oklahoma State Regents for Higher Education in 1969, the role of the community also received attention. This report cautioned Cameron to "broaden community support of the institution without community domination of the school." The report further added that "perhaps local support and enthusiasm for the college could be transferred from the community concept, to the idea of a state college controlled by its state board of regents."[82]

Several factors converged to complicate the relationship between Cameron and the commu-

Cameron Majorettes on the sidelines during a 1967 football game. *Courtesy Sally Soelle Collection, Cameron University Archives.*

nity it served, and somewhat ironically it seems to have in part been driven by the observations of North Central. While North Central described students and faculty as "enthusiastic" about the transition to a four-year institution and noted that "There appeared to be considerable pride in the institution," the criticisms made by North Central echoed divisively across campus for decades to come.[83] North Central repeatedly made note of the number of faculty who were from and educated in Oklahoma at the same time as they pointed out the need for greater academic rigor and more graduate training for a greater percentage of the faculty. In one instance North Central commented

that "the highly homogeneous character of both groups [students and faculty] tends to encourage provincialism."[84] They praised Cameron's use of a Title III education grant to allow current faculty to take a leave of absence to complete their degrees, but certainly this method met with some cynicism as the notion evolved that at Cameron sabbaticals were only given to people for completing graduate school rather than pursing extensive post graduate research, correspondent to the national norm in academia.

Cameron instructors who only held bachelor's degrees found themselves in a precarious position as the school became a four-year institution. In one rather public showdown three female Cameron instructors appealed to the Oklahoma Education Association (OEA) to investigate their dismissal from Cameron. F. E. Willington, the associate executive secretary of OEA indicated that "all three dismissed teachers held only bachelor degrees and that because the college is moving from a junior to a four-year status, teachers with higher degrees must be hired for accreditation reasons." The teachers, however, felt that they had been "singled out" without knowing why and correctly pointed out that other instructors with only bachelor's degrees still remained on staff at Cameron.[85] Increasingly, Cameron seemed to be struggling with both an image and identity problem; not good enough to be a real university but too good to employ locals with only bachelor's degrees. With the shift to four-year status Cameron simultaneously alienated some members of the community while undermining its long standing reputation as a fine junior college. Apparently fed up with "all the complainers and criticizers of the day," one Cameron student who described herself as a "busy homemaker" with two children who commuted from Frederick to attend classes at Cameron said "I am tired of the uninformed and overly-critical informed people belittling my school!" She added that there were "many outstanding, well qualified teachers at Cameron."[86]

As Cameron prepared for the start of its first semester of offering senior level classes to what would become Cameron's first baccalaureate graduating class, President Owen grappled with trying to shore up Cameron's academic standing. In hindsight, the closing of Cameron's dairy proved highly symbolic of the school's new mission. In fact, after the dairy had been dismantled and the equipment sold, Owen recommended that the $11,437.35 made from the sale be used to buy additional library books.[87] When President Owen initially proposed closing the dairy in the summer of 1969, he said that it cost the school more than $12,000 annually to operate and cited the fact that "the dairy program has not been used at all in relation to" student learning.[88] While Owen expressed concern that the matter be handled carefully "to attempt stopping as much conversation as possible which might arise with the thought that we might be de-emphasizing agriculture here at Cameron," the school did in

fact seem to be moving away from its agricultural roots.[89] That same summer a petition circulated across campus in support of changing the school's name from "Cameron State Agricultural College" to "Cameron State College." Owen wrote to Forrest McIntire requesting guidance on the matter. Owen said "Personally, the name as it is suits me" but added that he would "not be objectionable at all to seeing the name changed." He concluded by saying that he had "little interest in this matter" and that he had "no particular recommendation to make."[90]

Despite the seemingly bleak outlook following Cameron's withdrawal from North Central, things did in fact begin to turn around for the school rather quickly. President Owen applied again in the fall of 1969 for correspondent status and the association sent a visiting team in January and October of 1970 and again in April of 1971. On the whole, evaluators praised Cameron and President Owen for the progress made at the school. By 1971 enrollment reached 4,320

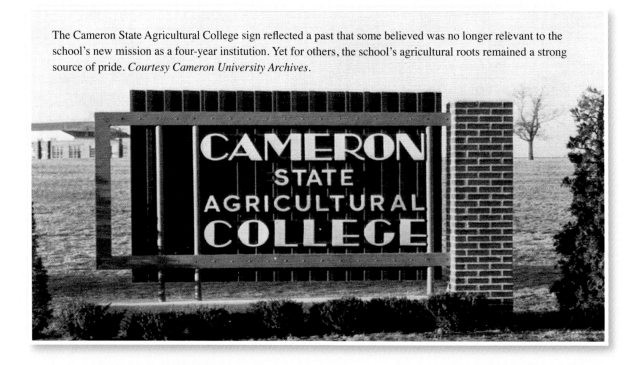

The Cameron State Agricultural College sign reflected a past that some believed was no longer relevant to the school's new mission as a four-year institution. Yet for others, the school's agricultural roots remained a strong source of pride. *Courtesy Cameron University Archives.*

Helen V. Casey came to Cameron in 1913 to teach English and mathematics. By the late 1920s she was regularly identified as the most senior instructor on campus. *Courtesy 1914 Wichita, Cameron University Archives.*

Helen V. Casey Cavanaugh Carney continued teaching math at Cameron until she retired in 1963, having outlived two husbands. Her tenure at Cameron spanned five decades, making her the longest serving faculty member in the school's history. *Courtesy 1963* Wichita, *Department of English and Foreign Languages.*

that progress had continued; of the 109 faculty teaching in bachelor degree granting departments, only one held just a bachelor's degree whereas 61 had master's degrees and 47 had doctorates. Of the other 20 faculty in non-bachelor degree departments, six had bachelor's degrees, thirteen had a master's degree, and one held a doctorate.[94] All told, this trend revealed a rather drastic turn around on campus.

By the mid 1970s, Cameron exhibited a thriving campus in many ways. The school had overcome its accreditation problems. An influx of young well-trained faculty from both within and outside the state converged on campus and left a profound mark on the institution. Faculty like Terral and Karen McKellips, Lynn Musslewhite, Mickey Cooper, and Josephine Rayburn came to Cameron in the 1960s and 1970s, stayed with the institution for decades and left a lasting imprint on Cameron. In the Department of Mathematics alone, one can find much of Cameron's history embedded in the lives of two individuals whose collective time at Cameron spanned nearly 90 years of the school's history. Helen V. Casey came to Cameron in 1913 to teach math and English. While she left for a few years toward the end of the decade, she married and had a son, she returned to Cameron as Helen Cavanaugh and taught math until she retired in 1963 as Helen Carney, having survived two husbands, and was the longest serving faculty member on campus. When Terral McKellips accepted a position in the math department five years after Carney's retirement, he likely did not anticipate the trajectory his own career at Cameron would take. While he officially retired in 2001 as provost of the university, he returned a year later to serve in interim administrative positions.

The transition to a four-year institution led to resentment, feelings of inferiority, anger, defensiveness, bewilderment, and tension among faculty and within the community. It also sparked

students, close to a 10% increase over the previous year.[91] In the January 1970 report, evaluators noted that Cameron's request to withdraw from North Central had transpired as a result, in part, of a "dialogue with officers of the Association," and they acknowledged the existence of tremendous tension on campus during their visit in February of 1969.[92] The evaluators described Burch as having been "most unhappy about the Board" replacing him and that his attitude "undoubtedly had a substantial impact on the judgment of N.C.A. examiners" in regard to the "perception of the degree of magnitude assigned to the problems." They were, however, quick to point out that this in no way meant that "the problems were or are any less real or severe."[93] They also noted improvements were headed in the right direction. An internal report a few years later, in October of 1972, revealed feelings of pride, a deeper appreciation of tradition, and a sense of accomplishment as Cameron continued to fulfill its fundamental mission to the community it served by providing quality education to those living in southwest Oklahoma. Out of the growing pains the campus experienced, a new enthusiasm emerged with the recognition that some of Cameron's best traditions remained intact. Cameron always had prided itself on the individual attention students received on the campus, and this had not changed. Nick Miller, whose father coached Cameron's basketball team to numerous victories attended classes at Cameron in the mid-1960s and he recalled a former classmate, Tony Miles, who arrived on Cameron's campus with only a "paper grocery sack" which held a single change of worn out clothes and a toothbrush. This 6-foot-7-inch basketball player weighed only 185 pounds but "Mac," who ran the cafeteria, made sure that he got as much to eat as he wanted and by Christmas Nick estimated that his friend had gained 30 much-needed pounds. Nick also remembered that when local people found out about Tony's situation, "they got him some clothes." He explained "that's the way it was on campus then, there were people that genuinely cared about you." [95]

Tony Miles Attended Cameron and at 6-foot-seven-inches tall, was a tremendous asset to the men's basketball team. *Courtesy 1966* Wichita, *Cameron University Archives.*

In 1931 President Coffey noted that no official records were kept of students employed on campus because he was personally acquainted with each and every one of them. The campus grew far too large for President Owen to make such a claim, but during his tenure, as in that of those who followed, substantial attention remained directed toward the one-on-one attention students received from faculty and staff. Cameron changed even more over the next few decades but there exists no more pivotal moment in the history of the school than the survival of the transition to becoming a bachelor degree granting institution.

CHAPTER FIVE

"CAMERON PRIDE": THE MATURATION OF AN INSTITUTION

Cameron Pride

*Give us truth to light the darkness and
Visions to pursue and faith to meet the
Challenges of a world we must renew
Cameron pride, Cameron pride, broader than the
Plains, for your guidance and your promise, our
Praise and thanks to you.* [1]

Cameron students enjoy taking a break from classes and homework to ride double on a bicycle around campus. *Courtesy Cameron University Office of Community Relations.*

Cameron evolved and matured throughout the 1970s and 1980s as the school—sometimes timidly and sometimes proactively—found its niche among universities in the state. As Cameron became increasingly accustomed to being a university, the culture of the school also transformed. Bob Ziegler came to Cameron in 1968 to teach in the biological sciences department and he recalled the transitional period and the youthful, inexperience on campus, saying, "We had a tremendously large number of faculty who really had no idea how a university operates," and who felt that "the institution didn't know what they were doing either" so that they "all kind of grew together."[2] Scherrey Cardwell who came to Cameron to teach English in 1971 also recalled the vibrant culture among the young faculty where life-long friendships developed and a "sense of faculty oneness" emerged that "went beyond departmental lines."[3] Tom Sutherlin arrived at Cameron the following year and he too recalled the strong sense of community that developed among the faculty as they attended "potluck suppers on the lawn by North Hall" and worked together to "scrounge" the equipment they needed to support the emerging programs on campus.[4] In fact many of these new faculty members became heavily involved in creating new curriculum for the four-year degree programs and they helped codify procedures for faculty governance, university committees, and in essence, participated in the establishment and growth of a university atmosphere.

Yet, the "extreme conservatism" identified by North Central persisted in many aspects of student and faculty life at Cameron and this certainly did not change over night. The feminist movement which emerged following the publication of Betty Friedan's best selling book, *The Feminine Mystique* in 1963, ushered in an era of dramatic changes in the role of American women.[5] The collective efforts of Friedan and other feminists opened up public dialogue on the legal, educational, and wage inequality of women. While this movement effected great change nationally, at Cameron, more conservative attitudes persisted, especially when it came to female attire and conduct. Mary Allen taught at Cameron from 1967 through 1994 and she recalled the strict dress code at Cameron. She explained that "no woman could come in the library with pants on."[6] Another faculty member, Josephine Rayburn, recounted an experience in which she had been working around her house and realized she needed to pick something up at the library but quickly found herself turned away at the door because her clothing did not adhere to the dress code.[7] When a librarian voiced his suspicions that female students brazenly crossed the threshold into the library braless, Karen McKellips said that her husband Terral and another faculty member facetiously proposed operating a "rent-a-bra" counter in the foyer of the library after which point the concerned librarian dropped the issue.[8]

President Don Owen oversaw much of the early process of curriculum development as Cameron expanded its four-year degree offerings. *Courtesy 1971* Wichita, *Department of English and Foreign Languages.*

Even in instances where no actual dress code existed, many female faculty members encountered a cultural expectation of what, at the time, characterized the prevailing assumption of how women on campus ought to dress. For instance, when Karen McKellips came to Cameron to interview for a position in the newly created teacher education program, she donned a conservative brown dress with a white lace collar, fully convinced that she would not have been hired had she shown up in a pants suit.[9]

After Karen McKellips got the job, however, she quickly decided to defy the norm and wear a pants suit. According to McKellips, this marked the first time a female faculty member wore pants to teach and upon returning to her office after class she found three other female faculty members congregated at her door, wanting to know who had given her permission to do such a thing. When she told them that no one had done so, they left but over the next few days, Karen noticed a number of other women also wearing pants suits. While no one granted McKellips permission to make such a daring move, she quickly pointed out that in her 33 years at Cameron, no one ever told her what to wear or what she could or could not say in the classroom. She added, however, that according to some of the other faculty, a handful of chairmen called meetings in which they expressly forbid women in their departments to wear pants to work. She recalled her own chair being told by other chairmen that he needed to put a stop to her unconventional attire. He refused to do so and for Karen McKellips, at least, the issue dropped and she wore what she wanted.[10]

Female students, however, continued to face a strict set of rules within the context of the school's conventional notions of gender roles. Charles Elkins, the Dean of Student Services, sent letters to the parents of female students whose names appeared in a petition published in the student newspaper in which the students called for "an open forum" between students and the administration regarding housing regulations on campus. While Elkins noted that the students had not indicated any specific complaints in the petition, he nonetheless took the petition as "a cry for help" and told the parents that he believed two specific rules lay at the root of their discontent. He proceeded to ask the parents to let him know how they felt about getting rid of "closing hours" for female students and allowing male visitation in female dorm rooms. He explained that current Cameron policy required female students to sign into their rooms by 11:30 p.m. during the week and by 1:00 a.m. on Friday and Saturday and added that males were not allowed in the women's dormitory rooms. His letter criticized the students for failing to follow proper procedure or talking to "any top-level administrator" about their concerns before going to the paper. He said that "We at Cameron want to help our students, but at the same time we recognize that they can be as thoughtless in their demands as we can be as parents or college administrators."[11] While the intent of Elkin's letter may have simply been to get input from parents, it nonetheless served a dual purpose by suggesting to these particular parents that in all likelihood their daughters coveted previously impermissible freedoms. In actuality, when the Shepler Hall Women's Executive Committee subsequently held a special meeting to take up the issue—thereby following proper procedure—only 9.9% of the students favored completely abolishing closing hours whereas 57.6% of them supported a weekday curfew of 12:30 a.m. and no curfew on Friday and Saturday nights.[12]

An interesting convergence of social conservatism and youthful challenges to authority created competing images on the school's campus throughout the 1970s. The tenth floor of the South Shepler dormitory included a sundeck for female students to sun bathe, but as the 1976-1977 *Residence Hall Handbook* explained, they had to "wear robes over sunbathing attire going to and from the sundeck" because "there may be visitors or workmen in the building."[13] While notions of morality, proper conduct, and dress codes changed over time it seems noteworthy that even in the mid 1970s, each individual department determined the dress code for their classes.[14] This undoubtedly meant that those departments with the strictest dress codes effectively set the tone for the rest of campus given the infeasibility of repeatedly changing clothing between classes. This, ironically, coincided with the phenomenon of streaking which became popularized on college campuses across the country and also came to Cameron in the mid 1970s. Danny Vardeman, a 1977 Cameron graduate recalled that he knew the "first person who ran across campus nude," even though he did not actually witness the incident. According to Vardeman, the male student in question "started at the dormitories and headed north." He also recalled that as streaking became more popular, campus security and the administration "would catch wind of what was going on" and "pretty much stopped it."[15]

Clearly, student life at Cameron had evolved considerably from when the first students took up residence on the campus in the early 1910s and held fierce competitions as to which class led the best, most vibrant chapel service. Students in the 1970s puzzled over the emphasis on school loyalty among earlier generations. The 1976 edition of the *Wichita* offered a retrospective on Cameron's history in which staff writers mused over the "strange" things like "class yells, class mottos, and even a class flower" that "students considered important back in the early 1900s." Yet, they also noted that such traditions served as "a uni-

fying element that contributed to a working cohesion for the betterment of Cameron," which they added, "is hard to find today."[16] In this particular edition, students lamented the decline in school activities, titling one section: "Welcome to where the action ain't...Cameron University." They asserted that the "burden of dull activities should not be placed solely on the administration," adding that more students needed to become involved in campus life.[17]

In a piece entitled "Homecoming Habit," the yearbook staff writers said the time had come for students to "dare to risk failure and try something new" and that they needed to "stop blindly following tradition." The piece described homecoming as discriminating against male students who "are denied club representative status on the basis of their sex," adding that "many female students feel the rejection of being 'unchosen' on the basis of looks alone." The "unfortunate females" who won the homecoming competition apparently had to struggle with "knowing they are only a symbol of winning politics and a cute rear end." While the piece concluded that students should spend their "time, energy, and money" on something more "worthwhile and constructive," than they apparently deemed homecoming, the same edition of the *Wichita* also criticized student apathy on campus.[18] All in all, such speculative criticism from students is hardly new; even at Cameron students

Despite the conservative dress code expectations which continued into the 1970s, female students had access to the Shepler sunbathing deck so long as they wore proper cover-ups as they came and went. *Courtesy Cameron University Archives.*

had historically and periodically decried the loss of school spirit, the spread of indifference, prevalence of bad manners, and other such signs of a civilization in perceived decline.

While student complaints voiced in the *Wichita* must be understood within the context of the anti-establishment rhetoric of the 1970s, and more general collegiate trends of critiquing the status quo, North Central concerns about censorship of campus publications were perhaps put to rest with the publication of this particular edition. In a rather daring move, students even "took on" the State Board of Regents, quoting Chancellor E. T. Dunlap in bold lettering as saying, about Cameron: "You get too damn much" funding already. The students took issue with this notion and pointed to the Cameron administration's contention that "the school was being underfunded by $180,000." The *Wichita* blamed the lag in planned construction projects and expansion on poor "funding and the regents." [19] Students also used the yearbook to voice complaints about parking on campus in a piece entitled "The North Forty," which described Cameron's "most unpopular PE [Physical Education] course." They labeled this "required course" as "Introduction to the North Forty 1115, Section 1," saying it consisted of "a $5.00 fee, a half mile walk to classes, and is mandatory for all students who drive" but added that this "independent study" carried with it no actual PE credits.[20] Student perspectives on campus life, traditions, funding, parking, and governance provide a useful lens through which to view the evolution of school culture during this transitional period. The point is not so much to either accept or reject the scathing—albeit satirical—nature of some of the comments but rather to gain insight into what it meant for the campus environment to have them expressed at all.

Leon Fischer, Bill Burgess, and Albert Johnson, Jr. all came to Cameron as students during the mid-1970s and their recollections of Cameron

Homecoming at Cameron gave student groups the opportunity to design and build their own floats and participate in the annual homecoming parade. *Courtesy Sally Soelle Collection, Cameron University Archives.*

life provide both insight into the history of the school and as a reminder of the divergent experiences among students. Leon came to Cameron in 1973 to study agriculture. While some students in the *Wichita* criticized the "homecoming habit," for Leon, who played an active role in the Aggie Club, this event stimulated camaraderie and school spirit. He in turn felt a strong connection to campus. After graduating from Cameron, he went to Oklahoma State University (OSU) for his

Students dancing to the music of Mike Thomas and his group. *Courtesy 1972 Wichita, Department of English and Foreign Languages.*

BELOW: The freshmen class officers were Kim Smith, George Wesley, Penny Reed, Bill Burgess, and Linda Swann. *Courtesy 1975 Wichita, Cameron University Archives.*

Ph.D. and later returned to Cameron as a faculty member in the agriculture department, of which he eventually became chair.[21] Bill Burgess came to Cameron in 1974 on a debate scholarship after having been recruited by Professor Tony Allison. He recalled feeling plugged into campus life. Burgess said that for financial reasons, he really had no other choice but to come to Cameron and initially envied his friends who went to larger, more prestigious schools. Yet, by the end of his first semester, Burgess had become active on campus and felt "proud of the education" he was getting at Cameron. Burgess lived on campus all four years and during his final two years served as class president and as a resident hall assistant.[22] Even as a freshman, Burgess recognized the need for community support. In the 1975 *Wichita*, he explained that "If we get people involved, donations will start rolling in," and he added "the more money, the better the school."[23] As a student, he played an active role and he became one of Cameron's strongest advocates, first as a proud alumnus and later as a state regent.

Like Fischer and Burgess, Albert Johnson,

Jr. eventually found his way back to Cameron when he became the vice president for university advancement nearly 30 years after graduating from the institution. However, in Johnson's case he could easily have been one of the uninvolved commuter students that writers in the *Wichita* complained about. Johnson played both golf and basketball, in addition to taking ROTC classes, but he lived at home while attending Cameron and said that he could not recall "attending a single dance" or other such social event. For him, the focus stayed on athletics and homework, leaving him little time for campus socials. Johnson's parents were well known in the community. Both Albert Johnson, Sr. and his wife Jo had played a key role in the integration of Lawton, and Albert, Sr. bore a large amount of responsibility for integrating the Lawton Public Schools. Albert, Jr.

recalled that his parents had joined the country club so that he would be able to play golf there, which is where he first met Jerry Hrnciar.[24] Ultimately, he enjoyed a strong collegiate golf career at Cameron but even though more than a decade had passed since the adoption of the 1964 Civil Rights Act, which among other things, prohibited discrimination in public accommodations and hiring, Johnson faced a jarring case of blatant discrimination in the world of golf, a world incidentally where very few black players entered.

In 1973 Hrnciar came to Lawton as the golf pro for the country club and two years after that he approached Cameron basketball coach, Red Miller, about starting a golf team at Cameron. Prior to this, Miller occasionally scrambled together a group of other athletes to play in a tournament here and there, but this was the extent of golf at

Cameron's men's golf team included Stan Ward, Albert Johnson, Jr., Mickey Botkin, Blake Allen, Randy Warren, and Coach Jerry Hrnciar. *Courtesy 1976* Wichita, *Cameron University Archives.*

Cameron. Hrnciar began coaching Cameron's golf team on a volunteer basis until being hired as the athletic director and golf coach by the university in 1989. He literally built the program from the ground up and spent more of his own money, he said, than perhaps he should have. Yet, he liked giving back to the community and it just so happened that for him it took the form of building and then subsidizing the golf program at Cameron. When Albert Johnson, Jr. graduated from high school that same year and began taking classes at Cameron, it seemed logical that he would join the golf team. Coach Hrnciar described Johnson as an "outstanding" athlete both on and off the course. Given his golf prowess, it came as no surprise when Johnson received an invitation to play at the Briarwood Tournament in Tyler, Texas during the summer of 1977. Coach Hrnciar received a phone call after the Briarwood golf pro received his application materials, saying that the board

had voted not to let Johnson play in the tournament because they had learned that he was black. Hrnciar recalled being "stunned" and that before he could even decide what to do, Albert Johnson, Sr. called him on the phone. The two agreed to let Albert, Jr. decide how he wanted to handle it and that they would support whatever he wanted to do.[25]

Albert Johnson, Jr. elected not to pursue any legal action against the country club in Tyler. Moreover, he did not want to show up at the course and try to play only to have the situation hanging over him. Johnson recalled his coach's support and offering to caddy for him if he decided to go to the tournament anyway.[26] From Hrnciar's perspective, Johnson handled himself well.[27] Yet, it must have been difficult for his parents who were such an integral part of the Lawton community, not to mention integration efforts, to watch their only child be denied access to a golf

The Civil Rights Movement brought racial discrimination to the forefront of national attention and facilitated a dialogue on cultural pride which in turn fostered interest in organizations such as Cameron's Afro-American Society. *Courtesy 1973 Wichita, Department of English and Foreign Languages.*

course simply because of the color of his skin, especially in the late 1970s. The civil rights movement led to marked change in race relations during the 1960s and 1970s, but they played out in a more gradual and subtle fashion in the relatively conservative town of Lawton, Oklahoma. Nevertheless, the fact that both Jerry Hrnciar and the Johnson family were surprised by the racism of the country club in Tyler illustrates the comparatively progressive relations in Lawton and at Cameron. In many ways the biggest obstacle for most people from southwestern Oklahoma remained financial, and in that sense Cameron represented its constituents well.

Much of what happened at the school during this period established the norm for what continued over the next few decades. One particular difficulty facing the school stemmed from the costly construction of the Shepler Complex which included two ten-story student dormitories. Despite President Burch's optimism that the facility would be filled to capacity after its completion in 1969, this turned out to be only wishful thinking. In a letter to Congressman Tom Steed, President Owen said that "it was a housing error that we have built too many housing units for the number of students desiring to live on campus." The new Shepler Center could house 1,172 students and total student housing space on campus could accommodate 1,500 students yet in the spring of 1970 only 365 students resided on campus. Owen said he was "at a loss as to why they [the previous administration] built so many facilities with so few students desiring their use." He added that of the "approximately 4,000 students on campus, 2,700 live in Comanche County, thus resulting in a very high commuting population or percentage." Owen also pointed out that Cameron had "borrowed $3,000,000 from the Federal Government" for the construction costs in addition to the $3,245,000 worth of revenue bonds the school sold as part of an agreement entered into by Cameron's regents

The Shepler Complex was completed in 1969. Initially the complex was intended to provide dormitory rooms for Cameron students but due to low demand for on-campus housing, much of the space was used for other purposes. *Courtesy Cameron University Office of Communications.*

We Are Not a 'Flagship' University: A Study of Cameron Football

by Kevin Chandler
History Major • Class of 2009

During its eighty-year tenure, the Cameron University football team experienced many peaks and valleys. In the inaugural season of 1912-1913, President R.K. Robertson officially coached the team, but quarterback Tom Stringer led most of the practices. In both the 1918-1919 seasons and the 1943-1946 seasons Cameron abandoned the program to support the war efforts in Europe. In the 1961-1962 campaign the Cameron team went undefeated and won the Junior Rose Bowl, only to be stripped of all their regular season victories by the Oklahoma Collegiate Junior College Conference for using ineligible players. The height of Cameron football was 1987, when the team avenged its 1986 National Association of Intercollegiate Athletics championship game loss with a 30-2 victory over Carson-Newman College. As one alumnus noted, "It was fitting and proper that this team could reach the pinnacle of their success before their own fans in their own stadium on their own turf. Saturday, December 12, 1987 was truly CAMERON's Day!" Yet, five years later, on December 11, 1992, President Don Davis recommended to the Board of Regents that the program be abolished. To comprehend the rapid demise of Cameron football, one must examine not only the factors specific to the Cameron program but also the role football generally plays within academic institutions.

By 1927, when Cameron became a junior college, football already had developed into a popular and increasingly profitable enterprise. Several interpretations as to why football proved so lucrative exist. Some, following the paradigm of football as an industrial game, believe the increase in leisure time and disposable income led many to the stadiums. Football displayed a form of theater, the tension building throughout the game and indeed throughout the entire season. Some historians argue that college athletics "reflect the commercial aspect of [America's] free enterprise system." Others feel college athletics, particularly football, epitomize many cultural values revered in American culture, such as meritocracy, hard work, and social equality. President Theodore Roosevelt believed football "fostered precisely the qualities of character necessary for success on the battlefield, which he...regarded as the supreme and necessary test of men and nations." Whatever the interpretation, it seems historians tend to attribute football's palatability as emotional in nature, heuristic instead of logical. Also, it is apparent scholars feel the game thrived in America by appealing to societal norms and beliefs.

Cameron football evolved in this environment, one which placed football at the head of athletic programs throughout the nation. Yet, for programs to receive unconditional support from university officials, they needed sustained success on the field. Although Cameron's team won the 1987 NAIA National Championship, the team enjoyed no similar success after transferring to the National Collegiate Athletic Association's Division II Lone Star Conference in 1988. For example, during their final season Cameron finished with only one win and nine losses. The team suffered setbacks early on that season when key players, including one junior college All-American transfer, were declared academically ineligible and others were injured. The team allowed an average of 36 points a game while scoring an average of only 11, placing them at the bottom of the conference. Lack of success on the field fueled an additional concern, plummeting ticket sales. Without suitable ticket revenues, the program proved difficult to support.

Some student and community responses reflected a generally ambivalent reaction to the disbanding of Cameron football, in contrast to the adamant protests of earlier fans. One area journalist thanked President Davis for "pulling the plug on a terminally ill patient." Brian Epperson, sports editor for *The Cameron Collegian* at the time the program was eliminated, stated "I'm glad he [Davis] recommended the cut. It's better to eliminate a program than to have it and refuse to back it." Even students closely linked with the football team, such as those in the Cameron

Pride marching band and drill team, expressed relief at the program's end. While some students expressed remorse and disagreed with the decision, the overall sentiment seemed markedly apathetic.

The termination of Cameron football in December of 1992 struck some with surprise while others saw it as the inevitable conclusion of the program's decline. Although the operating costs and lack of sufficient ticket sales figured prominently in the recommendation of President Davis and the ultimate decision of the Board of Regents, there were other elements at work. First, the unusual demographics of the institution hindered the appeal of football among the student body; most students were working professionals with little free time for campus social engagements or came to the area through an affiliation with Fort Sill and had little interest in regional football programs. Second, the loyalty of many football fans in southwest Oklahoma lay either with the University of Oklahoma or Oklahoma State University football teams,

which helps explain the empty bleacher phenomenon during Saturday afternoon home games. Next, President Davis followed an agenda for expanding both academic and student activity programs requiring the institutional resources previously dominated by the school's football program. Further, dissolution of the football program enabled Cameron officials to champion the university's compliance with the NCAA Title IX resolution mandating equal opportunities and resources for men's and women's athletic programs.

While opinions of what was lost and gained vary, what is clear is Cameron University did not need football to market the institution to prospective students. Affordable tuition rates, expanding academic programs at both the undergraduate and graduate levels and a sustained population of potential students at nearby Fort Sill helped Cameron University thrive without the glitz and pageantry of college football. While the football program at Cameron University did not survive, the institution did.

Just five years after Cameron's football team won the 1987 NAIA Championship, the football program was discontinued at the university. *Courtesy 1988* Wichita, *Cameron University Archives.*

and the Department of Housing and Urban Development.[28] In short, this left the school with a staggering debt which they could not pay on the basis of dorm revenue alone given the low demand for campus housing.

In an effort to generate the needed funds, Owen proposed an on-campus residency requirement for all full-time students who were single and under the age of 22 who had not completed 33 credit hours. The president explained that "The reason for this policy is simple, in that our auxiliary housing is under a revenue bond." He added that failure to make the required payment would adversely affect Cameron as well as other institutions hoping to make a similar arrangement.[29] The bond agreement required that Cameron make two annual payments of $125,000 for the Shepler Center and Owen faced enormous odds in finding a way to generate enough money to cover the expense.[30] By this time, no married student housing existed on campus, despite the demand Owen apparently believed existed. Perhaps cost prohibitive given the housing debt facing the school already, there appears to have been no consideration given to converting some of the existing dorm space into married student housing. Instead, Owen explored the arguably ill-conceived possibility of adding an "installation of a 40-unit trailer mobile home park" which would have set "directly west of the Shepler Center parking area." He believed that the addition of a trailer park would "solve the problem of transportation" for married students "who desire to live closer to campus."[31] While the plans failed to materialize, the effort to acquire the trailer park further underscores the difficulty Cameron faced of appropriately meeting both the amount and type of housing needs desired by the student body.

Even under the best circumstances, the transition from a two-year to a four-year educational institution would have been challenging but the added obstacles faced by Cameron were profound, to say the least. Inadequate funding

and the crushing debt of the partially occupied Shepler Center dampened campus enthusiasm and hampered the growth of the institution. Vernon Howell, former president of Cameron, chaired the Cameron College Committee in the early 1970s and he described well some of the problems facing the institution. In a letter to Representative Tom Steed he explained that Cameron was "still operating in the same instructional facilities as while a Junior College." To further illustrate Cameron's dire need for financial support, Howell pointed out that "a number of classes" were "being taught in old sheet-iron buildings" and that it had become "necessary to use the bottom floor of a dairy barn for the Art Department."[32]

Ultimately, the administration simply could not generate enough money to meet the bond payment schedule and so they began renting out space to non-campus entities, including the Federal Aviation Administration (FAA) in 1971. While this move stemmed from financial necessity, it could not help but alter the campus environment. In regard to leasing campus space to the FAA President Owen, point-blank, explained that "we are seeking more contracts in order that we keep our heads above water" because the school found it "increasingly difficult to maintain our entire bond payments."[33] By the mid-1970s only a small fraction of the student body lived on campus, which, coupled with the arrival of non-campus entities, meant that the campus took on an altogether different feel than what President Burch had aspired to when construction on the Shepler Complex first began and as the Cameron community, perhaps naively, looked forward to being a four-year school. As yearbook staff writers put it: "Cameron is no longer a farm school to transfer from—why some people have even begun to stay for four years. But, the hard part is yet to come."[34]

Cameron had, nevertheless, gained accreditation from North Central in 1973, and for the rest of that decade, faculty and administrators created a number of new programs and they worked tirelessly to codify campus policies and procedure. The state legislature officially changed Cameron's name to "Cameron University" in 1974.[35] More than anything else, the addition of "university" to Cameron's name seems to have solidified its change in status in the minds of students. The 1975 *Wichita*, which chronicled the events of the 1974-1975 school year hailed it as "Year One" for the institution as a university.[36] Another sign of changing times at Cameron was the athletic department's acceptance into the NCAA, Division II.[37] The university's official press guide for 1975 summed up the school's continued push for development in the depiction of a cowboy cartoon with a gun and the phrase "We're aiming higher in '75."[38] As a group, the faculty, staff, and administrators working under the leadership of President Owen deserve much credit for really making Cameron a university by the end of the decade.

While opinions of Owen varied across campus, his management style held the most significant implications for how the university operated during this critical period of program development and expansion. Terral McKellips described Owen as giving people whom he respected and trusted a good deal of freedom to do what they thought needed to be done. McKellips related a story from one of Owen's past positions to illustrate his approach to management. After replacing a superintendent who enjoyed a reputation as a "total micromanager," Owen had occasion to be sitting at his desk one day when a janitor came in to talk to him. The janitor informed him that the girl's bathroom needed more tampons and when Owen asked why the janitor thought it necessary to tell him this, the janitor replied that the previous superintendent kept the tampons in his desk drawer.[39] Owen, it seems, had no desire for that degree of oversight, which as it turned out did not entirely bode well for Cameron.

The maturation of Cameron as an institution

did not happen in a vacuum. By the mid-twentieth century, the State Regents for Higher Education had begun taking a more long-sighted approach to educational planning in the state and as projected enrollment for state colleges and universities continued to increase dramatically, this became all the more necessary. An important manifestation of this long-range planning came in the form of

During the 1970s, Cameron's nursing program was among one of the more popular on campus. *Courtesy Sally Soelle Collection, Cameron University Archives.*

the "Plan for the 70's" in which the State Regents addressed the role of the various state colleges and universities in the educational mission of the whole state. They wanted to make sure that the programs each institution offered were viable and appropriate to the school's mission. Chancellor Dunlap explained that this "set of guidelines and broad directions for the best use of Oklahoma's resources for higher education" was "designed to improve both the quantity and the quality of Oklahoma higher education."[40]

Cameron's Rifle Team provided students with an opportunity to hone their skills and engage in competitions. *Courtesy 1980* Wichita, *Department of English and Foreign Languages.*

Despite Chancellor Dunlap's assurance that the Regents sought to provide guidance rather than unilateral action, President Owen grew concerned over the implications of the plan for Cameron because it intimated that four-year schools might cease to offer associate degrees.[41] Alarmed at such a possibility, Owen quickly appealed to the Regents to reconsider. Given Cameron's very recent addition of upper class work, such a shift in mission would likely have dealt a death blow to the institution by gutting its enrollment. The Regents responded to Owen indicating that he had perhaps over-reacted. They pointed out that what the plan really called for was that institutions "review all programs currently offered" and then make recommendations as to "any programs which should be eliminated and any new programs which should be added." The Regents

further added that they had "no plans" to take any actions on programs prior to receiving institutional recommendations. The Regents said that they "had no intention of discontinuing associate degree programs at Cameron College until it was determined that people in the area had no need for such programs."[42] In actuality, Cameron appeared to be in no danger of losing its associate degree programs and the State Regents appear to have been baffled by Owen's reaction, especially because he prematurely involved both state politicians and the press in his unfounded concerns.

Nevertheless, Owen's tenure at Cameron resulted in growth and advancement in numerous areas. While some criticized his attempt to require students to live on campus as a way to generate revenue for the Shepler bond payment, he actively pursued ways to improve the economic outlook for the institution. In hindsight, however, the positive advancements for the school cannot help but be dwarfed by the scandal his administration became engulfed in just as he left office. In fact, his last several months at Cameron included a significant amount of friction with faculty and a growing discontent.

To be sure, the lead up to Owen's departure from Cameron included a good deal of faculty unrest. In August of 1979, President Owen "without input or recommendations from the faculty" changed the minimum teaching load from 13 to 15 hours. While only a little more than 30% of the faculty who responded to a survey handed out by the Faculty Affairs Committee indicated that their teaching load increased as a direct result of the policy, the damage to faculty morale seems much greater. More than 60% described faculty morale as "low" and the biggest issue for most seemed to be their frustration at not being included in the decision-making process. Of those responding to the survey, only two faculty members said that they had been contacted regarding the new policy, whereas 102 said that they were not contacted. All

105 responses to the survey answered "no" when asked if they knew "of any Governance committee which was contacted in regard to this change."[43]

When Owen discovered that the Faculty Affairs Committee had circulated the survey, he requested a meeting with the committee. After Dr. Ann Nalley, a chemistry professor and the chair of the committee, invited President Owen to talk to them, he "expressed his disappointment" and said that "the questions seemed designed to elicit a negative response." Members of the Faculty Affairs Committee defended their actions, saying the intent of the survey was to make the administration aware of the impact of such a decision on faculty morale. President Owen and the committee members failed to reach a consensus as to the extent to which he had asked for faculty input on the decision. From his perspective, he felt that he had clearly told the faculty that a decline in enrollment for the 1978-1979 school year, coupled with decreased appropriations, had necessitated some sort of drastic change.[44] The faculty, however, did not discover what that change would be until they reported back to campus in August.[45] Terral McKellips had been chair of the mathematics department for eleven years by this time and he said Owen's decision to increase faculty load across the board "was the beginning of the end" for him. Owen, it seems, "would not back down" which left him with "almost no way to recover."[46]

A story that appeared in the *Lawton Magazine* made the growing rift on Cameron's campus pub-

Cameron's Student Union provided a place for students to socialize and play games between classes. *Courtesy 1980* Wichita, *Department of English and Foreign Languages*.

lic knowledge. The front page of John Dickerson's story entitled "Cameron: A Troubled Institution?" included a copy of the survey conducted by the Faculty Affairs Committee, including the number of "yes" and "no" faculty responses to each question. Dickerson quoted a number of faculty comments from the survey as well as comments from Owen. Comments ranged from "Morale is horrible out here. I've been here since 1971 and I've never seen it worse" to "A fish stinks from its head, and that's where Cameron is beginning to smell."[47] Owen appeared quite out of tune with faculty sentiment when he responded that "there is no morale problem."[48] Dickerson described Cameron as "becoming a hotbox of controversy" increasingly characterized by an "iconoclastic faculty attacking an apparently deafened administration."[49]

While occasional faculty grousing constitutes the norm on any college campus, it nonetheless seems fair to say that the 1979 fall semester stands out as a particularly trying time, and it would get worse before it got better. A month after criticizing the Faculty Affairs Committee for conducting the survey, President Owen announced possible plans to request an unpaid leave of absence to potentially pursue political ambitions. He did so at a meeting with the Board of Regents for Oklahoma A & M Colleges and Oklahoma State University, and two days after the story appeared in The Oklahoman, he issued a memo to Cameron personnel telling them about his decision.[50] In the memo he said that he had "a definite commitment to become a candidate for the United States Congress, Fourth District" so long as the incumbent, Tom Steed, did not seek re-election. He added that he would "immediately inform" Cameron employees as soon as he reached a "final decision."[51] The following February Owen submitted his resignation, citing "personal rather than political reasons."[52] Yet, he maintained a commitment to run for office so long as Steed did not seek re-election.[53] Owen officially entered the congressional race in early

March saying that the country needed "increased attention to agriculture" and "a strong national defense system."[54] Effective April 7, 1980, the Regents appointed Cameron Vice President Richard Murray as interim president pending a search for Owen's replacement although he also retained his vice-presidential duties.[55] When Murray discovered that someone had nominated him as a candidate for the presidency, he wrote to the regents and requested that his name be removed. Murray said that he felt he could best serve the university by returning to his role as vice president following the selection of a new president. He argued this arrangement would provide for "continuity" while also allowing for the "objectivity which a new person could bring to the institution."[56]

By the time the search got underway for a new president, the son of former president Clarence Davis had come to play a significant role in advocating for Cameron in the State Legislature, and it is perhaps not surprising that he closely followed events at Cameron. Representative Don Davis spent part of his youth at Cameron. During his father's presidency, the family lived in the modest president's home located on campus. Don Davis was only 15 years old the summer his father died of a heart attack, an event which simultaneously devastated the Cameron community and the Davis family. Don Davis went on to graduate from Lawton High, attend college, and eventually graduated from law school before turning to a career in politics. Ironically, he and Don Owen seemed poised to trade careers as Owen wanted to get involved in politics and as Davis became interested in the presidency at Cameron. When Owen stepped down, Davis did indeed get the opportunity to follow in his father's footsteps to become Cameron's next president. The selection of Davis as president marked a substantial departure from previous searches. Every president prior to Davis had a background in public education and had served as a school superintendent prior to

President Don Davis was Cameron's fifteenth president. Following the resignation of President Don Owen, Vice President Richard Murray served as interim president until Davis took office in the summer of 1980. President Don Davis served as president for 22 years. *Courtesy Cameron University Archives.*

coming to Cameron. And every presidential search prior to this one had been conducted without faculty, student, or staff input. By the time Davis took office in 1980, the institution had come a long way from when it started as an agricultural high school, making superintendent experience much less relevant even than it had been a decade earlier when Owen became president. Equally important, this also marked the first time that the campus community played a meaningful role in the selection of a president. The Regents named

a search committee comprised of 21 members, including alumni, faculty, administrators, and students. The selection of Davis in June of 1980 bode well for the institution, and it came at a critical time because the presidential search already had become overshadowed as the biggest scandal in the history of the school.

There can be little doubt that President Owen's administration made extraordinary accomplishments toward the betterment of Cameron, and by extension the betterment of southwest Oklahoma. Yet, financial discrepancies that occurred during his administration resulted in a scandal that rocked the school and ended his political ambitions. A number of stories appeared in state newspapers on May 7, and they carried with them bad news for Cameron. One article detailed the decision of the Oklahoma State Bureau of Investigation (OSBI) to look into "allegations that materials and equipment purchased for Cameron University may have been diverted to the personal use of school employees." The same article indicated that while the investigation "reportedly doesn't focus on former Cameron president, Don J. Owen," that he had nonetheless decided to withdraw from the congressional race for "personal reasons" which, perhaps coincidentally, followed the circulation of "false rumors implicating him in wrongdoing at Cameron." Owen maintained that his decision to withdraw from the race "had nothing to do with" the OSBI investigation and rumors about his role.[57] As the investigation continued over the next few months, more charges emerged. On July 11, Bob Delver, who oversaw maintenance for the school, initially faced 88 counts of embezzlement, eight of which related to his alleged use of campus supplies and personnel to work on rental properties he owned. While a former employee had complained about this very problem and Owen said he looked into the matter but found no wrongdoing, the OSBI reached an altogether different conclusion.[58] Delver resigned

Greek organizations comprised an important part of campus life at Cameron and gave students the opportunity to forge lifelong friendships. *Courtesy 1984* Wichita, *Department of English and Foreign Languages.*

a few weeks later with the charges against him standing at "six embezzlement charges" which included allegations of "66 counts of embezzlement of university labor, supplies, equipment, and materials worth $70,000."[59]

By the following September, District Attorney Dick Tannery indicated that the case against former Cameron employees had expanded to include charges against two more individuals. Don Owen was charged with various counts of embezzlement, conspiracy to commit embezzlement, and obstruction of justice. J. R. Allison worked at Cameron from 1969 to 1977 as the food services director and he also faced charges for embezzlement and conspiracy to commit embezzlement. All told, the case against Owen, Delver, and Allison alleged a substantial amount of misappropriation of funds, the use of university equipment, employees, property, and supplies for personal gain, outright pocketing of university cash, and even the use of Cameron food for poker parties at the Owen ranch.[60] After substantial publicity and months of what must have been an agonizing ordeal for the entire campus community, the three men faced prosecution. Bob Delver pleaded guilty to the embezzlement charges against him and received immunity for "any further statements he might make"

and his name appeared on the state witness list to testify against both Allison and Owen. Yet when questioned by Assistant District Attorney Robert Perrine, his testimony "apparently differed from sworn statements given during his arraignment on June 2, 1980."[61] A number of Cameron employees testified as the preliminary hearing progressed resulting in varying—but largely consistent—degrees of evidence supporting the charges against Owen and Allison. Owen, however, refused to testify against Allison and repeatedly pleaded the fifth during his questioning.[62]

Resolution came slowly and could not help but overshadow the positive things going on at Cameron. Ultimately, Bob Delver received "five years suspended sentences on each complaint" and had to "pay $4,500 in restitution."[63] In March of 1982, two years after the initial OSBI investigation, a jury found J.R. Allison guilty of two of the four charges against him and recommended he be sentenced to six years in prison. The jury found him guilty of "embezzling the use of a food services employee as a house maid for his personal use" as well as for Owen's personal use. They also found him guilty of "embezzling about $4,000 from the university's catering fund." The jury did, however find him not guilty of two other embez-

In an era that predated cellular phones, Cameron student Cheryl Johnson made use of a campus pay phone. *Courtesy 1987* Wichita, *Department of English and Foreign Languages.*

changes occurred in the creation of two top level posts—the vice president for Academic Affairs and the vice president for University Operations—both of whom reported directly to the president.[77]

Over the next few years, the school benefitted from a smoother administrative structure yet problems of declining enrollment, low retention, and poor funding persisted. The Center for Advisement and Student Development (CASD) undertook extensive exit interviews between July and December of 1983 to get a better handle on retention problems facing the school. As a result of interviewing 201 students, the CASD found that 57 students withdrew for job-related reasons and 40 for personal problems and 173 of the 201 students responded that "nothing could be done to help them remain at Cameron." Not surprisingly, over half of the students who withdrew from courses had below a 2.0 Grade Point Average (G.P.A.). While the CASD recommended developing greater support programs for the three groups of students who held the highest drop rates—high risk students with a less than a 2.0 G.P.A., undecided majors, and brand new incoming freshmen—enrollment and retention problems continued.[78] An analysis of enrollment trends for the years 1983 through 1985 revealed a decline in freshmen enrollment of 29%. Other areas of concern included the need to streamline and coordinate financial aid and

scholarships and to "consider implementing more retention actions."[79]

For the most part, student life at Cameron continued to flourish even as school officials fretted over problems typical to academia. Jake Brownlow came to Cameron in 1984 because one of his friends received a football scholarship to play for Cameron and he hoped to "walk on" and do the same. After three days of practice, he succeeded in securing a scholarship offer from the coaches and went on to play for the next four years. He recalled being "awed about the stadium" because it had astro turf, which "was a big thing." The crowning achievement of Brownlow's football career at Cameron came when the team won the 1987 National Championship, described as one of his most "memorable experiences."[80] Despite the football team's success on the field, financial problems plagued the program. President Davis looked into the possibility of disbanding the program in the early 1980s because of budget cuts but the final decision to cut the program did not come for another decade. While this remains an emotional and contentious issue in many respects, a number of people including Tom Sutherlin, Terral McKellips, and Don Sullivan, all of whom described themselves as avid football fans and supporters of Cameron's football program, hailed Davis' decision to drop the football program as "courageous" and the right thing to do for the university.[81] However, Jerry Hrnciar, the athletic director and men's golf coach, felt blindsided by the decision and the way in which Davis chose to implement it.[82]

Many critical things happened in the trajectory of advancing the university under Davis' administration and he faced some difficult decisions which benefitted Cameron in many ways, yet strained his relationship with the Lawton community. By the mid-1980s, the school needed more space on campus. While overall college and university enrollment in Oklahoma increased in the

Cameron Cheerleaders along with school mascot, Ole Kim, fostered school spirit at pep rallies and sporting events. *Courtesy 1990* Wichita, *Department of English and Foreign Languages*.

fall of 1986, Cameron enjoyed the largest enroll-ment increase of public institutions in the state.[83] The increase in enrollment at Cameron coincided with the looming expiration of the FAA contract, which had brought considerable income to the school and since the early 1970s had proved vital to the economic health of the institution. In 1986 alone, Cameron received $1.9 million dollars for leasing space to the FAA Management Training School. With the FAA's lease scheduled to expire in September of 1986, the field of interest in who housed the program exploded. Cameron, along with a number of other interested parties put in

bids for the FAA school. Cameron's bid, however, consisted of a proposal to build new facilities to house the FAA in order to free up space in dormitories, the student union, and the business building which the FAA occupied at the time. Joe Carter, the information director for Cameron, told the press that one factor in the school's decision stemmed from North Central guidance indicating that Cameron "needed more room for our own students."[84]

The need for more space on campus meant that President Davis had a difficult task on his hands because the community strongly supported having, and keeping, the FAA school in Lawton. According to one estimate, the training school yielded an economic impact of between $10 to $15-million a year through the combined "income from the government, spending by the students in the locality and other business stimulated by the presence of the school." [85] Terral McKellips pointed out that Davis did not oppose having the FAA on campus per se, but rather he grew concerned over the lack of space necessary to accommodate both their needs and the needs of students. Anxious to keep the school in Lawton, the Board of Trustees of the Lawton Metropolitan Airport passed a resolution in support of moving the FAA school from Cameron to the airport so that it would stay local. The resolution recognized "the significant contribution made to the City of Lawton, Oklahoma, by the presence" of the school and indicated that the board of trustees wanted to "publically proclaim its willingness to cooperate

in any way possible in the efforts being made to retain" the school in the Lawton community.[86] Ultimately, the FAA decided to move the school to Florida. Cameron's "loss" of the training school did not sit well with some of the locals and McKellips described this event as "the first major damage to Davis' relationship with the community." [87] Yet, from a physical plant standpoint, Harold Robinson described the FAA's departure as "a good day" for the university because Cameron's maintenance workers spent considerable time responding to the needs and complaints of FAA employees on campus.[88]

Despite the damage, President Davis accomplished a notable feat in that he found a way to remove the Shepler bond debt while simultaneously increasing the availability of space on campus. What Davis lacked in experience as an academician, he made up for in experience as a bond attorney. Davis recalled that "Oklahoma's booming

Historically, Cameron has had a significant number of Native American students who have participated in cultural awareness events such as the Cameron Pow Wow sponsored by the Cameron Native Intertribal Council. *Courtesy 1991* Wichita, *Department of English and Foreign Languages.*

economy" in the early 1980s gave Cameron "an opportunity to free" itself from its "bonded indebtedness." Davis explained that if Cameron could come up with $2 million and invest it at 18% then the school "could establish an escrow that would pay off the $6 million" Cameron owed and so he "set out to gather up $2 million." Davis drafted the legislation which gave Cameron, along with Northeastern and Northwestern, both facing similar problems as Cameron, permission "to use earnings from one of the state's surplus accounts to satisfy bond payments" at each of the three schools. Money from the surplus account was then used "to purchase a $50 million certificate of deposit from First National Bank in Oklahoma City." After which point the bank "immediately prepaid approximately $6 million in interest which would become due on the CD at a future date." In turn, that money was then used "to purchase United States Government bonds, which were paying 18%, for use by the three universities." Following this, "The bonds were put in trust and Cameron was debt-free, and had $1 million in reserves released from the original bond issue," explained Davis.[89] In this instance Cameron clearly benefitted both from Davis' work as a bond attorney and his political connections.

Much happened at Cameron during the 1980s and as the next decade rolled around, Cameron again faced another North Central accreditation visit. By this time Terral McKellips had become the chief academic officer at Cameron and he described North Central's 1991 visit as one of the most important events in the history of the school. Ever since the state legislature changed Cameron's function to that of a four-year institution in 1966, followed by the State Regent action the following year, Cameron had grappled to find its academic footing. The long term result of this less than smooth transition amounted to what McKellips called an "inferiority complex." While Cameron had succeeded in gaining accreditation a number

of times by 1991, they had yet to do so without strings attached. That is to say, without a list of vital or critical areas of concern that needed immediate attention and caused the school to receive shorter terms of conditional accreditation rather than the standard ten-year span given to institutions who passed free and clear. The 1991 experience, however, changed the campus climate.[90]

McKellips recalled that when the North Central evaluators completed their report, they gave President Davis the option of having a closed or open session and Davis opted to make the session open to the campus community. When the evaluators read their report and indicated that Cameron had earned the full ten years of accredited status, free of conditions, McKellips said that faculty "stood up, cheered, and clapped" and that the North Central evaluators later told him that they had never seen anything like it. In essence, the unconditional accreditation validated all of the hard work that faculty, staff, and administrators had undertaken over the past few decades. McKellips said that the atmosphere changed on campus and that people grew less timid about trying new things and pursuing innovations because they now had a clear mandate. McKellips summed up this pivotal moment, saying simply that "the inferiority complex dissipated and a new spirit of optimism and enthusiasm ensued."[91] While the journey took much longer than Presidents Burch, Owen, and Davis could have possibly hoped for, Cameron finally reached maturation as a four-year institution. If the Shepler bond payments constituted the "financial albatross" around the neck of the institution, then the failed and conditional North Central accreditations were the academic equivalent. And as president, Don Davis succeeded in removing both, and setting Cameron firmly on the path to a healthier, more secure future.

The decade that followed brought renewed challenges for the institution and for Davis' administration. He brought an end to Cameron football which simultaneously strained his relationship with some members of the community while winning him praise from others. Don Sullivan recalled that the reaction he saw in his position as director of university advancement was "largely positive."[92]

Similarly, English faculty member Leigh Holmes recalled that he and other members of his department viewed the decision as a good one.[93] Yet, McKellips explained that when Davis acted to disband the team, it "cost him a lot of community support."[94] Some members of the community equated football with university; even if they did not attend the games or financially support the program, they somehow expected them to continue. All told, reaction varied considerably as those in the Cameron community expressed varying degrees of indifference, relief, gratitude, or anger to news that Davis had succeeded in ending the football program. Whatever the individual reactions, Bill Burgess, who had become an active alumnus, community leader, and close friend of Davis by this time recalled that it "took a lot of guts" to get rid of the program and that "it cost Davis" substantially.[95] Davis, however, did not seem to shy away from making tough decisions and more often than not, the institution benefitted from his rather bold maneuvering. As Davis led Cameron into the last decade of the twentieth century, the campus faced new challenges and enjoyed increased opportunities. Cameron had succeeded in becoming a university.

Nance-Boyer Hall dates back to 1930 and is the oldest remaining building on campus. It is named after two politicians who strongly advocated for the school, Representative Jim Nance and Senator Dave Boyer. *Photograph by Jim Horinek.*

Completed in the fall of 2009, the Bentley Gardens sit on 2.6 acres and includes the Tom and Monica McCasland Family Pond which provides a beautiful gathering place for the whole Cameron community. *Photograph by Jim Horinek.*

CHAPTER SIX

"LET THE WORLD HEAR OF CAMERON"

Whatever our fate may be in the future, we are all well pleased with the work which we have done here. And will always have a good word for Cameron.

We hope to see Cameron prosper in the future and its enrollment greatly increased. There is no reason why it should not, for we have everything that is necessary for a good school, and the faculty cannot be beaten. If everyone only knew what a good school we have, we would soon have to have more buildings.

Whatever we may do let us remember that, "Not failure but low aim is crime." Have a purpose in life, aim high and shoot promptly. Let the world hear of Cameron School and you. [1]

— Loy Dykes, Class of 1916

When Loy Dykes imagined the bright prospects for Cameron's future in 1914 he could not have foreseen the trajectory of Cameron over the next several decades but the pride and optimism of his words proved well-founded. With the growth of technological advances and computing, the world would indeed "hear of Cameron." The school became a university and reached institutional maturity under the leadership of President Don Davis, who led Cameron from 1980 to 2002. During his 22 years in office he achieved a number of significant accomplishments and left office after a term that spanned almost one fifth of Cameron's history, longer than any other president in the history of the school.

One of the most notable changes under Davis came with the shift in its governing board from the A & M and OSU Board of Regents to OU's Board of Regents in 1992. Perspectives varied on the change at the time. On one hand, the shift took Cameron away from its agricultural roots and the board that had governed it since the transfer from the Oklahoma State Board of Agriculture in the 1940s. On the other, there existed a pervasive sense on campus that OSU's Board of Regents micromanaged Cameron and gave the institution very little autonomy to pursue its educational mission. To escape, Davis described how he and OU Regent Vic Williams "concocted a plan to transfer governance of Cameron from the A&M Board of Regents to the OU Board." Davis said that he "drafted the legislation affecting the transfer" and then had OU legal counsel review it before Representative Sid Hudson "inserted it in a conference committee report which could be voted up or down, but not amended, by the entire house and senate." The measure passed and then Governor David Walters "signed the bill into law on the Cameron campus."[2]

The move was generally well received on campus, particularly among those who oversaw academic programs and the physical plant. On the academic side, Terral McKellips recalled that one frustration with the OSU board had stemmed from the fact that they governed a number of other regional institutions and the board tended to lump them all together. Whenever Cameron wanted permission to try something new, for example, the board felt that it "had to consider the possibility that all the other schools they governed might want to do the same thing." Another problem concerned the amount of oversight the board provided, which seemed to be at the heart of frustration for many on Cameron's campus. When Terral McKellips first came to Cameron, for example, the board had to approve all out-of-state travel, even to Wichita Falls, Texas which was less than an hour away from Lawton.[3] Harold Robinson re-

The presence of fraternities and sororities on campus contributed to a more vital student life through the sponsorship of events such as the Greek Council tug of war competition. *Courtesy 1991* Wichita, *Department of English and Foreign Languages.*

called the difficulty in completing repair projects on campus because even in the mid 1980s, all purchase orders over $250.00 required advance approval from the board. While that amount increased over time, from his perspective at least, things worked much better under the University of Oklahoma's Board of Regents because they gave Cameron considerably more leeway.[4] Cindy Ross, who later replaced Davis as president, also praised the move toward governance by the University of Oklahoma's Board of Regents, which eventually expanded to govern Cameron, Rogers State University, and the University of Oklahoma.[5]

Without question, the transfer of governance marked the beginning of a series of key events in the early 1990s that allowed Cameron to grow in new directions. The elimination of football, while extremely controversial, freed money for other sports programs on campus and brought Cameron into compliance with Title IV legislation in terms of equitable funding for women's sports. The clean North Central accreditation in 1991 gave the campus community a sense of accomplishment and security to pursue innovation. The shift to a new governing board gave Cameron a clean slate, not to mention a good deal more freedom. All of these factors shaped the campus environment throughout the decade and played a role in creating a climate conducive to harnessing innovation, technology, and ultimately altering the learning process both on campus and at remote sites and through distance education.

Perhaps the biggest and most far reaching academic change on Cameron's campus which occurred during the Davis administration was the rapid evolution of computers and classroom technology. Cameron had two computer science courses in the catalogue as early as 1968, but even two decades later many faculty members considered computers "a fad." As a result, Terral McKellips recalled a good deal of faculty opposi-

Cameron's Women's volleyball team has historically been among the strongest athletic teams on campus. *Courtesy 1993 Wichita, Department of English and Foreign Languages.*

tion to his efforts to equip all faculty offices with computers. Some compared them to overhead projectors and predicted they would be a short-lived innovation only to be replaced by something else. McKellips, however, correctly ascertained that computers would become an integral part of academic life. He spent a significant amount of time researching computing and technology in his capacity as the division head, later changed to dean of science and technology, and then as the vice president for Academic Affairs, later changed to provost and back again. He firmly believed that computerizing the campus had been paramount to sustaining and growing the institution's mission.[6]

Without question, technology fundamentally altered course delivery in a variety of ways. By the mid-1980s, Cameron offered instruction through pre-packaged video tapes coupled with professor feedback in telecourses that reached "approximately 200-300 students per semester." Then came "the addition of talk-back television," which involved the sending of live audio and television transmissions of courses from one site, usually the main campus, to others, usually high schools or other educational institutions, and allowed Cameron to "expand its electronic delivery" and offer "entire programs to some remote sites."[7] While telecourses and Interactive Television (ITV) courses grew in popularity, especially among non- traditional and concurrently enrolled high school students, even greater technological changes awaited. By the early twenty-first century, Cameron began offering online courses through the internet at both the undergraduate and graduate level, a phenomenon which grew increasingly important to Cameron's enrollment in the decade that followed.

Online courses capitalized on the revolutionary promise of the internet, which reached Cameron in March of 1995 when the world wide web service was installed on campus and Greg Duncan designed the first home pages for the university. His wife, Julie Duncan, soon took on the task of maintaining and updating those pages, and the dramatic expansion of the internet on campus was underway.[8] Cameron's home pages and campus web capabilities expanded tremendously over the next decade, and the new technology fundamentally altered and enhanced how people access information about the university. Eighty years after Loy Dykes admonished his classmates to "let the world hear of Cameron," he no doubt would have been amazed by how literally possible and easy that task had become.[9]

Computing technology and the internet reshaped many aspects of modern American life as the world became more connected and information more accessible than ever before. What transpired at Cameron is important not for its uniqueness but for how much it changed the atmosphere of communication, data access, and student learning. Karen Hardin served as the first director of online education at Cameron and oversaw the development of the first online courses. In 1999 Hardin, McKellips, and others began working to lay the foundation for online course offerings and looked at a variety of internet based servers for courses before settling on Blackboard. The first online courses were largely in the area of general education classes and included such topics as speech, American Federal Government, American History, and Philosophy. This first group of courses was offered in the fall of 2001 and the demand for online classes has grown significantly since that time. By the fall of 2002, Cameron offered 34 online classes and that number increased to 49 by the spring of 2007.[10]

Despite the proliferation of new forms of course delivery, the physical campus remained the primary location for student learning, and as such routine maintenance and building improvements played a crucial role in student and faculty perceptions of the learning environment. As president, Davis oversaw a number of new construction projects during his time at Cameron, including the Fitness Center and the Sciences Complex, though that construction was not without its share of growing pains. While the Fitness Center eventually became a tremendous asset to the whole campus community, construction proved costly and fraught with errors. Harold Robinson, who came to Cameron in 1983 and served as Assistant Head of Grounds and Physical Plant operations before becoming the director in 1987, recalled how difficult the project became. The swimming pool constituted one of the biggest problems with the Fitness Center, and Robinson recalled that at one time it "leaked about 1,100 gallons of water a day." The pool eventually had to be completely torn out and rebuilt. Repairs to the Fitness Center in the first year following its completion totaled

Communications Professor Steve Adams provided a hands-on demonstration of how to use radio equipment to Cameron broadcasting students. *Courtesy 1992* Wichita, *Department of English and Foreign Languages.*

BELOW: Cameron's state-of-the-art Sciences Complex was built in the mid-1990s and a decade later remained one of the most attractive buildings on campus. *Courtesy Cameron University Archives.*

more than half of the initial construction cost.[11] Construction of the Sciences Complex, however, proceeded much more smoothly and it quickly emerged as one of the most impressive buildings on campus. In fact, Glen Pinkston, the vice president for Business and Finance, who eventually came to oversee the physical plant, has noted that even after 16 years the building required "very little" attention.[12]

Construction and renovation meant to en-

hance Cameron's ability to serve southwest Oklahoma was hardly confined to the main campus in Lawton. It was also evident in Duncan, where residents had long sought an institution of higher learning that could serve the city and negate the need for residents to commute to and from Lawton for classes. Cameron addressed this need initially by offering classes at the Duncan High School in 1972 to both concurrent high school students and to non-traditional students who wanted to continue their education by taking night classes. By the early 1990s, however, growing enrollment and a strong desire for a designated space for college courses emerged. Community leaders and officials from Halliburton, Duncan's largest employer, began seriously exploring the possibility of establishing a facility or campus of their own.

State Representative Ed Apple wrote to Oklahoma State Regents Chancellor Hans Brisch in hopes that he might support Duncan's effort to create a higher education center. Apple explained that there was "considerable interest from the community in Duncan in support of establishing a higher education center, or eventually, a junior college." He requested guidance from Brisch and asked for his recommendations as to how best to proceed.[13] Brisch responded by telling Apple that the University of Oklahoma had received authorization to offer courses for a Master of Education in Secondary Education and that Cameron had received authorization to offer an associates degree in Interdisciplinary Studies. He added that the University of Science and Arts of Oklahoma, located in Chickasha, would "be asked to serve" in the case of "any lower division courses Cameron University is unable to offer." The chancellor concluded by assuring Representative Apple that the State Regents remained "interested in the needs of the citizens in Duncan." He also indicated that Cameron had agreed to undertake a needs assessment study in Duncan to determine the appropriate course of action for expanding educational offerings in the area.[14]

While Brisch seemed sympathetic to the desire for greater access to higher education in Duncan, the issue of building a new facility in which to house these courses remained problematic. In a letter to Oklahoma State Senator Cliff Marshall, Brisch indicated that while he remained committed "to meeting the Duncan higher education need" he pointed out that the House Joint Resolution (HJR) 1053 of 1978 opposed the

"establishment of additional higher education centers," and that both the Council of Presidents and the State Regents had endorsed the resolution in 1989. Brisch also pointed out that Oklahoma higher education was "only funded 60 cents on the dollar" thus making it "indefensible to contemplate additional bureaucratic structures that would further dilute higher education services."[15] What for many communities would have likely consti-

Siblings Ryan and Robin Griffith at Cameron's 5th annual mud volleyball game. *Courtesy 1992* Wichita, *Department of English and Foreign Languages.*

tuted an end to ambitions for their own higher educational facility seemed to spark even greater determination in Duncan, and so they set out to find another way to construct their own building.

Throughout the early 1990s, the Duncan community, with the support of Cameron President Don Davis, persisted in efforts to establish a higher education facility. Susan Camp, who became the very first employee of the center

cousin, Don Davis, and said, "Well, where should we build this thing?"[16] The determination of the Duncan community to have their own higher education facility resembled that of the Lawton community in the early twentieth century when they took it upon themselves to raise the money necessary for the establishment of Cameron, and their subsequent support that contributed greatly to the university's ability to survive numerous ef-

The Duncan Higher Education Center building was constructed in 1994 and became an official branch campus of Cameron University a decade later. *Courtesy Cameron University Office of Community Relations.*

when it opened in August of 1994, recounted the famous, or infamous depending on one's perspective, exchange leading up to the establishment of the facility. After meeting with community leaders and politicians in Duncan, Hans Brisch reportedly told the delegation in no uncertain terms that there would be no more higher education centers in Oklahoma. As Brisch's plane took off, Duncan Mayor Wayne Holden reportedly turned to his

forts to close its doors.

While the Duncan community certainly encountered obstacles along the way, they nevertheless succeeded in accomplishing their plans for the educational center. The Duncan City Council voted to use money from the Duncan Economic Development Trust to build the new facility on 20 acres of land donated by the Duncan Civic Auditorium Foundation.[17] J. E. Jackson and his family

Theater students Shannon Zura and Darold Kowalke in a production of "Seascape" directed by Cameron Professor Scott Richard Klein. *Courtesy 1993* Wichita, *Department of English and Foreign Languages.*

A tepee erected on campus during Native American Spirituality Week was sponsored by Cameron Campus Ministry. *Courtesy 1993* Wichita, *Department of English and Foreign Languages.*

originally gave the land to the city for purposes of building an auditorium, but with the construction of the Simmons Center nearby the need no longer existed and so the Jacksons agreed that the land could be used for the higher education center.[18] Construction began soon after and was complete in 1994.

When Susan Camp started her new job at the newly-christened Duncan Higher Education Center that August, she had no idea what to expect. She had a bachelor's degree in chemistry from Cameron and had taught high school but felt intrigued by the opportunity to be a part of the new center. While the Duncan community had put together the funding for the building, Camp recalled that "no funds had been budgeted for furnishings."

Just before the start of the first classes she went to Duncan High School and posted signs to let students know that the college classes would be held at the new education center, which had only three furnished classrooms when the semester began. Although Camp did not even have her own desk when she started the job, she recalled the excitement among the students when they first came for classes, saying that "their eyes lit up when they first saw their new building."[19] Enrollment grew steadily in Duncan and ten years after the opening of the higher education center, it became an official branch campus of Cameron University.

By the late 1990s Cameron students could boast of access to a wide array of class formats, degree programs, and scholarship opportunities. President Davis established the President's Leadership University Scholars (PLUS) program in 1981 to attract high school students with strong leadership potential to campus, and it quickly became one of the most prestigious scholarship programs at Cameron. By the 1990s, the reputation of the scholarship had grown considerably and played a definitive factor in the decision of a number of students to attend Cameron. Recipients of this scholarship had to maintain an overall G.P.A. of 3.0, be involved in a student organization on campus, attend university events, and perform service hours in the community. In exchange, they received free tuition and campus housing. A number of impressive students graduated from Cameron as a result of the program and many of the PLUS scholars have gone on to play an active role in the Cameron alumni organization.

Among those PLUS students was Jennifer Barnett Holland. When she contemplated her college options with her parents in the spring of 1996 as she prepared to graduate from Frederick High School, Cameron did not make the top of her list. Like many students, she hoped to get farther away from home and she had no particularly strong impressions of Cameron. When she toured cam-

pus, however, she recalled being impressed by the newly completed Sciences Complex and surprised by how much she saw going on at the campus. When Jennifer received notification that she had received the PLUS scholarship, she and her parents decided that going to Cameron made the most amount of sense. Jennifer had two siblings already at college and as an added incentive, her father told her that she could go to any school she wanted, but that she would only have a car if she went to Cameron.[20]

Like scores of other students who enrolled after Cameron began offering four-year degree programs, Jennifer planned to only stay for a year or two so that she could get some of her general education courses out of the way, and to have the car. Yet Jennifer found what many other Cameron students have found over the years; that the longer she stayed at Cameron and the more active she became on campus, the more she felt connected to the place, and the harder it became to contemplate leaving. She eventually settled on communications as a major and did so, in part, because she increasingly found herself drawn to public relations opportunities and because she had gotten to know her professors and felt that she had found her academic niche with them. As a PLUS scholar, Jennifer had many opportunities on campus and had administrators like Louise Brown and Don Sullivan as PLUS advisors. She worked in President Davis's office, the Fitness Center, and in the community relations office with Keith Mitchell. Her experiences at Cameron are unique in some respects in that after getting her bachelors and masters degrees at Cameron she went on to work as the Student Activities Director, the director of Student Development, and then Dean of Student Services. She married her college boyfriend, Todd Holland, who played baseball at Cameron and went on to become the head baseball coach. The larger significance of Jennifer's personal story, however, is that it provides insight into the process

Cameron Baseball:
The Transformation of a Team
to a Program

by Tyson Moll
History Major and Cameron baseball player • Class of 2009

By the 1920s Cameron baseball had evolved into an informal sport, sometimes intramural in nature and others with pick-up games between assorted Cameron players and players from either Fort Sill or Lawton High. In 1958, however, the Cameron baseball team made a name for themselves, both on and off campus, while competing in the NJ-CAA (National Junior College Athletic Association) despite having only minimal facilities and equipment. At its start of competitive play, Cameron had no organized baseball team and the focus was on basketball and football. The athletes having no season in the spring decided to start a baseball

team. Member of the 1958 team and recent inductee into the Aggie Hall of Fame Jackie Martin recalled having to talk basketball coach Ted Owens into coaching the team. Martin said, "We had a bunch of guys who wanted to play. We didn't have a field, uniforms, or anything" so they practiced on the grass "north of North Hall which isn't even here anymore."

In 1958, the Cameron team reached the regional competition which they won against schools from New Mexico and Arizona. The team then went on to win Cameron's first official National Championship. Coach Owens managed to acquire their uniforms from a Fort Sill team that got new ones the year before. The team tore off the logos and played with blank uniforms. Even while playing in the national tournament, most of the players wore different hats. When the news arrived in Lawton that the team had won the National Championship, most students and community members did not even know that Cameron had a team. The team never received championship rings or even a rally or

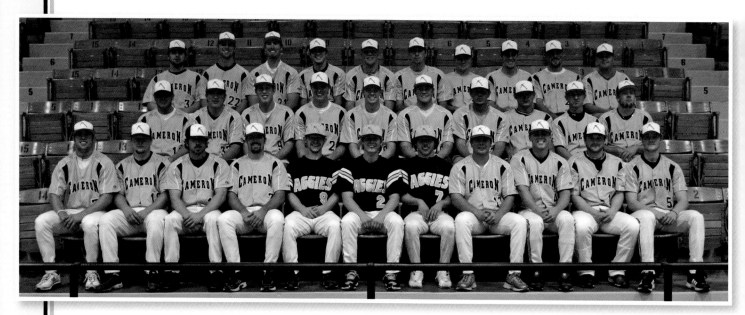

Cameron's 2008 baseball team, including Tyson Moll (top right), enjoyed a successful season under the leadership of head coach and former Cameron baseball player, Todd Holland. *Photograph by Craig Martin. Courtesy Cameron University Office of Sports Information.*

CIS was" at the time, but these two faculty members seemed to believe in her, and so she decided to give it a try. She graduated in 1989 and left Cameron to work at Halliburton. When a friend told her about a job opening in the Testing Center at Cameron in 1994, which Dr. Phillips oversaw by this time, she applied and got hired for the position. In her job at the testing center, Linda came into contact with a number of students who reminded her of herself when she first returned to college. Her own experience allowed her to connect with both traditional and non-traditional students who felt out of place or fearful that they could not succeed in college.[23]

After Linda began working at Cameron, Don Phillips again shaped her educational fortunes by telling her that she needed to get her master's degree so that she could advance at the university. By the time she completed her master's degree in 1998, much of Linda's career had been shaped by the advice of Don Phillips and the interest he had shown in her. Linda went on to serve as Assistant Registrar and then Registrar and found herself in a position of being able to reassure nervous students and advise them that they could get a quality education at Cameron from faculty who really cared about them. She recalled that Don Phillips frequently came to refer to her as his daughter even though they were not related but shared the same last name. That a timid student who described herself as a "small town girl with no exposure to anything cultural" found a mentor like Don Phillips and went on to become the head Registrar speaks volumes about Cameron's relationship to its students.[24] While every story has unique aspects, in many ways Linda Phillips' story seems more representative than exceptional. She, like many students who came to Cameron and even returned there to work, found a connection through the individual attention Cameron faculty and staff traditionally provided for students, regardless of whether they attended the high school, the junior

During a welcome back party Cameron students celebrated the new term by dancing in the Fine Arts Courtyard. *Courtesy 1994* Wichita, *Department of English and Foreign Languages.*

college, or the university.

While Cameron continued to serve traditional and non-traditional students alike, a new and significant challenge manifested itself at the dawn of the twenty-first century. The terrorist attacks against the United States on September 11, 2001 shocked much of the world and had profound ramifications for Cameron in the years that followed. Given the substantial military population at Cameron, it eventually meant a sharp decline in enrollment among soldiers and their dependents. Linda Phillips recalled that the number of special requests from soldiers increased in the first few years following the attack as soldiers sometimes received orders to deploy overseas with virtually no notice or time to withdraw from classes.[25] Cameron's administration worked to try to alleviate the strain on military families by expediting the special requests and offering support where they could, but the impact of so many withdraw-

147

President Don Davis addressed faculty, staff, students, and members of the Lawton community at Convocation during the mid-1980s. *Courtesy Cameron University Department of English and Foreign Languages.*

als and transfers on enrollment proved enormous. As a consequence, when Dr. Cindy Ross became president in 2002, she eventually faced a need to increase enrollment among traditional age college students to offset the declining population of military students and dependents. In the fall of 2001, Cameron's enrollment included 808 active duty military personnel and 673 military family members, which equaled more than 20% of overall enrollment. By the fall of 2008, those numbers had decreased to 673 active duty students and 313 family members, which constituted a significant enrollment decline resulting in large part from the War on Terror which followed the 9-11 terrorist attacks on the United States.[26]

Not long after the attacks, on January 29, 2002, President Davis called a general faculty and staff meeting in which he announced his plan to submit his "request for retirement to the board of regents" later that afternoon and draw to a close more than two decades of service to the university. Davis indicated that he wanted his retirement to become effective June 30, 2003 and that he wanted the new president to take over on January 1, 2003, giving Davis some sort of "off campus"

assignment for his final semester. He also wanted to be "designated as President Emeritus" upon his retirement. He provided the faculty and staff with an overview of some of the important events that occurred during his administration before saying that "The most significant are those events which take place daily between faculty and students in classrooms and laboratories and staff and students in advisement, activities, and athletics." He added that "This is where visions are shared, minds are molded, confidence is instilled [built], and dreams are made reality." Davis concluded by telling those in attendance that "You in this room make possible the miracle of higher education."[27] Whatever plans or hopes President Davis had for how his retirement might play out, the regents decided to appoint a new president effective less than six months later, on July 1, 2002.

After having served as president for 22 years, Don Davis left behind a more mixed record than perhaps he would have liked. Yet, as Cindy Ross later observed, no decision a president makes goes without some criticism.[28] Without question, Davis accomplished a great many things for the institution. No small task exists in trying to boil down the contributions of a president whose tenure spanned more than two decades, but among his most vital achievements for Cameron were getting the school out from under the enormous Shepler Complex debt, shifting Cameron to the OU Board of Regents, establishing KCCU as a National Public Radio station on campus, creating a graduate school in 1987, promoting the growth of technology on campus, maintaining the school's accreditation, implementing academic festivals every three years, and starting both the President's Partners donor program and the PLUS scholarship. In reflecting on his presidency, Davis cited establishing Cameron as an interactive university and providing cultural opportunities to students through the study abroad program, academic festivals, and KCCU programming, as among the most gratifying achievements.[29]

Back when he first became president in 1980, Davis was perceived by many as the personification of a "home town boy done good."[30] However, by the time he left campus Cameron's relationship with the community had grown tepid at best. The departure of the FAA training school from Cameron's campus, the abolition of the football team, and perhaps the simple passage of time all served to complicate Davis's relationship with the community as well as some alumni and donors. While Davis had a reputation for being both charming and courageous, he also had a reputation for being indecisive and quick-tempered.[31] Whatever Davis's strengths and weaknesses as a president, the sum total of his career at Cameron nevertheless reveals that he left the institution in better shape than he found it. He had, it would seem, much to be proud of from the time he spent at Cameron.

Shortly after Davis concluded his retirement announcement, the search for a new president began in earnest. Cindy Ross, who had worked in the Office of the Vice President for Academic Affairs at Oklahoma State University before going

on to serve as the chief academic officer for the Oklahoma State Board of Regents for twelve years, decided to apply for the position. As a fifth-generation Oklahoman and a graduate of OSU, Ross' background made her an interesting candidate for the position. She grew up in a small rural community with only 30 students in her high school graduating class. Though she started college at OSU as a traditional student, she left to start a family and returned later to finish her bachelor's degree, eventually earning her doctorate in higher education administration.[32]

Ross' work with the State Regents afforded her a good deal of familiarity with all of the public institutions of higher education in Oklahoma, but she remembered Cameron standing out because of the emphasis on strong relationships with students, the very thing that had historically kept people like Jennifer Holland, Linda Phillips, and countless others on Cameron's campus. Ross said that she "had no real expectation" that she would get the job at Cameron. She was one of five finalists, including Provost Don Sullivan and former speaker of the state House of Representatives Lloyd Benson, who interviewed for the position. At the end of a long day of interviews, Ross spent the night in a Lawton hotel waiting for the phone

President Cindy Ross became Cameron's sixteenth president when she took office in the summer of 2002. She replaced President Don Davis and has continued to govern the institution into its second century. *Courtesy Cameron University Archives.*

to ring so that she would know if she had been selected for the position or not.[33] When the phone call confirming her selection finally came, Ross accepted the position as president at Cameron and said "I'm excited; ready to roll up my sleeves and get started." During the search much speculation ensued as to whether or not Cameron would have another former politician, like Benson, as president, a situation which had become a common trend in Oklahoma higher education. Yet, Chancellor Hans Brisch "applauded the unanimous decision" to appoint Ross as Cameron's president, saying "It is customary in higher education that academic folk have the opportunity to knock on the door of a college presidency."[34]

OU Regent Jon R. Stuart had just been appointed to his post when he came to Lawton to interview the three finalists for the presidency at Cameron. He recalled that Ross quickly gained his support because during her interview she repeatedly emphasized the importance of students and student learning. She also impressed him with her "complete and total knowledge of where Lawton and Cameron fit in the state." Stuart explained that Ross understood the situation at Cameron and "knew the strengths and weaknesses" of the institution.[35] In fact, Dr. Gilbert "Gib" Gibson, a longtime community leader and Cameron supporter, said that while he initially favored another candidate, after Ross became president, he quickly became impressed with her keen understanding of the issues facing southwest Oklahoma and the role Cameron could play in addressing those issues, such as economic development and support for the military.[36]

Cindy Ross began preparations for the move to Lawton in the summer of 2002, just as a number of recent high school graduates contemplated their futures and finalized their college plans. One of those students was Lawton native Frank Myers. He grew up knowing he would go to college. He came from a middle-class background, but like

Students walking across campus from Nance Boyer, the oldest building on campus, toward the Sciences Complex have the opportunity to enjoy the attractive small-campus environment. *Courtesy Department of English and Foreign Languages.*

so many students he needed financial assistance to make attending college a reality. He applied to three schools but only Cameron offered him a full ride when they awarded him the PLUS scholarship. Like Jennifer Holland, Myers planned to stay at Cameron for the first year or two but then he made connections to people on campus and his plans changed. He received an opportunity to become a student worker in Holland's office in

Student Activities. He described this as a "turning point" because he became very active in campus life by getting involved in the Program Activities Council (PAC) and student government. Myers recalled that "everything changed so much" after he went to work for Holland. He went on to serve as PAC co-chair and in his senior year served as the student government president. This, in turn, put him into direct contact with administrators on campus. He got to know President Ross and sat on committees with other administrators and faculty members. Frank recalled how Glen Pinkston, the vice president for Business and Finance, always made him feel like his opinion mattered. He also worked as an Aggie Ambassador, giving campus tours and helping out with campus events. All of these experiences gave Myers the same sense of being connected to Cameron as they had Jennifer Holland during the previous decade.[37]

Myers' decision to attend Cameron and then to stay made him a third generation Cameron graduate following in the footsteps of both his mother and grandmother. When he explained that he "fell in love with Cameron" because "the university will give you as much as you put into it," his comments echoed that of his grandmother, Alice Fullerton Watson, a 1928 graduate.[28] She reflected fondly on her time at Cameron saying that "it was just a joy to be" at the school where she was surrounded by people who cared.[39] For both Myers and his grandmother nearly 60 years earlier, the positive experience at Cameron came down, in large part, to the personal relationships forged between students and their mentors. After graduating, Myers returned to Cameron to work as a recruiter in the admissions office and eventually as the coordinator of prospective student services, putting him in direct contact with the next generation of Cameron students.

Frank Myers' story offers a compelling glimpse into the attitude transformation that began to emerge on Cameron's campus following President Ross' arrival. After coming to Cameron, Ross continually emphasized that she wanted Cameron to be the "University of Choice" in southwest Oklahoma. While some students no doubt still enter Cameron with plans to transfer, increasing numbers of students are drawn to the institution because of the low cost, small classes, and individual attention they receive from faculty and staff. Ann Morris, for example, graduated from high school in 2005 and came to Cameron, just as her two older sisters had done. She received the PLUS scholarship, which she described as "one of the major aspects" in making her want to come to Cameron. Like Jennifer Holland and Frank Myers, Morris became very involved on campus, which certainly gave her that same sense of feeling connected that the others articulated. However, by the time she had watched her two older sisters go through Cameron and all the things they were involved with, Cameron was her university of choice. She described her experiences at Cameron, saying "it is amazing to see the changes" and "to be a part of" all that happened during her time on campus.[40] As a member of the 2009 centennial graduating class, Ann Morris reflected well President Ross' desire to revitalize the enthusiasm and spirit of a traditional college campus.

For President Ross, the connections described by Jennifer Holland, Frank Myers, and Ann Morris comprised one of Cameron's greatest assets, and she worked to strengthen support for similar connections and for students in general after arriving at Cameron. When President Ross first came to Cameron, the university's reserve fund contained less than one month's operational funds. Just six weeks into her presidency, Ross received word that due to a shortfall in state revenue, Cameron faced a budget cut and over the next year, more cuts followed.[41] In November of 2002 Cameron faced its second budget cut following Ross' appointment as president and had to "cut an additional $325,000 for [from] the school's budget." This additional cut of 1.66% came only two months after a 4.34% cut had been implemented.[42] The following January, Cameron again faced a budget cut of 2%, creating a seemingly insurmountable challenge for the school.[43] To further complicate matters for the new president, Cameron employees had been promised raises by the previous administration. Given the budget problems, President Ross had no choice but to cancel the raises. She praised the employees though, saying that she "received no complaints."[44]

Over the next several years, Cameron faced continued budget challenges and even as enrollment peaked in 2004, President Ross redoubled private fund-raising efforts to offset declining state appropriations to higher education. In fact, Ross oversaw the first comprehensive fundraising campaign in the school's history with the $8.5 million Changing Lives campaign. The campaign far exceeded even President Ross' expectations as the final count totaled $12,567,327, which dramatically surpassed the original goal. Money raised during this campaign went to fund creation of the Bentley Gardens, the McMahon Centennial Complex, endow faculty positions, improve landscaping, and increase the number of student scholarships. Of this venture President Ross said, "Three years ago we had a dream, and that dream led us to embark on a historic and ambitious fundraising campaign," and added that "Today we know that dreams do come true. The dream of Cameron's Centennial Changing Lives Campaign came true because of the overwhelming generosity of the donors who are providing a solid foundation for Cameron's second century."[45] Indeed, it proved to be the largest three-year fundraising campaign of any regional university in the history of the state.[46]

Many aspects of Ross' administration have, in one way or another, focused on community outreach and a restoration of tradition. When Ross came to Cameron, she began spending considerable time out in the community. She met

The ground-breaking ceremony for the McMahon Centennial Complex marked an exciting time for Cameron because this new building, which includes a student union and banquet facility, will be the center of campus life for decades to come. *Photograph by Jim Horinek.*

with superintendents and community leaders and looked for opportunities to make Cameron available to the people of southwest Oklahoma. Ross described Cameron as "an integral part of southwest Oklahoma" and added that the university had a responsibility to "provide leadership to help the community thrive." As such, she wanted Cameron to "be first in people's minds when a problem needs to be solved."[47] So, for Ross, the role of Cameron continued to be that of providing a quality education to the people of southwestern Oklahoma and also playing a strong leadership role within that community. John McArthur, who came to Cameron in July of 2004 as the dean for the School of Science and Technology and then became the vice president for Academic Affairs in 2006, described Ross as being "everywhere in the community" and added that this has made her "a great advocate for Cameron."[48] Gib Gibson also recognized Ross' presence in the Lawton community as well as in surrounding areas. He said that Ross "understands Cameron's role in providing leadership in southwest Oklahoma" and that she also has "been very involved with the military and providing support to military families."[49]

Ross extended her visibility within the Lawton community to that of Duncan as well. Susan Camp recalled shortly after Ross took office, she went to Duncan, visited with community leaders, and spent considerable time going over Cameron operations in Duncan. Camp said that President

Ross "made herself very available to the Duncan community."[50] Over the next few years, the relationship between the Duncan Higher Education Center and Cameron continued to grow, and Ross began talking with community leaders about the possibility of Duncan becoming an official branch campus. In May 2004, Governor Brad Henry signed House Bill 2624 which made the designation official. In January of 2005, the City of Duncan formally donated the land and the building to Cameron University. Ross praised the Duncan community as being "fully committed to higher education" and said simply that "the presence of a higher education institution is an absolute necessity for economic development."[51] President Ross also credited then-Representative Jari Askins for her strong advocacy of designating Duncan as a branch campus, saying that Askins worked tirelessly to support the effort.[52] Duncan enroll-

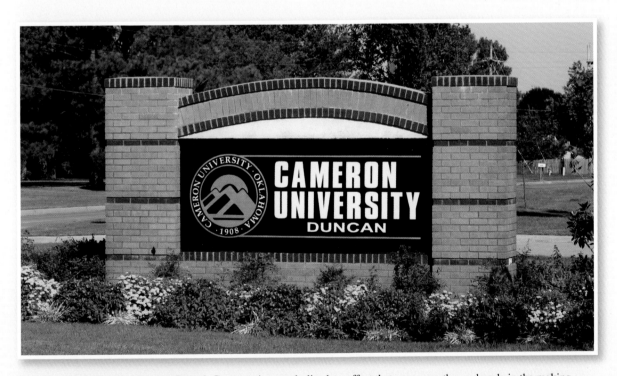

The Cameron University Duncan Branch Campus sign symbolized an effort that was more than a decade in the making, which was for the Duncan community to have their own official branch campus. *Courtesy Cameron University Office of Community Relations.*

ment skyrocketed following its official designation as a branch campus, increasing 40% in the fall of 2004, and Camp noted that in just ten years time, they had gone from offering nine classes to 90 in the Duncan facility.[53]

The legislature's decision to make Duncan a branch campus made a tremendous impact on the Duncan community, but met with some criticism in the state. An editorial in *The Oklahoman* suggested that there already were ample higher education institutions in the state and then said that "college students have no shortage of choices." The editorial went on to point out that Lawton was "just 30 miles from Duncan."[54] President Ross responded to the editorial by explaining that the significant increase in enrollment in Duncan and the move to make Duncan a branch campus came "at no additional cost to Oklahoma taxpayers."[55] Susan Camp recalled how surprised she had been after assuming her duties at the Duncan campus by just how important it had been as "an access point to education" for people in that area.[56] While 30 miles may not seem like a lot, for some potential students, it absolutely meant the difference between whether they ever attempted to attend college or not.

Providing access to both affordable and quality higher education historically constituted the most important role of Cameron in southwest Oklahoma, and Ross continued that mission as she also looked to restore tradition to the school. Perhaps the best example of restoring campus traditions during Ross' administration occurred with the revival of the school's mascot, Ole Kim. For decades, Cameron students had vacillated

Despite debates over the past few decades as to whether Cameron should adopt a new mascot or retain its traditional one, Ole Kim prevailed and today is the chief ambassador of school spirit and pride. *Courtesy Cameron University Office of Community Relations, 2007.*

between celebrating the school's traditions and wanting to focus on the newer, more modern aspects of the evolving institution. Students in 1966, for example, wrote that "Without tradition, a school has no foundation."[57] Ten years later, students asserted that Cameron had "finally lost the reputation of being an 'aggie school,'" which they described as having "brought about the main source of jokes that plagued CU."[58] By the time President Ross came to Cameron, the school no longer fit the traditional model of an agricultural institution and in fact, seemed to still be searching for its identity. While institutional maturity mattered much to the strength of the school's academic mission, a rallying cry for school spirit, it was not. And so, wherever one came down on the old versus new debate, one clear factor seemed indisputable: the school needed something around

which to organize and foster school spirit.

The administration made plans to unveil Cameron's new mascot at the 2004 homecoming pep rally. Ross noted that "traditions are the threads that link a university's past—and its alumni—with the current student body and with future growth." In keeping with that, Ole Kim returned as Cameron's mascot and school officials announced that Cameron would remain "the Aggies."[59] Lawton Mayor Cecil Powell proclaimed February 27, 2004 "Cameron Aggies Day" in recognition of this decision. According to the official proclamation, Cameron first "gave its mascot life when student Jeanne Desautel Foster dressed as Ole Kim and rode in the 1964 homecoming parade."[60] Ole Kim appeared at the 2004 pep rally in a "professionally produced mascot costume" and has continued to regularly appear at university events since that time.[61]

Any effort at identifying a sitting president's legacy lends itself to, at best, incompleteness. In the case of Ross, one might well assume that hers will have some connection to improving the physical appearance of Cameron. Cameron Village, a state-of-the-art student housing complex, and the CETES building were completed in 2005 and were the first major construction projects following her arrival at Cameron. However, much more than anyone could have reasonably hoped for followed. The McMahon Centennial Complex, CETES Phase II, and a new business building thoroughly showcase the school's growth and the president's commitment to improving the campus. Another significant improvement to the campus beautification efforts occurred through a gift from OU Regent Jon R. Stuart who donated hundreds of trees, many of which now line the perimeter of campus. Completion of the 2 ½-acre Bentley Gardens has further enhanced the appearance of the institution and its grounds.

While preventative maintenance seldom tops anyone's list of why they choose to work or go

The opening of Cameron Village in 2005 provided students with access to modern apartment-style living quarters adjacent to the beautifully designed McMahon Living and Learning Center. *Courtesy Cameron University Archives.*

to school at a particular university, it nonetheless plays a vital role in the daily experiences of those who inhabit a given institution. Glen Pinkston said that from his perspective "the perfect repair is the one that is done before something breaks, not after," and this has informed his approach to campus maintenance. For Pinkston, taking care of the campus entails doing things like making sure the reading room in the library has enough light to actually read and correcting problems well before even a perception of neglect arises. Virtually all presidents who serve in their position very long oversee some construction on their campuses, but Ross' approach has been more systematic than that of some. In fact, Pinkston credited President Ross with really "establishing an architectural pallet" for the school.[62] For example, new construction blends with older buildings through the use of the same color of brick and other architectural consistencies.

In the same way that Ross pursued an "architectural pallet" for the university, she also diligently oversaw larger campus plans for advancing the school's mission. During her administration, both Plan 2008 and Plan 2013 created cohesive, albeit flexible, five-year blueprints for improvements in all aspects of university life and attempted to encourage a greater degree of awareness of how

individual programs, faculty research, and campus initiatives should work in concert with Cameron's aim to foster diversity, pursue innovation, and educate new generations of students. Significantly, both plans emphasized putting student learning first and recognized that even amidst change and progress, Cameron's central commitment to educating its' students remains at the forefront of ongoing innovation.[63]

For Ross, however, "the evolution of culture at Cameron" constituted her most important goal after coming to the campus. She expressed a strong desire to increase pride in the institution. Increasing student activities on campus, maintaining and restoring school traditions, improving alumni relations, and supporting the unique needs of both traditional and non-traditional students all have

The new School of Business was completed in 2009 and includes classrooms equipped with the latest technological equipment. *Photograph by Jim Horinek.*

Under the direction of head cheerleading coach Robin Martin, Cameron's cheerleading team has flourished, winning the top leadership award in 2008 and 2009 at the Universal Cheerleaders Association (UCA) competition. *Photograph by Bennett Dewan.*

been a part of this effort. Additionally, showcasing both faculty and student accomplishments and literally opening the doors of the university to the community have served to improve the relationship of Cameron to Lawton and the surrounding communities. After Cameron's difficult transition to a four-year institution, for many it became "the school of last resort," but under Ross' leadership, the reputation of Cameron has improved significantly. Albert Johnson, Jr., the vice president for university advancement, recalled how different the culture is now than when he was a Cameron student in the late 1970s.[64] Certainly this change has manifested itself in numerous ways but one example can been seen in campus attire. Ross said that it frustrated her when she first arrived on campus to see how many students wore t-shirts from universities other than Cameron.[65] One creative way of addressing this particular problem came simply from allowing Cameron students to trade in their old t-shirts for new Cameron shirts, a move which eventually transformed not only the t-shirt culture, but the level of school spirit on campus.

Student athletes play a profound role in foster-

ing school spirit and at Cameron, the men's and women's sports teams have, on the whole, enjoyed a good deal of success. Athletic Director Jim Jackson credited Ross for her strong support of the athletic programs and his approach to community outreach has complimented hers well. The athletes engage in numerous hours of community service and during the 2008-2009 school year alone, student athletes completed over 2,500 hours of community service. This does not, however, include the occasional call Jackson receives from someone who requests that he send a few of the athletes over "to help a little old lady move a television set" or some such thing, a request, which he says the athletic department gladly honors. This, in turn, cannot help but generate a positive image of the university. Jackson said, "This is a good time to be at Cameron."[66] The baseball team is thriving and the softball team continues to improve its record despite several coaching changes in recent years. Both the men's and women's basketball teams have considerable promise for the coming year. The women's volleyball team has historically had a very strong record. The golf program has

Cameron basketball player Dave Smith led the Aggies to a winning regular season, scoring a total of 435 points during the 2008-2009 season. *Photograph by Bennett Dewan.*

Cameron's nationally-ranked women's and men's tennis teams have enjoyed a good deal of success under head coach James Helvey. Cameron tennis player Sara Flores competed during the 2009 season. *Photograph by Bennett Dewan.*

continued to enjoy a healthy record under Coach Hrnciar's leadership and Coach James Helvey has led the tennis teams to countless victories. Even Cameron's cheerleading squad has grown in visibility and strength in recent years. Indeed, the relationship of athletic programs to the community remains particularly important in generating support for the teams and the overall campus and the Aggie Gold Club demonstrates well the public support for Cameron athletics.

When Jamie Glover came to Cameron in February of 2003, Cameron's recruiting staff had just doubled from two to four, and she recalled the challenges she and the others faced. In years past, recruiters had not always felt that they received either the funding or "the tools to do recruiting

that they needed." Glover recalled that early on she met with counselors and students at job fairs who said "We have never had someone from Cameron come here before." While she pointed out that "it takes time to change an image," she also added that Cameron enjoys a good deal more recognition now than when she first started. Now, as associate vice president for Enrollment Management, Jamie Glover regularly hears from principals and counselors who want their students to come to Cameron. For her, the key to ensuring long term change lies in "providing consistency in publications" and other venues such as the website. In addition to the "consistent message" that Cameron provides a quality and affordable "personalized education," another core component of recruiting success stems from being able to offer a more "comprehensive scholarship program." [67] In fact, financial assistance to students has grown significantly under Ross' administration and new money for student scholarships from the Centennial Changing Lives Campaign alone totaled more than $1.9 million. [68]

As Cameron prepared to celebrate its centennial year during the 2008-2009 academic year with the guidance of the Centennial Commission, which included distinguished alumni, President's Partners, regents, and community leaders, the Cameron community explored many aspects of the school's roots. The kick-off event for the centennial celebration included a concert by the Oakridge Boys and fireworks, but perhaps the most notable part of the event was how closely it resembled the "Cameron Day" tradition established early in the school's history in which the campus periodically opened its doors to feed and entertain the community. While well-known speakers like George Will and Al Roker came to campus as part of the year-long celebration, in many ways the most gripping part of the year came in the form of the centennial moments, aired on the KCCU Radio station as part of their centennial oral history project.

As the year-long centennial festivities came to an end, President Ross announced new plans for the school's future with the "Every Student. Every Story" campaign in recognition of Cameron's long history of putting students first. In the twenty-first century, Cameron students come from a much more diverse background than they once did. Eighty-one percent of Cameron students still come from Oklahoma but 14% are from another state or territory and 5% are from a foreign country. Sixty percent of Cameron students are female and Cameron has one of the most diverse college campuses in Oklahoma with only about 55% of the student body identifying themselves as "white," and a large number of African American, Hispanic, and Native American students in attendance. [69] The stories of Cameron students will continue to take on greater diversity both culturally and geographically, as just one of the many manifestations of living in an increasingly global society. Yet, the common thread expressed in the philosophy behind "Every Student. Every Story" remains Cameron's commitment to fostering individual relationships with its students. Another aspect of the announcements included a commitment to increased opportunities for healthier living with such additions as greater recycling efforts, a new mile-long walking path on campus, healthy eating options in campus dining facilities, and a new community garden that opened in the spring of 2009. As Cameron prepares to enter its second century the emphasis remains on students, but with new attention to healthy living, something that early Cameron students took as a given.

With the announcement of these new innovations on Cameron's campus at the close of the centennial year, one cannot help but be struck that the institution has indeed come full circle. The agriculture program no longer occupies center stage at Cameron, yet, with five faculty members and the number of majors ranging from 110 to 130, the program continues to offer a vital service to the people of southwest Oklahoma. Leon Fischer attended Cameron as a student in the 1970s before returning to teach in the agriculture department in 1991. Now serving as chair, he noted how far removed most of the students, including agriculture majors, are from the farm. Cameron still operates a farm and offers applied programs in animal science and agricultural business. Fischer explained that most of Cameron's agricultural majors end up working in either the science or the business side of the industry rather than as strictly farmers, as many assume.[70]

Early Cameron students came to the agricultural high school to learn practical skills that they could take back to the farm with them but their learning experience extended far beyond learning how to cook or judge livestock. These students spent considerable time learning to think critically; to debate, write poetry, take music classes,

Vice President for Finance Glen Pinkston and Vice President for Academic Affairs John McArthur prepared the Cameron Executive Committee's garden plot in the new community garden, 2009. *Photograph by Leon Fischer. Courtesy Cameron University.*

engage in athletics, and put on drama productions. In essence, their education at Cameron made them well-rounded people who possessed more than just the practical skills needed for successful housewifery or farming. Much has changed in the past 100 years and Cameron now offers an altogether different kind of education in terms of the varied degree programs students have to choose from, but with the addition of the community garden, there is in fact, a restoration of tradition; for now there has emerged an opportunity to acquire practical skills while receiving a college education. Fischer said he has been amazed at the interest in the community garden and the overall "go green" movement that much of the country has become fixated on.[71] While agricultural students once came to Cameron to hone their practical skills while learning to write poetry, university students majoring in everything from art to accounting, not to mention faculty, staff, and administrators, can now take advantage of the campus garden plots.

The story of Cameron is ongoing and by no means has this been a story of the school's inevitable progression to viability or success; while change may be inevitable, greatness is not. At many junctures in Cameron's history, the school has struggled for a sense of identity and purpose. At times it has lacked a clear vision for future growth which often contributed to a sort of innovation in a vacuum that hampered consistent procedures from being implemented and maintained across the institution. Yet, the growth of Cameron and the strength of the educational programs it offers happened not by chance or the simple passage of time but because of the dedication of past and present administrators, faculty, staff, and ultimately, the students who have chosen to come to Cameron. To be sure, Cameron has come a long way since President Liner first greeted students in their basement classroom in downtown Lawton or when male students proudly pitched their tents on the grounds of the new campus in the sweltering heat of the late summer. In 1931, President Coffey affirmed his belief that any student willing to work should have access to education.[72] At a press conference nearly 80 years later, on June 23, 2009, President Ross echoed that very same sentiment in introducing Cameron's latest efforts to ease the financial burden on students as she said that she believed no student should be denied an education for financial reasons. She proudly noted that Cameron remains the second least expensive university in the state and that *US News and World Report* ranked Cameron number one nationally for its students having the least amount of debt upon graduation.[73] And so, as Loy Dykes wrote in 1914, "whatever the future may hold" there is indeed good reason to be "well pleased with the work which we have done here."[74]

The McMahon Centennial Complex will open in the spring of 2010 and its balcony will overlook the Bentley Gardens. *Photograph by Jim Horinek.*

CHAPTER ONE

1. "Dear Old Cameron" appears in the last line of the school's original Alma Mater which ends with "Dear Old Cameron, Hail to thee," by Flora Belle Robertson, class of 1922, 1921 *Wichita*. Unless otherwise noted, the *Wichitas* were accessed in the Cameron University Archives (hereafter CUA).

2. "Cameron School Song," 1925 *Wichita*, p. 69.

3. "Three Years Ago Today the Townsite Was Bare Prairie," *Lawton News Republican*, 7 September 1904, p. 1. Unless otherwise noted, the newspapers refereced were accessed in the CUA.

4. "Cost of Living in a Good Town," *Lawton News Republican*, 20 April 1905, p. 2.

5. Senate Bill 109, Chapter three, article III on Agriculture Education, in "Session Laws of Oklahoma, 1907-08," Cameron History, Folder 12, Box 2, CUA.

6. Hugh Corwin, "Cameron State School of Agriculture, 1909-1927," *The Southwestern Oklahoma Historical Society*, January 1976, Vol. 12, No. 3, p. 130. According to Corwin local businessmen got together and purchased eighty acres which they sold at a profit allowing them to buy 160 acres for the school and farm.

7. Paul Frederick Orr, "Class History," *1912 Class Soubenir*, Folder 1, Box 2, Alumni Collection, CUA; "Informal Reception at Agricultural School," *Daily News Republican*, 27 March 1910, p. 1.

8. According to *The Oklahoman*, a case of smallpox prevented the State Board of Agriculture's first choice for the school's president from holding that position; "Agricultural School at Lawton to Open Nov. 16," *The Oklahoman*, 5 November 1909, p. 10.

9. Mrs. Dora Cox Frye taught mathematics, Miss Cecil Kirkpatrick taught Domestic Science, Miss Jane Edwards taught English, and A. H. Chapman taught Agriculture during Cameron's first year. Corwin, "Cameron State School of Agriculture, 1909-1927, p. 132.

10. Ibid., 133.

11. "Large Crowd at Reception," *Daily News Republican*, 29 March 1910, p. 1.

12. Orr, "Class History."

13. Ibid.

14. "Aggy School Is Growing," *Lawton Constitution Democrat Weekly*, 2 February 1911, p. 1.

15. Ibid.

16. "Aggies in New Home," *Lawton Constitution Democrat Weekly*, 11 March 1911, p. 1.

17. Ibid.

18. Cameron State School of Agriculture January Expenditures, 27 December 1911, Folder 1, Box 1, Oklahoma State Board of Agriculture Minutes Collection (hereafter OSBA Collection), Special Collections and University Archives, Oklahoma State University Libraries (hereafter OUS Archives).

19. "Third Annual Announcement: The Cameron State School of Agriculture," p. 6, 1911, Alumni Collection, CUA.

20. Ibid., p. 8

21. Ibid., p. 6.

22. Ibid., p. 9.

23. Ibid.

24. "Oklahoma Butter: Gotham's Choice," *The Oklahoman*, 20 May 1912, p. 4.

25. Ibid.

26. Letter to "My Dear Pupils" from J. A. Liner, 9 April 1912, Folder 32, Box 1, Alumni Collection, CUA.

27. "Liner Quits School of Agriculture," *Lawton Constitution Democrat Weekly*, 30 May 1912, p. 4.

28. "Cameron's New President Here," *Lawton Constitution Democrat Weekly*, 6 June 1912, p. 6.

29. Ibid.

30. "Three Thousand Film Feet Advertise Cameron School," *Lawton Constitution Democrat Weekly*, 18 July 1912, p. 4.

31. "Cameron School Is Saved," *Lawton Constitution Democrat Weekly*, 13 June 1912, p. 4.

32. "Must Have Pupils or No School," *Lawton Constitution Democrat Weekly*, 20 June 1912, p. 10(a).

33. "Dormitory Is Practically Assured Now," *Lawton Constitution Democrat Weekly*, 4 July 1912, p. 2.

34. "Delay Opening for Dormitory," *Lawton Constitution Democrat Weekly*, 22 August 1912, p. 8.

35. "Three Thousand Film Feet Advertise Cameron School," *Lawton Constitution Democrat Weekly*, 18 July 1912, p. 4.

36. "Cameron Opens: Fifty Students," *Lawton Constitution Democrat Weekly*, 19 September 1912, p. 1.

37. "Operating Cameron's Dormitory," *Lawton Constitution Democrat Weekly*, 24 October 1912, p. 10.

38. Corwin, "Cameron State School of Agriculture, 1909-1927," p. 147.

39. "Consider Cameron," *Lawton Constitution Democrat Weekly*, 21 November 1912, p. 6.

40. "To Abolish 5 Schools in State?," *Lawton Constitution Democrat Weekly*, 30 January 1913, p. 5.

41. "Aggie Schools Given a Knock in Committee," *Lawton Constitution Democrat Weekly*, 6 February 1913, p. 1; "Funds for Cameron Approved," *Lawton Constitution Democrat Weekly* 1 May 1913, p. 8.

42. "Students Self Governed Here," *Lawton Constitution Democrat Weekly*, 9 January 1913, p. 1.

43. "Hennessey Talked to Graduates," *Lawton Constitution Democrat Weekly*, 29 May 1913, p. 1 (a).

44. "Robertson Out; Frost President," *Lawton Constitution Democrat Weekly*, 10 July 1913, p. 2.

45. Corwin, "Cameron State School of Agriculture, 1909-1927," p. 150.

46. "Change at Cameron," *Lawton Constitution Weekly*, 29 January 1914, p. 3.

47. Ibid.

48. To State Board of Agriculture from R. P. Short, 30 November 1914, Folder 14, Box 1, OSBA Collection, OSU Archives.

49. "Cameron's 1st Annual," *Lawton Constitution Weekly*, 21 May 1914, p. 6 (a).

50. "Introduction," 1914 *Wichita*.

51. Frank Ikard, President, Athletic Association, "Athletics," 1914 *Wichita*.

52. Ibid.

53. Corwin, "Cameron State School of Agriculture, 1909-1927," p. 152.

54. Ibid., p. 155.

55. "Crisis in Affairs of Cameron School: Pres. Gault Is Here," *Lawton News*, 2 November 1915, p. 1. Gault was president of the State Board of Agriculture, Cameron's governing board.

56. Ibid., p. 5.

57. "Cameron College Praised," *Lawton Constitution* 10 February 1916, p. 1.

58. Lulu M. Gray, "Junior Class History," 1914 *Wichita*.

59. 1915 *Wichita*.

60. "Enrollment at Cameron Greatest in History of the School," *Lawton Constitution*, 21 January 1915, p. 1 (a).

61. "Aggie School Opens Sept. 11," *Lawton News*, 31 August 1916, p. 1 (b).

62. Woodrow Wilson, "The President's Message to You," 1917 *Wichita*.

63. Kitchen Mechanics poem, 1918 *Wichita*.

64. Dedication, 1918 *Wichita*.

65. "Cameron School Over Crowded," *Lawton Constitution*, 17 September 1919, p. 1 (a).

66. Ibid., p. 1 (b).

67. "The Cameron Truck," 1920 *Wichita*, p. 89.

68. "Matron Alleged to Have Accused Pupils Falsely," *The Oklahoman*, 4 March 1920, p. 1. The current Shepler Complex which includes both male and female dorms was named after Ned Shepler, a relative of Agusta Shepler.

69. Ibid.

70. Corwin, "Cameron State School of Agriculture, 1909-1927," p. 163-167.

71. Ibid., p. 163. Corwin's contentions may indeed be correct but it should also be noted that Farley repeatedly asked for more money to expand the school and that the lack of dormitory space in the fall of 1919 clearly hurt the school's growth as students had to be turned away.

72. Ibid., p. 167. According to Corwin, the cost of room and board at Cameron was $10.00 a month for several years.

73. Ibid., p. 162-163.

74. Ibid., p. 168.

75. "Savage Praises Cameron State School After Visit," *Lawton Constitution*, 3 March 1922, p. 1.

76. "Wickizer Boosts Cameron School," *Lawton Constitution*, 15 March 1922, p. 1.

77. "Cameron School is Aggressive," *Lawton Constitution*, 28 December 1922, p. 1 (a).

78. To "Dear Cameronite" from President A. E. Wickizer, Summer 1922.

79. Paul Bowman, Video-taped interview, Alumni Weekend, October 1987, CUA.

80. Vivian Hay Buckwell, Video-taped interview, Alumni Weekend, October 1987, CUA

81. 1923 *Wichita*, p. 71.

82. Corwin, "Cameron State School of Agriculture, 1909-1927," p. 181.

83. Ibid., p. 71.

84. Ibid., p. 179.

85. W. E. Armstrong, 17 December 1925, 1925 Cameron State School of Agriculture Time Capsule letter, CUA.

86. Harry Hammond, Video-taped interview, Alumni Weekend, October 1987, CUA.

87. 1925 *Wichita*, p. 64.

88. Ibid.

89. Ibid., p. 65.

90. Ibid.

91. 1924 *Wichita*, p. 61.

92. Ibid.

93. Alice Fullerton Watson, Video-taped interview, Alumni Weekend, October 1987, CUA.

94. Payroll of Cameron State School of Agriculture 5 January 1925; 2 September 1926, OSBA Collection, OSU.

95. Lewis "Les" Faulkner, Video-taped interview, Alumni Weekend, October 1987, CUA.

96. Ibid.

97. Corwin, "Cameron State School of Agriculture, 1909-1927," p. 173.

98. Clinton Far and Harry Hammond, Video-taped interview, Alumni Weekend, October 1987, CUA.

99. Ernie Crain, Video-taped interview, Alumni Weekend, October 1987, CUA.

100. Oakle Best Hilbert, Video-taped interview, Alumni Weekend, October 1987, CUA.

101. Ellie Morrison and Oakle Best Hilbert, Video-taped interview, Alumni Weekend, October 1987, CUA.

102. "The Kitchen Force" 1925 *Wichita*, p. 84.

103. Ibid.

104. W. R. Rice, "A Farm," *The Oklahoman*, 30 March 1924, p. 45.

105. Ibid.

106. "Introduction," 1914 *Wichita*.

107. Corwin, "Cameron State School of Agriculture, 1909-1927," p. 187.

CHAPTER TWO

1. "It's Cameron College," 1931 *Wichita*, p. 20.

2. "Cameron School Trains Boys and Girls to Make the Most of Farm Life," *Lawton Constitution*, 25 January 1927, p. 8.

3. "College Work at Cameron, Plan," *Lawton Constitution*, 18 February 1927, p. 3.

4. "Cameron School Fares Well in Legislature," *Lawton Constitution*, 25 March 1927, p. 1.

5. "Cameron Hit by Johnston Pen; Fund Cut," *Lawton Constitution*, 10 April 1927, p. 1.

6. "Cameron Gets 79,000 Fund," *Lawton Constitution*, 11 April 1927, p. 4. The paper broke down the budget as follows: "Year 1927-28: Salaries, $27,250; support and maintenance, $8000; repairs and buildings, $2500; sidewalks and paving $5000; total $42,750; Year 1928-29: Salaries, 27,500; support and maintenance, $8000; repairs, $1000; total, $36,500."

7. "State Board to Visit Cameron School on Friday" 3 February 1927, p1;"Board Begins School Probe" 4 February 1927, p.1;"Cameron School Hearing Closes," 6 February 1927, p. 1; *Lawton Constitution*

8. "New Cameron School Head Is Appointed," *Lawton Constitution*, 2 May 1927.

9. "State Senator Visits Cameron," *Lawton Constitution*, 4 August 1927, p. 1.

10. "Governor Talks," *Lawton Constitution*, 25 August 1927, p.1 (b).

11. "Registration Sets Record," *The Cameron Collegian*, 9 September 1927, p. 1.

12. "Campus Rules," *The Cameron Collegian*, 9 September 1927, p. 2.

13. Jim Thorne, "The College Class," 1928 *Wichita*, p. 34.

14. "Petty Quarles," *The Cameron Collegian*, 3 November 1927, p. 2.

15. "Hell Hounds," 1928 *Wichita*, p. 91.

16. Ibid;"Review of Football Season," 1928 *Wichita*, p. 69.

17. "Pep Pirates," 1928 *Wichita*, p. 87.

18. "Girls Basketball Review," 1928 *Wichita*, p. 78.

19. "Student Senate," 1928 *Wichita*, p. 83. The student senate included representatives for the 5 grades (four high school and one college class) plus two other at large senators during its first year.

20. "Our Hashers," *The Cameron Collegian*," January 1928, p. 4.

21. Vivian Hay Buckwell, Video-taped interview, Alumni Weekend, October 1987,CUA

22. "Cameron State School of Agriculture Junior College,"1928 *Wichita*, p. 125.

23. "To Parents of School Children," *The Cameron Collegian*, 27 February 1929, p. 2.

24. "Cameron Leads Junior College by 94 Students; Still Growing," *The Cameron Collegian*, 7 February 1929, p. 1.

25. "Letter to the Editor," *The Cameron Collegian*, 21 November 1928, p. 2.

26. "Cameron College Looking Forward to Most Successful Year in History, Twenty-Second Catalog Indicates," *Lawton Constitution*, 17 June 1930, p. 1.

27. "Prospects of Big Cameron Year Bright," *Lawton Constitution*, 10 August 1930, p. 1.

28. "Cameron Offers Splendid Opportunities to College Students in All Lines in Which They May Be Interested; Best of Instructors," *The Cameron Collegian*, 9 September 1930, p. 3.

29. "Lack of Room Causes Much Doubling Up," *Lawton Constitution*, 29 January 1931, p. 1.

30. "Cameron is U.S. Third Largest Junior College," *The Cameron Collegian*, 4 March 1931, p. 1.

31. Schiller Scroggs, Director of Administrative Research, Oklahoma A & M, "A Partial Survey of Cameron State School of Agriculture Made for the Oklahoma State Board of Agriculture," March 1931, p. 2

32. John L. Coffey, "Opportunity," 1931 *Wichita*, p. 13.

33. "The Case of Coffey," *The Oklahoman*, 5 May 1931, p. 6

34. Ibid.

35. "John L. Coffey Appointed Head of State Board," *The Cameron Collegian*, 20 January 1937, p. 1.

36. "Dedication" 1931 *Wichita*.

37. "C. M. Conwill," *The Oklahoman*, 6 May 1931, p. 15.

38. "Cameron Will Not Publish Yearbook" 1931, unidentified newspaper clipping, Cameron History, Folder 8, Box 2, CUA.

39. "Second Semester Enrollment Shows Increase; Record," *The Cameron Collegian*, 28 January 1932, p. 1.

40. "Unemployment's Greatest Enemy Found to be Education, Aggie Instructor Says" *Lawton Constitution*, 5 January 1933, p. 1. These unemployment figures are particularly problematic because the occupation of "housewife" is not part of the paid labor force so it is not included in unemployment statistics.

41. "Co-Eds Get Less Chance to Marry Than Other Girls, One Survey Says," *The Cameron Collegian*, 5 October 1932, p. 1

42. "Home Economics," 1931 *Wichita*, p. 125.

43. Susan Ware, *Holding Their Own: American Women in the 30's*, (New York: MacMillan Publishing Company, 1984).

44. Sara Hend, "Nonfeminist," 1931 *Wichita*, p. 137.

45. "Cameron Pupils Will Receive Aid from CWA Work," *Lawton Constitution*, 16 February 1934, p. A3.

46. "'New Deal' Found Interesting and Helpful Here Now," *The Cameron Collegian*, 28 February 1934, p. 1.

47. "Work Begun on Athletic Field for Cameron," *Lawton Constitution*, 15 March 1934, p. 1.

48. "Cameron Sets Record as 132 Will Graduate," *Lawton Constitution*, 15 April 19345, p. 1.

49. "President Conwill—Cameron's Best Friend," *The Cameron Collegian*, 11 April 1934, p. 2.

50. "Cameron Largest of Oklahoma's 23 Junior Colleges," *The Cameron Collegian*, 31 October 1934, p. 2.

51. Ibid.

52. "Cameron FERA Project Made by Local Head," *Lawton Constitution*, 18 September 1934, p. 5.

53. "Cameron Pupils Get Federal Aid," *Lawton Constitution*, 21 September 1934, p. 1 (a).

54. "Work Sought for Aggie Students," *Lawton Constitution*, 23 August 1933, p. 6.

55. "Cameron Cash Unaffected By Hopkins Action," *Lawton Constitution*, 10 September 1935, p. 1.

56. "Application for $100,000 Loan for Erection of Two New Dormitories at Cameron College Now Being Studied," *Lawton Constitution*, 13 December 1933, p. 1.

57. "Only Eight Students at Cameron in 1934 Are Without Jobs," *Lawton Constitution*, 8 February 1935, p. 5.

58. "Farming Is First of Occupations Among Parents," *The Cameron Collegian*, 4 November 1936, p. 1.

59. "John L. Coffey Appointed Head of State Board," *The Cameron Collegian*, 20 January 1937, p.1.

60. "Schools Rally to Plans for Garden Plots," *The Oklahoman*, 21 January 1937, p. 15.

61. "NYA and State Aid Places 253 Aggies on Roll," *The Cameron Collegian*, 3 November 1937, p.1.

62. "200 Acres Planted in Garden Crops by Aggies, NYA," *The Cameron Collegian*, 30 March 1938, p.1.

63. "NYA Girls to Have Projects for Community," *The Cameron Collegian*, 11 October 1939, (The page number listed in the paper is page 2 but the actual number is 4).

64. "Two New Tennis Courts to Be Finished Soon," *The Cameron Collegian*, 27 April 1938, p. 3.

65. "5,000 Aggie NYA Shops Building Will Be Erected," *The Cameron College Collegian*, 3 November 1938, p. 4.

66. "NYA Youths to Do All Work on Aggie Building," *Lawton Constitution*, 13, April 1938, p. 5.

67. "Distinct Advantages Are Discovered In 'Back-To-Nature' Roads of Cameron Campus," *The Cameron Collegian*, 20 December 1939, p. 5.

68. "Cameron the Beautiful," *The Cameron Collegian*, 6 December 1939, p. 2.

69. "Phone System Installed In Aggie Offices," *The Cameron Collegian*, 9 September 1936, p. 1.

70. "Pep Problem Solution," *The Cameron Collegian*, 3 November 1937, p.2.

71. "Hell Hounds Enjoy Nice Evening Meal," *The Cameron Collegian*, 18 March 1942, p. 4.

72. "Roosevelt Field to Be Dedicated at Game Friday," *The Cameron Collegian*, 6 October, 1937, p. 4.

73. Lloyd Mitchell, KCCU Interview, Oral History Project, 17 March 2008.

74. Robert S. Johnson with Martin Caidin, *Thunderbolt!* (New York, Ballantine Books, Inc., 1959), p. 25-26.

75. "We're Awful Glad You're Here," *The Cameron Collegian*, 8 September 1937, p. 1.

76. "Cameron German Club Is Formed," *Lawton Constitution*, 2 October 1935, p. A6; "Cameron Boasts First Indian Club," Lawton Constitution, 10 October 1935, p. B3.

77. "Indian Pupils Form New Club" *The Cameron Collegian*, 9 October 1935, p. 3.

78. Charles Graybill, KCCU Interview, Oral History Project, 14 March 2008.

79. "Is Chivalry [A] Thing of Past?" *The Cameron Collegian*, 13 March 1935, p. 4.

80. "Bring A Date Or Not To Bring A Date, Question," *The Cameron Collegian*, 13 March 1935, p. 4.

81. "Blondes Bewail as Chemistry Havocs Their Complexions," *The Cameron Collegian*, 2 January 1936, p.4.

82. "Can Men Cook? Only 22 Out of 70 On Cameron Campus Say They Cannot, We'll Take Ma's Cooking Any Time," *The Cameron Collegian*, 2 January 1936, p.4.

83. "So You Think You're Starved, Eh?—Read This," *The Cameron Collegian*, 22 November 1939, p. 2.

84. "Little Piggies of Cameron Don't Go to Market," *The Cameron Collegian*, 20 December 1939, p. 8.

85. "Enrollment at Cameron Sets Record of 919," *The Cameron Collegian*, 27 April 1938, p. 4.

86. "Recorded Enrollment Now on File Comes to 736, Slight Decrease from Last Year's," *The Cameron Collegian*, 27 September 1939, p. 1.

87. "Number of Those on NYA Program Cut 40 Per Cent," *The Cameron Collegian*, 13 September 1939, p. 4.

88. "Cameron Faces Slice in Budget," *The Cameron Collegian*, 19 April 1939, p. 1

89. Ibid., p. 2.

90. "Cameron Funds Sliced $2,192," *Lawton Constitution*, 3 October 1939, p. 1.

91. Homer Specht, "Is the World Safe for Democracy?" *The Cameron Collegian*, 29 November 1933, p. 4.

92. "17 Years Ago," *The Cameron Collegian*, 6 November 1935, p. 2.

93. "Let War Come, She's Ready" *The Cameron Collegian*, 24 April 1935, p. 4.

94. "An Aggie Student Decrees We Would Not Fight Unless Faced by Invasion," *The Cameron Collegian*, 8 March 1939, p.4.

95. "Student Survey on War Opinions Is Conducted," *The Cameron Collegian*, 11 October 1939, p. 1.

CHAPTER THREE

1. "We're From Cameron," Cameron History, Folder 8, Box 2, CUA. The school paper often included the words to the school songs in its first edition of each academic year to promote school spirit.

2. "College to Drop Its High School Course in 1941," *Lawton Constitution*, 6 January 1941, p. 2.

3. "Nation Is Moving Toward War, Aggie Students Are Told," *Lawton Constitution*, 22 May 1941, p. 5.

4. "College Salary Increase Likely," *Lawton Constitution*, 28 March 1941, p. 1 (b); "Cameron Streets to be Paved Next Month, Ozmun says[s]," Lawton Constitution, 24 July 1941, p. 1.

5. "Cameron College Has Grown Rapidly," *Lawton Constitution*, 5 August 1941, p. 1.

6. "France's Fall," *The Cameron Collegian*, 3 December 1941, p. 2.

7. "Let's Get Serious Aggies," *The Cameron Collegian*, 24 September 1941, p. 3.

8. "Changing Times," *The Cameron Collegian*, 8 October 1941, p. 3.

9. "Attention Americans!" *The Cameron Collegian*, 5 February 1941, p. 2.

10. "Student Opinion on Current International Problems Is Given in English Essays," *The Cameron Collegian*, 5 February 1941, p. 2

11. "Attention Americans!" *The Cameron Collegian*, 5 February 1941, p. 2

12. "What Is an American?" *The Cameron Collegian*, 22 October 1941, p. 3

13. "Does America Face War?" *The Cameron Collegian*, 5 November 1941, p.2. Lend-Lease marked a clear departure from the Neutrality Acts as the U.S. moved to lend war materials to any country whose national defense was in the best interest of the United States. This also included the use American ships to transport goods to allies.

14. Johnson, *Thunderbolt!*, p. 43-44.

15. "Former Aggie Dies in Action," *Lawton Constitution*, 18 December 1941, p. 1.

16. "Cameron loses 32 Percent of its Enrollment," *Lawton Constitution*, 10 March 1942, p. 3.

17. "'Shoot 'Em and Get It Over with," 28 December 1941, p. 1.

18. "87 Former Aggie Students Serve in Armed Forces," *Lawton Constitution*, 4 March 1942, p. 8 (b).

19. "College Students Should Remain in School—Conwill," *The Cameron Collegian*, 7 January 1942, p.1.

20. "Defend Your Country," *The Cameron Collegian*, 21 January 1942, p. 2.

21. "College Students Should Remain in School—Conwill," *The Cameron Collegian*, 7 January 1942, p.1.

22. "Aggie Plans Are Outlined by President" *The Cameron Collegian*, 7 January 1942, p.1.

23. "Aggie Students Sign Pledge to Aid in Defense," *Lawton Constitution*, 21 January 1942, p. 2.

24. "Collegians Can Do Their Part," *The Cameron Collegian*, January 7 1942, p.3.

25. "Aggies Have a Part in War Effort Too," *The Cameron Collegian*, 6 October 1943, p.1.

26. "Ninth Cameron Instructor Goes into War Service," *Lawton Constitution*, 29 April 1942, p. 2 (a).

27. "Cameron Paper First of State Junior Colleges," *Lawton Constitution*, 12 May 1942, p. 3 (a).

28. "Pep Pirates' Formal Banquet and Dance Honor Football Men," *The Cameron Collegian*, 7 January 1942, p. 3.

29. "Hellhound Slime Says Initiation Worth His Time," *The Cameron Collegian*, 4 November 1942, p. 1.

30. "History Class Shows Pride in Its Citizenship," *The Cameron Collegian*, 29 April, 1942, p. 1.

31. "Cameron College Offers Defense Summer Course," *The Oklahoman*, 8 April 1942, p. 10.

32. "Capt. Breedlove Arrives in London," *Lawton Constitution*, 7 July 1942, p. 5.

33. Johnson, *Thunderbolt!*, p. 18

34. "Exchanges Gloves for Marine Riffle," *Lawton Constitution*, 3 August 1942, p. 3.

35. "Former Cameron Student's Plane Shot Down in Sea," *Lawton Constitution* 21 August 1942, p. 2.

36. "Former Cameron Student Is Killed," *Lawton Constitution*, 11 November 1942, p.1.

37. "Cameron to Graduate 51," *Lawton Constitution*, 21 March 1943, p. 1 (a).

38. "Colleges Strive to Remain in Tact, Conwill Explains," *Lawton Constitution*, 15 April 1943, p. 2 (a).

39. "Former Cameron Athlete Stars as Navy Flyer," *Lawton Constitution*, 29 March 1943, p. 5.

40. Robert Olds, *Helldiver Squadron: The Story of Carrier Bombing Squadron 17 with Task Force 58*, (New York: Dodd, Mead, and Company, 1944), p. 10.

41. "Cameron College Graduate Pilots Bomber Back From Bremen After 3 Motors Knocked Out, Cable Damaged," *Lawton Constitution* 19 April 1943, p. 5.

42. "Three Aggies Decorated in Air Heroism," *Lawton Constitution*, 24 June 1943, p. 1.

43. "Feature Role," *Lawton Constitution*, 3 January 1945, p. 5 (b).

44. "Three Former Cameron Students Are Given Captains' Commissions Same Date in Same b-26 Marauder Group," *Lawton Constitution*, 23 February 1945, p. 2.

45. "Cameron Buddies Are in Same Unit," *Lawton Constitution*, 22 March 1945, p. 9 (b).

46. "War Casualty," *Lawton Constitution*, 9 March 1945, p. 5.

47. "C.M. Finnigan Killed on Iwo," *Lawton Constitution*, 7 March 1945, p. 1.

48. "Former Cameron Student Killed," *Lawton Constitution*, 6 January 1944, p.7.

49. "Former Cameron Student Killed," *Lawton Constitution*, 10 January 1945, p. 3.

50. "Cameron Seeks Army Air Unit," *Lawton Constitution*, 10 August 1939, p. A6.

51. "Cameron College Is Recognized," *Lawton Constitution*, 12 September 1939.

52. Lloyd Mitchell, KCCU Interview, Oral History Project, 17 March 2008.

53. Johnson, *Thunderbolt!*, p. 10.

54. Ibid., p. 20; 32.

55. Ibid., p. 33-34.

56. Ibid., p. 6; 8.

57. Congressional Medal of Honor Society, http://www.cmohs.org/medal-history.php.

58. From President Franklin D. Roosevelt, "Den's Book," CUA.

59. "Keathley, George D." in "Den's Book, "CUA.

60. In March of 1962 Keathley's wife and mother came to Cameron for the ceremony in which Cameron's ROTC drill team officially became the Keathley Riffles, "Den's Book," CUA.

61. "Cameron, State's Largest Junior College, Faces Slump in Enrollment," *Lawton Constitution*, 5 August 1943, p. 2

62. "Cameron's Cost Lowest in State," *Lawton Constitution*, 3 September 1943, p. 1. The article placed expenses for the other schools as follows: Northeastern: $114.42; Connors: $98.42; Eastern: 138.72; Murray: $110.84.

63. "Cameron Enrollment Steadily Growing," *Lawton Constitution*, 6 October 1943, p. 2 (b).

64. "Cameron College Funds to be Cut," *Lawton Constitution*, 4 March 1943, p. 4 (a).

65. "Year's Closing Exercises Set at College," *Lawton Constitution*, 22 April 1945, p. 4.

66. "School Opened at Cameron for Army Men," *Lawton Constitution*, 18 January 1943, p. 1.

67. "Rationing Brings Sharp Revision of Cameron's Menus," *Lawton Constitution*, 23 March 1943, p. 6.

68. "Football Dropped for the Duration," *The Cameron Collegian*, 7 April 1943, v. 16, n. 2, p. 4.

69. "Canning Will Be Easy at College," *Lawton Constitution*, 4 August 1943, p. 3.

70. "Across the Campus," *The Cameron Collegian*, 8 November 1944, p. 2.

71. "Conwill Named President Again," *The Cameron Collegian*, 16 May 1945, p.1

72. Johnson, *Thunderbolt!*, p. 221-222.

73. "Cameron College Founded in 1909; Future Is Bright," *Lawton Constitution*, 6 August 1945, p. 8 (a).

74. "New Term Will Open at Cameron College Sept. 10," *Lawton Constitution*, 19 August 1945, p. 14 (a).

75. "Enrollment Totals 218 at Cameron," *Lawton Constitution*, 17 September 1945, p, 2,

76. "100 Vets Enroll at Cameron for Second Semester," *Lawton Constitution* 1 February 1946, p. 3.

77. "Those Cameron Students Consume a Lot of Food," *Lawton Constitution* 25 October 1946, p. 8

78. "ROTC Unit May Be Trained at Cameron; New Gym Set," *Lawton Constitution*, 1 January 1946, p. 1.

79. "It's Strictly a 'He-Man' Campus at Aggie College," *Lawton Constitution*, 18 October 1946, p. 12 (c).

80. "Conwill Dies in California," *Lawton Constitution*, 20 September 1946, p. 1.

81. Ibid.

82. "Breedlove Gets Legion of Merit," *Lawton Constitution*, 15 June 1944, p. 8

83. "Breedlove Asks Regents to Visit Cameron to Determine Increased Enrolment Needs," *Lawton Constitution*, 11 August 1946, p. 1.

84. "Cameron Gets Flight Course," *Lawton Constitution*, 28 August 1946, p. 1 (a).

85. "Cameron Enrolment Reaches 702 Today," *Lawton Constitution*, 11 September 1946, p. 1.

86. Regents Vote Approval of 35 Per Cent Increase for Cameron's Operation Costs," *Lawton Constitution*, 24 November 1946, p. 1.

87. "College Plans Are Outlined," *Lawton Constitution*, 6 December 1946, p. 1.

88. Roy P. Stewart, no title, *The Oklahoman*, 4 May 1947 p. 70.

89. "Howell Reports on Progress at Cameron College," *Lawton Constitution* 21 August 1947, p. 2.

90. "Cameron Dormitories Are Full, Record Enrollment Predicted," *Lawton Constitution*, 3 September 1947, p. 12.

91. "Vernon Howell," *Lawton Constitution*, 5 October 1947, p. 4 (b).

92. Ibid.

93. "Cameron to Build College Infirmary," *The Oklahoman*, 7 August 1947, p. 30.

94. "Aggie Students Given Holiday," *Lawton Constitution*, 24 November 1947, p. 1.

95. "High Flying Aggies Selected to Represent East in Colorful West Coast Classic Dec. 13," *Lawton Constitution*, 28 November 1947, p. 1 (b).

96. "Aggie Students Given Holiday," *Lawton Constitution*, 24 November 1947, p. 1.

97. High Flying Aggies Selected to Represent East in Colorful West Coast Classic Dec. 13," *Lawton Constitution*, 28 November 1947, p. 2.

98. "Aggie Boosters Gather Today," *Lawton Constitution*, 30 November 1947, p. 1.

99. "Aggies State Rose Bowl Trek Monday," *Lawton Constitution*, 3 December 1947, p.1.

100. Ibid.

101. 1948 *Wichita*.

102. Ibid.

103. "35 Aggie Gridmen Given 'O' Jackets," *Lawton Constitution*, 6 January 1948, p. 6 (a).

104. "Cameron Dethroned As Loop Champ," *Lawton Constitution*, 13 January 1948, p. 1 (a).

105. "Pep Rally Set at Cameron Tonight," *Lawton Constitution*, 15 September 1948, p. 9.

106. "Rose Bowl Film Showing Slated," *Lawton Constitution*, 16 May 1948, p. 10 (c).

107. "Aggies Make '47 Cage Debut with Carnegie," *Lawton Constitution*, 30 November 1947, p. 13.

108. See, for example, 1948 *Wichita*.

109. "Cameron Sees Banner Term," *Lawton Constitution*, 29 August 1948, p. 2.

110. "Cameron Senior Total Is Record," *Lawton Constitution*, 10 March 1948, p. 1.

111. "Booklet Showing Cameron Campus Life Prepared," Lawton Constitution, 15 April 1948, p. 17; "Optimistic Report Given on Cameron," *Lawton Constitution* 23 April 1948, p. 1.

112. "Draft May Affect College Students," *Lawton Constitution*, 27 July 1948, p. 1.

113. "Cameron College's Enrollment Drops," *The Oklahoman*, 24 October 1948, p. 21.

114. Pep Rally Set at Cameron Tonight," *Lawton Constitution*, 15 September 1948, p. 9.

115. "'Vigorous Democracy' Urged As Cameron Graduates 152," *Lawton Constitution*, 26 May 1949, p. A 14.

116. "President's Message," 1950 *Wichita*.

117. "Dedication," 1951 *Wichita*, p. 2.

118. "Ag Enrollment Figures Decline," *Lawton Constitution*, 22 January 1951, p. 1.

119. "The Constitution for the Student Association of Cameron State Agricultural College," p. 2, Cameron History, Folder 1, Box 1, CUA.

120. "Ibid., p. 6

121. "Cameron College Sets Record Enrollment," *The Oklahoman*, 27 February 1955, p. 60.

122. Peggy Long, KCCU Interview, Oral History Project, 15 March 2008.

123. Eugene Thompson, KCCU Interview, Oral History Project, 30 March 2008.

124. "A Loss for Cameron," unidentified newspaper clipping, 13 January 1957, Cameron History, Box 1, Folder, 9, CU Archives.

CHAPTER FOUR

1. Lulu Gray, "The Campus," 1914 *Wichita*, CUA.

2. "Howell Quits Cameron Job, Takes Bank Post," *Lawton Constitution*, 10 January 1957, p1.

3. Clarence Davis, "Letter from Aggie President," *The Cameron Collegian*, 22 May 1957, p. 1.

4. Clarence Davis, "President Welcomes Students," *The Cameron Collegian*, 13 September 1957, p. 1.

5. Clarence Davis, "Letter from Aggie President," *The Cameron Collegian*, 22 May 1957, p. 1.

6. "1173 Students Are Enrolled In Cameron," *The Cameron Collegian*, 3 November 1956, p. 1. The article also placed the ratio of male to female students at 4 to 1.

7. "Student Survey Attracts 497," *The Cameron Collegian*, 23 May 1956, p. 1.

8. "Commission Makes Survey of Facilities at Cameron," *The Cameron Collegian*, 30 April 1958, p. 1.

9. "Harris Proposes Four-Year Status for Cameron College," *Lawton Constitution*, 9 November 1958, p. 27.

10. Don Davis, Interview with the author, 14 August 2009.

11. "A Good Year Closes," *The Cameron Collegian*, 28 May 1958, p. 2.

12. Clarence Davis, "Letter from Aggie President," *The Cameron Collegian*, 28 May 1958, p. 1.

13. "Faculty Members Resign Ag Post," *The Cameron Collegian*, 28 May 1958, p. 1.

14. Clarence C. Davis, Information for the Fifth Edition of the American Junior Colleges Report, Folder 13, Unprocessed Presidential Papers, CUA.

15. Clarence Davis, "President Welcomes Students," *The Cameron Collegian*, 24 September 1958, p. 1.

16. "Will Cameron Make It?" *The Cameron Collegian*, 29 October 1958, p. 2.

17. Clarence Davis, "Letter from the President," *The Cameron Collegian*, 21 January 1959, p. 2.

18. Bill Crawford, "Cameron to Try for Accreditation Again in Two Years," *Lawton Constitution*, 29 April 1959, p. 8b.

19. Ibid., 8a.

20. Clarence C. Davis, Information for the Fifth Edition of the American Junior Colleges Report, Folder 13, Unprocessed Presidential Papers, CUA.

21. "Letter to the Editors," *The Cameron Collegian*, 21 January 1959, p. 2.

22. "Body and Mind," *The Cameron Collegian*, 27 February 1957, p. 2.

23. "Athletics Are for Everyone," *The Cameron Collegian*, 29 April 1959, p. 2; "Be Alert Or Be Conquered," The Cameron Collegian, 29 April 1959, p. 2.

24. "Remarks of Chancellor E.T. Dunlap to the Meeting of Governing Board Members and State Regents of the Oklahoma State System of Higher Education" 22 July 1963, p. 1, Unprocessed Presidential Papers, Folder 12, CUA.

25. "Cameron Teacher Attends Computer Classes at OU," *Lawton Constitution*, 15 October 1959, p. 30.

26. "Noted Consultant Visits Cameron," *Lawton Constitution*, 18 September 1959, p. 18.

27. "Cameron College President Dead," *The Oklahoman*, 13 July 1960, p. 33.

28. Minutes from the A & M Board of Regents Meeting, 14 July 1960, Unprocessed Presidential Papers, Folder 7, CUA.

29. Minutes from the A & M Board of Regents Meeting, 2 August 1960, Unprocessed Presidential Papers, Folder 7, CUA.

30. Minutes from the A & M Board of Regents Meeting, 10 September 1960, Unprocessed Presidential Papers, Folder 7, CUA.

31. Minutes from the A & M Board of Regents Meeting, 5 May 1961, Unprocessed Presidential Papers, Folder 7, CUA.

32. Don Davis, Interview with the author, 14 August 2009.

33. "Cameron College Dean Quits Post," *The Oklahoman*, 11 April 1962, p. 31.

34. "Cameron Quiet after Protests," *The Oklahoman*, 12 April 1962, p. 40.

35. David Madsen, Associate Secretary, to President Burch, 2 April 1962, Unprocessed Presidential Papers, Folder 19, CUA.

36. "Regents Order Lawton College Athletics Probe," *The Oklahoman*, 6 May 1962, p. 12.

37. "Cameron Vows to Fight Back With Top Clubs," *The Oklahoman*, 1 July 1962, p. 116.

38. "Cameron Grid Coach to Stay On," *The Oklahoman*, 20 June 1960, p. 44.

39. "Cameron Vows to Fight Back With Top Clubs," *The Oklahoman*, 1 July 1962, p. 116.

40. "The 1964 Cameron Aggies,"1965 *Wichita*, p. 167.

41. Foreword, 1965 *Wichita*, p. 3.

42. "State College Rolls Swelled," *The Oklahoman*, 5 March 1964, p. 47

43. To the Board of Regents for Oklahoma Agricultural and Mechanical Colleges From Lawton area leaders, 6 November 1963, Unprocessed Presidential Papers, Folder 28, CUA.

44. "School Unmoved By Four-Year Talks," *The Oklahoman*, 4 February 1965, p. 33.

45. To Dr. Richard Burch, President From E. T. Dunlap, Chancellor, Oklahoma State Regents for Higher Education, 2 March 1967, Unprocessed Presidential Papers, Folder 16, CUA.

46. Oklahoma State Regents for Higher Education Resolution No. 423, Unprocessed Presidential Papers, Folder 16, CUA.

47. "A Look at Cameron," 1967 *Wichita*.

48. 1967 *Wichita*, p. 17.

49. "Black, Gold, and Beautiful, *The Cameron Collegian*, 7 October 1969, p. 2

50. "Who Is Cameron?" *The Cameron Collegian*, 21 October 1969, p. 2.

51. Interview with James Mickey Cooper, KCCU Centennial Oral History Project, 16 April 2008.

52. Minutes from the A & M Board of Regents Meeting, 3-4 March 1967, Unprocessed Presidential Papers, Folder 3, CUA.

53. Minutes from the A & M Board of Regents Meeting, 9-10 May 1968, Unprocessed Presidential Papers, Folder 4, CUA.

54. To President Richard Burch From Terral McKellips, 11 December 1968, Unprocessed Presidential Papers, Folder 5, CUA.

55. Terral McKellips, Interview with the author, 12 June 2009.

56. Student Senate Minutes, 3 November 1969, Unprocessed Presidential Papers, CUA.

57. Ibid.

58. To J. P. McLemore, Chair, Disciplinary Committee From Betty Roundtree, 26 February 1969; To Students From President Richard Burch, 5 March 1969, Unprocessed Presidential Papers, Folder 48, CUA.

59. 1967-68 Disciplinary Committee Meeting Minutes, Unprocessed Presidential Papers, Folder 48, CUA.

60. "Resolution of the Board of Regents for the Oklahoma State University and Agricultural and Mechanical Colleges, 4 November 1967, Unprocessed Presidential Papers, Folder 77, CUA.

61. "Bartlett Urging Stand for Unity," 15 October 1969, *The Oklahoman*, p. 21.

62. Student Senate Meeting Minutes, 3 November 1969, Unprocessed Presidential Papers, CUA.

63. Interview with James Mickey Cooper, KCCU Centennial Oral History Project, 16 April 2008.

64. Bob Ruggles, "Heads for Lawton," *The Oklahoman*, 7 February 1969, p. 37.

65. "Report of a Visit to Cameron State College, Lawton, Oklahoma, 10-11 February 1969 for the Commission on Colleges and Universities of the North Central Association of Colleges and Secondary Schools," p. 13, President Don Owen Papers, Folder 14, Box 2, Accession 1, CUA.

66. Ibid., p. 14.

67. Ibid., p. 15.

68. Ibid., p. 1.

69. "Report of a Visit to Cameron State College, Lawton, Oklahoma, 13-14 May 1968 for the Commission on Colleges and Universities of the North Central Association of Colleges and Secondary Schools," p. 3, Owen Papers, Folder 14, Box 2, Accession 1, CUA.

70. "Report of a Visit to Cameron State College," 10-11 February 1969, North Central, p. 2, Owen Papers, Folder 14, Box 2, Accession 1, CUA.

71. Ibid., p. 4.

72. Bob Ruggles, "Heads for Lawton," *The Oklahoman*, 7 February 1969, p. 37.

73. "Report of a Visit to Cameron State College," 10-11 February 1969, North Central, p. 6-7, Owen Papers, Folder 14, Box 2, Accession 1, CUA.

74. To Burke W. Healey, Chairman, Board of Regents for the Oklahoma Agricultural and Mechanical Colleges From John M. Murphy, Chairman, Faculty Affairs Committee, 14 January 1969, Cameron History, Folder 1, Box 1, CUA.

75. Terral McKellips, Interview with the author, 12 June 2009.

76. "Chance at Cameron," *Oklahoma City Times*, 16 January 1969, Cameron History, Folder 2, Box 1, CUA.

77. "20 Seeking Presidency at Cameron," Unidentified Newspaper Clipping, Cameron History, Folder 2, Box 1, CUA.

78. Ed Carter, "Fletcher Native to Take reins at Cameron College, *Lawton Constitution*, 9 February 1969, Cameron History, Folder 2, Box 1, CUA.

79. To President Richard Burch From Norman Burns, Executive Secretary, North Central Association of Colleges and Secondary Schools, 1 April 1969, Owen Papers, Folder 14, Box 2, Accession 1, CUA.

80. To Dr. Joseph Semrow, Associate Executive Secretary, North Central Association of Colleges and Secondary Schools From Don Owen, 28 May 1969, Unprocessed Presidential Papers, Folder 56, CUA.

81. "Report of a Visit to Cameron State College, Lawton, Oklahoma, 13-14 May 1968 for the Commission on Colleges and Universities of the North Central Association of Colleges and Secondary Schools," p. 1, Owen Papers, Folder 14, Box 2, Accession 1, CUA.

82. "Accreditation Report to the Oklahoma State Regents for Higher Education Relative to Cameron State Agricultural College, 15-16 May 1969," Unprocessed Presidential Papers, Folder 21, CUA.

83. "Report of a Visit to Cameron State College, Lawton, Oklahoma, 13-14 May 1968 for the Commission on Colleges and Universities of the North Central Association of Colleges and Secondary Schools," p. 3, Owen Papers, Folder 14, Box 2, Accession 1, CUA.

84. Ibid., p. 6.

85. "OEA Investigates Dismissal of Three Cameron Teachers," *The Oklahoman*, 8 September 1968, p. 7, CUA.

86. "Public Forum," Unidentified Newspaper Clipping, Cameron History, Folder 2, Box 1, CUA.

87. To Dr. E.T. Dunlap, Chancellor, Oklahoma State Regents of Higher Education, From President Don Owen, 13 February 1970, Owen Papers, Folder 47, Box 3, CUA.

88. To "Regent Members" From President Don Owen, 26 August 1969, Owen Papers, Folder 38, Box 2, Accession 20, CUA.

89. To "Regent Members" From President Don Owen, 26 August 1969, Owen Papers, Folder 38, Box 2, Accession 20, CUA.

90. To Forest McIntire From President Don Owen, 3 July 1969, Owen Papers, Folder 43, Box 2, Accession 20, CUA.

91. Don Owen, Report covering from 1970-1972, Presidents Office, 1971-74, CUA.

92. "Report of a Visit to Cameron State Agricultural College, Lawton, OK 7-9 January 1970, for the Commission on Colleges and Universities of the North Central Association of Colleges and Secondary Schools, p. 1, President's Office, 1971-74, CUA.

93. Ibid., p. 2-3.

94. "Administration and Faculty, Cameron College, 1972-73," Owen Papers, Folder 9, Box 1, Accession 1, CUA.

95. Nick Miller, KCCU Interview, Oral History Project, 15 March 2008.

CHAPTER FIVE

1. "Cameron Pride" was composed by two Cameron faculty members and still serves as the university's official Alma Mater. Scherrey Cardwell wrote the lyrics and Gene Smith composed the music.

2. Bob Ziegler, KCCU Interview, Oral History Project, 30 April 2008.

3. Scherrey Cardwell, KCCU Interview, Oral History Project, 6 May 2008.

4. Tom Sutherlin, Interview with the author, 9 October 2008.

5. Betty Friedan, *The Feminine Mystique*, (New York: W. W. Norton & Co., 1963).

6. Mary Allen, KCCU Interview, Oral History Project, 16 April 2008.

7. Josephine Rayburn, KCCU Interview, Oral History Project, 16 April 2008.

8. Karen McKellips, Interview with the author, 3 June 2009.

9. Ibid.

10. Ibid.

11. To Parents From Charles Elkins, Dean of Student Services, 25 February 1971, Owen Papers, Folder 7, Box 1, Accession 27, CUA.

12. To Student Affairs Committee From Judy Coombs, President, Shepler Hall Women's Executive Council, Owen Papers, Folder 7, Box 1, Accession 27, CUA.

13. Residence Hall Shepler Center Handbook, 1976-77, p. 13, CUA.

14. Ibid.

15. Danny Vademan, KCCU Interview, Oral History Project, 25 March 2008.

16. 1976 *Wichita*, p. 13.

17. Ibid., p. 19.

18. Ibid., p. 31.

19. Ibid., p. 71.

20. Ibid., p. 66.

21. Leon Fischer, Interview with the author, 30 June 2009.

22. Bill Burgess, Interview with the author, 10 July 2009.

23. Bill Burgess, 1975 *Wichita*, p. 29.

24. Albert Johnson, Jr., Interview with the author, 22 June 2009.

25. Jerry Hrnciar, Interview with the author, 1 July 2009.

26. Albert Johnson, Jr., Interview with the author, 22 June 2009.

27. Jerry Hrnciar, Interview with the author, 1 July 2009.

28. To Congressman Tom Steed From President Don Owen, 13 March 1970, Folder 43, Box 2, Accession 20, CUA.

29. To All Cameron College Employees From President Don Owen, 26 February 1970, Owen Papers, Folder 52, Box 2, Accession 27, CUA.

30. To Forest McIntire From President Don Owen, 27 October 1969, Owen Papers, Folder 43, Box 2, Accession 2, CUA.

31. To Mayor Wayne Gilley From President Don Owen, 20 April 1970, Owen Papers, Folder 43, Box 2, Accession 20, CUA.

32. To Congressman Tom Steed From C. Vernon Howell, Chairman, Cameron College Committee, 3 March 1972, Tom Steed Collection (hereafter Steed Collection), Folder 19, Box 47, Carl Albert Congressional Research and Studies Center Congressional Archives, University of Oklahoma (here after Carl Albert Center, OU).

33. To Dr. Thurman J. White, Vice President, University of Oklahoma, From President Down Owen, 5 March 1976, Tom Steed Collection, Folder 15, Box 67, Carl Albert Center, OU.

34. 1976 *Wichita*, p. 3.

35. Memorandum to The State Regents, Presidents of Institutions, and Members of Governing Boards From E. T. Dunlap, Chancellor, 16 August 1974, Owen Papers, Folder 20, Box 3, Accession, 1, CUA.

36. 1975 *Wichita*.

37. Cameron Report, 1974/75-1975-76 school years, Owen Papers, Folder 11, Box 2, Accession 1, CUA.

38. Cameron University Press Guide for 1975, Owen Papers, Folder 8, Box 1, Accession 1, CUA.

39. Terral McKellips, Interview with the author, 12 June 2009.

40. To Representative Don Davis From E. T. Dunlap, Chancellor, Oklahoma State Regents for Higher Education, 18 November 1971, Owen Collection, Folder 20, Box 3, Accession 1, CUA.

41. "Plan for the 70's" Oklahoma State Regents for Higher Education, Owen Collection, Folder 23, Box 3, Accession 1, CUA.

42. To President Don Owen From E. T. Dunlap, Chancellor, Oklahoma State Regents for Higher Education, 1 December 1971, Owen Collection, Folder 20, Box 3, Accession 1, CUA.

43. John Dickerson, "Cameron: A Troubled Institution?" *Lawton Magazine*, January 1980, p. 46, Cameron History, Folder 5, Box 2, CUA.

44. Proposed Minutes of the Faculty Affairs Committee, 23 October 1979, Don Owen Papers, Unprocessed, CUA.

45. John Dickerson, "Cameron: A Troubled Institution?" *Lawton Magazine*, January 1980, p. 46, Cameron History, Folder 5, Box 2, CUA.

46. Terral McKellips, Interview with the author, 12 June 2009.

47. John Dickerson, "Cameron: A Troubled Institution?" *Lawton Magazine*, January 1980, p. 47, Cameron History, Folder 5, Box 2, CUA

48. Ibid., p. 48.

49. Ibid., p. 46; 49.

50. "Lawton University Chief Eyes Congress," *The Oklahoman*, 17 November 1979, p. 15.

51. To All Cameron University Employees From President Don Owen, 19 November 1979, Don Owen Papers, Unprocessed, CUA.

52. "Cameron President Resigning," *The Oklahoman*, 9 February 1980, p. 47.

53. "6 show Interest in Campaigning for Steed Seat," *The Oklahoman*, 14 February 1980, p. 13.

54. "Former Cameron President Enters Congressional Race," *The Oklahoman*, 9 March 1980, p. 17.

55. To All Faculty and Administrative Staff From Dr. Richard Murray, 8 April 1980, Don Owen Papers, Unprocessed, CUA.

56. To Mr. Edwin Ketchum, Chairman, Screening Committee, Board of Regents, From Richard Murray, Interim President, 14 May 1980, Don Owen Papers, Unprocessed, CUA.

57. Judy Fossett, "OSBI Probing Cameron Use of Equipment," *The Oklahoman*, 7 May 1980, p. 37.

58. "Letter Alleging Criminal Acts Bypasses Board," *The Oklahoman*, 20 July 1980, p. 7.

59. "Cameron Staffer Resigns in Wake of Allegations," *The Oklahoman*, 25 July 1980, p. 103.

60. "School's Ex-President Charged," *The Oklahoman*, 24 September 1980, p. 1.

61. Joann Thompson, "Cameron Workers on Leave," *The Oklahoman*, 7 October 1981, p. 47.

62. Joann Thompson, "Ex Cameron President Mum When Questioned About Co-Defendant," *The Oklahoman*, 9 October 1981, p. 114.

63. "Trial Testimony to Start," *The Daily Oklahoman*, 19 March 1982, www.infoweb.newsbank.com.

64. Joann Thompson, "Former College Official Guilty on Two Counts," *The Daily Oklahoman*, 25 March 1982, www.infoweb.newsbank.com. .

65. "Conviction Upheld; Another Overturned," *The Daily Oklahoman*, 14 December 1983, www.infoweb.newsbank.com.

66. "Former President of University Denies Embezzling Conspiracy," *The Daily Oklahoman*, 10 September 1982, www.infoweb.newsbank.com.

67. Lynn Fisher, "Ex-University Head Innocent," *The Daily Oklahoman*, 11 September 1982, www.infoweb.newsbank.com.

68. Karen McKellips, Interview with the author, 3 June 2009.

69. Harry Holloway, *Bad Times for Good Ol' Boys: The Oklahoma County Commissioner Scandal*, with Frank S. Myers, (Norman: University of Oklahoma Press, 1993).

70. To Representative Tom Steed (no date); From Representative Tom Steed, 30 April 1975, Steed General Collection, Folder 15, Box 67, Carl Albert Center, OU.

71. "Letter Alleging Criminal Acts Bypasses Board," *The Oklahoman*, 20 July 1980, p. 7.

72. Joann Thompson, "Ex-Chief Testifies in Cameron Case," *Daily Oklahoman*, 24 March 1982, www.infoweb.newsbank.com.

73. Terral McKellips, Interview with the author, 12 June 2009.

74. Jim Myers, "Cameron's New Don: A Journalist-Turned-Lawyer-Turned-Politician Takes on the World of Academia," *Lawton Magazine*, September 1980, p. 38, Cameron History, Folder 5, Box 2, CUA.

75. Ibid., p. 39.

76. "School Official to Lose Job in Cameron Shake-Up," *The Oklahoman*, 11 April 1981, p. 86.

77. To Dr. Ann Nalley, Chairman, Cameron Council From President Don Davis, 15 June 1982, Sally Soelle Collection, Folder 1, Box 2, CUA.

78. Withdraw Report Based on Exit Interviews, July 5, 1983 – December 2, 1983, Center for Advisement and Student Development, Charles Smith Papers, Unprocessed, CUA.

79. Enrollment Trends Summary, Sally Soelle Collection, Folder 14, Box 13, CUA.

80. Jake Brownlow, KCCU Interview, Oral History Project, date not recorded.

81. Tom Sutherlin, 9 October 2008; Terral McKellips, 12 June 2009; B. Don Sullivan, 7 October 2008; Interviews with the author.

82. Jerry Hrnciar, Interview with the author, 1 July 2009.

83. Jim Killackey, "College Enrollment Rises, *The Daily Oklahoman*, 23 October 1986, www.infoweb.newsbank.com.

84. James Johnson, "Cameron Ponders FAA School Move," *The Daily Oklahoman*, 2 March 1986, www.infoweb.newsbank.com.

85. James Johnson, "Cameron Ponders FAA School Move," *The Daily Oklahoman*, 2 March 1986, www.infoweb.newsbank.com.

86. Resolution, Lawton Metropolitan Area Airport Authority, 21 February 1985, Dave McCurdy Collection, Folder 10, Box 16, Carl Albert Center, OU.

87. Terral McKellips, Interview with the author, 12 June 2009.

88. Harold Robinson, Interview with the author, 16 June 2009.

89. Don Davis, to the State to Board of Regents, 29 January 2002, Don Davis Unprocessed Papers, CUA.

90. Terral McKellips, Interview with the author, 12 June 2009.

91. Terral McKellips, Interview with the author, 12 June 2009.

92. B. Don Sullivan, Interview with the author, 7 October 2008.

93. Leigh Holmes, Interview with the author, 10 October 2008.

94. Terral McKellips, Interview with the author, 12 June 2009.

95. Bill Burgess, Interview with the author, 10 July 2009.

CHAPTER SIX

1. Loy Dyke, "A Lecture Written and Lost by a Freshie," 1914 *Wichita*.

2. Don Davis, Statement to Board of Regents, 29 January 2002, p.3, Don Davis Unprocessed Papers, CUA.

3. Terral McKellips, Interview with the author, 12 June 2009.

4. Harold Robinson, Interview with the author, 16 June 2009.

5. Cindy Ross, Interview with the author, 7 November 2008.

6. Terral McKellips, Interview with the author, 12 June 2009.

7. Karen Hardin, Interview with the author, 29 June 2009; online course report, courtesy of Karen Hardin.

8. http://www.cameron.edu/~greg/webdesign/

9. Loy Dykes, "A Lecture Written and Lost by a Freshie," 1914 *Wichita*.

10. Karen Hardin, Interview with the author, 29 June 2009; online course report, courtesy of Karen Hardin.

11. Harold Robinson, Interview with the author, 16 June 2009.

12. Glen Pinkston, Interview with the author, 2 June 2009.

13. To Chancellor Hans Brisch from State Representative Ed Apple, 4 October 1989, Susan Camp, Office files, Duncan Branch Campus.

14. To State Representative Ed Apple from Chancellor Hans Brisch, 18 October 1989, Susan Camp, Office files, Duncan Branch Campus.

15. To State Senator Cliff Marshall from Chancellor Hans Brisch, 25 October 1989, Susan Camp, Office Files, Duncan Branch Campus.

16. Susan Camp, Interview with the author, 22 June 2009.

17. "Duncan Proposes Building Higher Education Facility," unidentified newspaper clipping, Susan Camp, Office Files, Duncan Branch Campus.

18. Susan Camp, Interview with the author, 22 June 2009.

19. Ibid.

20. Jennifer Barnett Holland, Interview with the author, 19 June 2009.

21. Ibid.

22. Linda Phillips, Interview with the author, 30 June 2009.

23. Ibid.

24. Ibid.

25. Ibid.

26. Military Enrollment Statistics, courtesy of Tom Sutherlin.

27. Don Davis, Statement to Faculty and Staff, 29 January 2002, Don Davis Unprocessed Papers, CUA.

28. Cindy Ross, Interview with the author, 7 November 2008.

29. Don Davis, Interview with the author, 14 August 2009.

30. Tom Sutherlin, Interview with the author, 9 October 2008.

31. Terral McKellips, Interview with the author, 12 June 2009.

32. Cindy Ross, Interview with the author, 7 November 2008.

33. Ibid.

34. Mick Hinton, "Regents Skip ex-lawmaker for Cameron," *The Daily Oklahoman*, 20 June 2002, www.infoweb.newsbank.com.

35. Jon R. Stuart, Interview with the author, 7 August 2009.

36. Gilbert "Gib" Gibson, Interview with the author, 6 August 2009.

37. Frank Myers, Interview with the author, 21 October 2008.

38. Ibid.

39. Alice Fullerton Watson, Video-taped interview, Alumni Weekend, October 1987, CUA.

40. Ann Morris, Interview with KCCU, Centennial Oral History Project, date unrecorded.

41. Cindy Ross, Interview with the author, 7 November 2008.

42. "Cameron Told to Cut Budget by $325,000," *The Daily Oklahoman*, 21 November 2002, www.infoweb.newsbank.com.

43. Steve Lackmeyer, "Job Outlook at Colleges in State Bleak, Budget Cuts Force Schools to Prepare for Worst," *The Daily Oklahoman*, 13 January, 2002, www.infoweb.newsbank.com.

44. Cindy Ross, Interview with the author, 7 November 2008.

45. Janet Williams, "Cameron University Announces Final Talley of Centennial Changing Lives Campaign," 23 July 2008, Press Release, Office of Community Relations.

46. Cameron has been especially fortunate to receive financial support from both the McMahon and McCasland Foundations. By the summer of 2009, the McMahon Foundation had donated more than $15 million to Cameron and the McCasland Foundation had donated more than $2.9 million to the university.

47. Cindy Ross, Interview with the author, 7 November 2008.

48. John McArthur, Interview with the author, 3 June 2009.

49. Gilbert "Gib" Gibson, Interview with the author, 6 June 2009.

50. Susan Camp, Interview with the author, 22 June 2009.

51. Adam Callaway, "Cameron University Accepts Donations of Land, Building from City of Duncan and DEDTA," Cameron University of Government and Community Relations Press Release, 25 January 2005.

52. Cindy Ross, Interview with the author, 6 August 2009.

53. Susan Camp, Interview with the author, 22 June 2009.

54. "Branching Out: Where Does Higher Ed Expansion Stop?" *Daily Oklahoman*, 3 May 2004, www.infoweb.newsbank.com.

55. Cindy Ross, "Duncan in Unique Partnership," *Daily Oklahoman*, 5 May 2004, www.infoweb.newsbank.com.

56. Susan Camp, Interview with the author, 22 June 2009.

57. 1966 *Wichita*.

58. 1976 *Wichita*, p. 3.

59. To Cameron University Faculty and Staff from Keith Mitchell, Government and Community Relations, 17 March 2004, Cameron History, Folder 18, Box 2, CUA.

60. Keith Mitchell, "Mayor Proclaims, 'Cameron Aggies Day' in Lawton, 27 February 2004, Cameron History, Folder 18, Box 2, CUA.

61. To Cameron University Faculty and Staff from Keith Mitchell, Government and Community Relations, 17 March 2004, Cameron History, Folder 18, Box 2, CUA.

62. Glen Pinkston, Interview with the author, 2 June 2009.

63. Plan 2008 authored by Lance Janda; Plan 2013 authored by John Morris.

64. Albert Johnson, Jr., Interview with the author, 22 June 2009.

65. Cindy Ross, Interview with the author, 7 November 2008.

66. Jim Jackson, Interview with the author, 10 June 2009.

67. Jamie Glover, Interview with the author, 7 July 2009.

68. Cindy Ross, Interview with the author, 6 August 2009.

69. "Cameron University College Portrait," http://www.collegeportraits.org/OK/CU/characteristics.

79. Leon Fischer, Interview with the author, 30 June 2009.

71. Ibid.

72. John L. Coffey, "Opportunity," 1931 Wichita, p. 13.

73. Cindy Ross, Press Conference, Cameron University, 23 June 2009.

74. Loy Dyke, "A Lecture Written and Lost by a Freshie," 1914 *Wichita*.

INDEX